Urbicide

The term 'urbicide' became popular during the 1992–95 Bosnian War as a way of referring to widespread and deliberate destruction of the urban environment. Coined by writers on urban development in America, urbicide captures the sense that this widespread and deliberate destruction of buildings is a distinct form of violence.

Using Martin Heidegger's notion of space and Jean-Luc Nancy's idea of community, Martin Coward outlines a theoretical understanding of the urban condition at stake in such violence. He contends that buildings are targeted because they make possible a plural public space that is contrary to the political aims of ethnic-nationalist regimes. Illustrated with reference to several post-Cold War conflicts – including Bosnia, Chechnya and Israel/Palestine – this book is the first comprehensive analysis of organised violence against urban environments. It offers an original perspective to those seeking to better understand urbanity, political violence and the politics of exclusion.

Martin Coward is a lecturer in International Relations at the University of Sussex, UK. His research focuses on the nexus of identity, violence and territory. Currently, he is investigating the manner in which this nexus is exhibited in the contemporary relationship between city and war.

Routledge Advances in International Relations and Global Politics

1 **Foreign Policy and Discourse Analysis**
France, Britain and Europe
Henrik Larsen

2 **Agency, Structure and International Politics**
From ontology to empirical enquiry
Gil Friedman and Harvey Starr

3 **The Political Economy of Regional Co-operation in the Middle East**
Ali Carkoglu, Mine Eder and Kemal Kirisci

4 **Peace Maintenance**
The evolution of international political authority
Jarat Chopra

5 **International Relations and Historical Sociology**
Breaking down boundaries
Stephen Hobden

6 **Equivalence in Comparative Politics**
Edited by Jan W. van Deth

7 **The Politics of Central Banks**
Robert Elgie and Helen Thompson

8 **Politics and Globalisation**
Knowledge, ethics and agency
Martin Shaw

9 **History and International Relations**
Thomas W. Smith

10 **Idealism and Realism in International Relations**
Robert M. A. Crawford

11 **National and International Conflicts, 1945–1995**
New empirical and theoretical approaches
Frank Pfetsch and Christoph Rohloff

12 **Party Systems and Voter Alignments Revisited**
Edited by Lauri Karvonen and Stein Kuhnle

13 **Ethics, Justice & International Relations**
Constructing an international community
Peter Sutch

14 **Capturing Globalization**
Edited by James H Mittelman and Norani Othman

15 **Uncertain Europe**
Building a new European security order?
Edited by Martin A Smith and Graham Timmins

16 **Power, Postcolonialism and International Relations**
Reading race, gender and class
Edited by Geeta Chowdhry and Sheila Nair

17 **Constituting Human Rights**
   Global civil society and the society of
   democratic states
   Mervyn Frost

18 **US Economic Statecraft for Survival
   1933–1991**
   Of sanctions, embargoes and economic
   warfare
   Alan P. Dobson

19 **The EU and NATO Enlargement**
   *Richard McAllister and Roland
   Dannreuther*

20 **Spatializing International Politics**
   Analysing activism on the internet
   Jayne Rodgers

21 **Ethnonationalism in the
   Contemporary World**
   Walker Connor and the study of
   nationalism
   Edited by Daniele Conversi

22 **Meaning and International
   Relations**
   *Edited by Peter Mandaville and
   Andrew Williams*

23 **Political Loyalty and the Nation-
   State**
   *Edited by Michael Waller and Andrew
   Linklater*

24 **Russian Foreign Policy and the CIS**
   Theories, debates and actions
   Nicole J. Jackson

25 **Asia and Europe**
   Development and different dimensions
   of ASEM
   Yeo Lay Hwee

26 **Global Instability and Strategic
   Crisis**
   Neville Brown

27 **Africa in International Politics**
   External involvement on the continent
   *Edited by Ian Taylor and Paul
   Williams*

28 **Global Governmentality**
   Governing international spaces
   *Edited by Wendy Larner and William
   Walters*

29 **Political Learning and Citizenship
   Education Under Conflict**
   The political socialization of Israeli
   and Palestinian youngsters
   Orit Ichilov

30 **Gender and Civil Society**
   Transcending boundaries
   *Edited by Jude Howell and Diane
   Mulligan*

31 **State Crises, Globalisation and
   National movements in North–East
   Africa**
   The Horn's dilemma
   Edited by Asafa Jalata

32 **Diplomacy and Developing Nations**
   Post-Cold War foreign policy-making
   structures and processes
   *Edited by Justin Robertson and
   Maurice A. East*

33 **Autonomy, Self-governance and
   Conflict Resolution**
   Innovative approaches to institutional
   design in divided societies
   *Edited by Marc Weller and Stefan
   Wolff*

34 **Mediating International Crises**
   *Jonathan Wilkenfeld, Kathleen J.
   Young, David M. Quinn and Victor
   Asal*

35 **Postcolonial Politics, The Internet
   and Everyday Life**
   Pacific traversals online
   M. I. Franklin

36 **Reconstituting the Global Liberal Order**
Legitimacy and regulation
Kanishka Jayasuriya

37 **International Relations, Security and Jeremy Bentham**
Gunhild Hoogensen

38 **Interregionalism and International Relations**
Edited by Heiner Hänggi, Ralf Roloff and Jürgen Rüland

39 **The International Criminal Court**
A global civil society achievement
Marlies Glasius

40 **A Human Security Doctrine for Europe**
Project, principles, practicalities
Edited by Marlies Glasius and Mary Kaldor

41 **The History and Politics of UN Security Council Reform**
Dimitris Bourantonis

42 **Russia and NATO Since 1991**
From Cold War through cold peace to partnership?
Martin A. Smith

43 **The Politics of Protection**
Sites of insecurity and political agency
Edited by Jef Huysmans, Andrew Dobson and Raia Prokhovnik

44 **International Relations in Europe**
Traditions, perspectives and destinations
Edited by Knud Erik Jørgensen and Tonny Brems Knudsen

45 **The Empire of Security and the Safety of the People**
Edited by William Bain

46 **Globalization and Religious Nationalism in India**
The search for ontological security
Catrina Kinnvall

47 **Culture and International Relations**
Narratives, natives and tourists
Julie Reeves

48 **Global Civil Society**
Contested futures
Edited by Gideon Baker and David Chandler

49 **Rethinking Ethical Foreign Policy**
Pitfalls, possibilities and paradoxes
Edited by David Chandler and Volker Heins

50 **International Cooperation and Arctic Governance**
Regime effectiveness and northern region building
Edited by Olav Schram Stokke and Geir Hønneland

51 **Human Security**
Concepts and implications
Shahrbanou Tadjbakhsh and Anuradha Chenoy

52 **International Relations and Security in the Digital Age**
Edited by Johan Eriksson and Giampiero Giacomello

53 **State-Building**
Theory and practice
Edited by Aidan Hehir and Neil Robinson

54 **Violence and Non-Violence in Africa**
Edited by Pal Ahluwalia, Louise Bethlehem and Ruth Ginio

55 **Developing Countries and Global Trade Negotiations**
Edited by Larry Crump and S. Javed Maswood

56 **Civil Society, Religion and Global Governance**
Paradigms of power and persuasion
Edited by Helen James

57 **War, Peace and Hegemony in a Globalized World**
The changing balance of power in the 21st century
Edited by Chandra Chari

58 **Economic Globalisation as Religious War**
Tragic convergence
Michael McKinley

59 **Globalization, Prostitution and Sex-trafficking**
Corporeal politics
Elina Penttinen

60 **Peacebuilding**
Women in international perspective
Elisabeth Porter

61 **Ethics, Liberalism and Realism in International Relations**
Mark D. Gismondi

62 **Law and Legalization in Transnational Relations**
Edited by Christian Brütsch and Dirk Lehmkuhl

63 **Fighting Terrorism and Drugs**
Europe and international police cooperation
Jörg Friedrichs

64 **Identity Politics in the Age of Genocide**
The Holocaust and historical representation
David B. MacDonald

65 **Globalisation, Public Opinion and the State**
Western Europe and East and Southeast Asia
Edited by Takashi Inoguchi and Ian Marsh

66 **Urbicide**
The politics of urban destruction
Martin Coward

Urbicide

The politics of urban destruction

Martin Coward

Routledge
Taylor & Francis Group

LONDON AND NEW YORK

First published 2009
by Routledge
2 Park Square, Milton Park, Abingdon, Oxon, OX14 4RN

Simultaneously published in the USA and Canada
by Routledge
270 Madison Avenue, New York, NY 10016

Routledge is an imprint of the Taylor & Francis Group, an informa business

© 2009 Martin Coward

Typeset in Times New Roman by Pindar New Zealand (Egan Reid) Ltd
Printed and bound in Great Britain by Biddles Digital, King's Lynn

British Library Cataloguing in Publication Data
A catalogue record for this book is available from the British Library

Library of Congress Cataloging in Publication Data
A catalog record for this book has been requested

ISBN 10: 0-415-46131-6 (hbk)
ISBN 10: 0-203-89063-9 (ebk)

ISBN 13: 978-0-415-46131-3 (hbk)
ISBN 13: 978-0-203-89063-9 (ebk)

For Alis and Erin

Contents

Preface and acknowledgments   xii

Introduction: The destruction of shared space   1

1 Interpreting destruction of the built environment   17

2 The logic of urbicide   35

3 The built environment and shared spatiality   54

4 The nature of heterogeneity: From *Mitsein* to *the inoperative
  community*   72

5 The political stakes of urbicide   91

6 The conceptual stakes of urbicide   108

Conclusion   122

Notes   138
Bibliography   147
Index   156

Preface and acknowledgments

Theory and the political gesture

In the preface to *When Victims Become Killers*, Mahmood Mamdani criticises area studies' 'methodological assumption' that 'facts speak for themselves' (Mamdani 2001, xiii). Area specialists, Mamdani argues, have linked 'expertise to the search for new facts' and, in doing so, have developed a 'profoundly antitheoretical' outlook that views theory as a 'deadening' force that 'manipulates the fact[s]' (*Ibid.*). Mamdani critiques this assumption, arguing that 'facts need to be put in context, and interpreted; neither is possible without theoretical illumination' (*Ibid.*). The methodological assumption that 'the empirical is detached and … in opposition to the theoretical' is thus, according to Mamdani (*Ibid.*), profoundly misguided.

I note these comments in order to indicate the general thrust of the argument that follows. Accounting for urbicide cannot be done through the amassing of empirical evidence alone. Indeed, the empirical facts are, I would contend, already reasonably well known. As such then, my argument, like Mamdani's, relies on the reportage and empirical investigations of others 'better to stand on their shoulders … the more to see beyond the horizon where their sights came to rest' (Mamdani 2001, xiv). My argument is thus 'more than just an attempt to dig up new facts … it is an attempt to rethink existing facts in light of rethought contexts, thereby to illuminate old facts and core realities in new light' (*Ibid.*).

The purpose of this argument is thus to delineate a conceptual understanding of acts of widespread and deliberate destruction of the built environment. The argument elaborates a conceptual proposition about the politics of destroying buildings. In this sense, this book is a work of political theory which takes as its subject matter a number of instances already reasonably well documented. Though the phenomenon of destruction of the built environment is often treated as secondary to more anthropocentric concerns, the examples under discussion are a matter of public record. I do not, therefore, intend for this argument to uncover instances of destruction that are hitherto undocumented.

This is not to say that the argument will not bring to light previously unconsidered aspects of political violence. Indeed, I would contend that the understanding of the nature of urban destruction that I will outline in this book is a novel recasting of the nature of political violence. At the core of the argument is the assertion that such a recasting forces us to approach the destruction of the built environment in a manner that recognises its role in negating plural communities and constituting homogeneous, exclusionary political programs. Whilst I do not claim to air previously undocumented evidence then, I do claim that my argument comprises a novel understanding of such evidence which, if followed, urges a fresh ethos of critical reflection on the political questions posed by the destruction of the built environment.

This argument thus considers several well-documented cases of widespread and deliberate destruction of the built environment: Yugoslavia, Chechnya and Israel/Palestine. The selection of cases was not designed to offer comprehensive empirical proof of particular patterns of destruction. Rather it was designed to offer evidence to ground and illustrate a set of conceptual reflections on the nature of such destruction. In this sense, the argument is somewhat phenomenological in trajectory: the cases provide a provocation to thought. My response to such provocation – the theory of urbicide I elaborate – comprises a conceptual framework to understand what is at stake, politically and conceptually, in the destruction of buildings. This framework is, I believe, generalisable across the spectrum of widespread and deliberate destruction of the built environment. I hope others evaluate it in light of other cases. Ultimately, as the framework embodies an ethos of critical reflection on the non-anthropocentric dimensions of political violence, it is its appropriation, not its universal validation against the facts, that is important. Generalisability must then be understood not in terms of a classical correspondence theory of truth, but rather in terms of providing a conceptual framework through which to start to understand the multiple cases of the deliberate and widespread destruction of the built environment that I have been unable to comment on here.

It is also worth noting that this conceptual framework, and attendant ethos of critical reflection, is itself a politically inflected gesture. Why or how could we engage with the question of political violence without that engagement comprising a political gesture itself? Scholars provide many accounts of the abstractions and reifications that justify regarding their expertise as in some sense separated from the domain of the political. However, I find these accounts ultimately unconvincing. The conceptual framework I present here is oriented towards revealing the dynamics of urban destruction precisely so that these may be contested. My critique of anthropocentrism is advanced precisely because I believe that this perspective disempowers political thought from understanding the material dimensions of existence and, thus, the full range of political violence(s). Ultimately this argument is infused with a sense that the plurality that it sees as being threatened by urbicide is worth defending. It is in this sense that the argument that follows is inspired by William Connolly's 'ethos of pluralisation' (Connolly 1995).

Elements of this argument have been previously published as: 'Community as Heterogeneous Ensemble: Mostar and Multiculturalism', *Alternatives*, 27:1 (2002), copyright (c) 2002 by Lynne Rienner Publishers; 'Urbicide in Bosnia' in S. Graham, (ed.), *Cities, War and Terrorism: Towards an Urban Geopolitics* (Oxford: Blackwell, 2004), pp. 154–171, copyright (c) 2004 by Blackwell Publishing;

'Against Anthropocentrism: The Destruction of the Built Environment as a Distinct Form of Political Violence', *Review of International Studies*, 32:3 (2006), pp. 419–437, copyright (c) 2006 by Cambridge University Press.

The writing of this book has been made possible through the support and critical engagement of a number of people. The ideas in this argument have been developed over a number of years and contexts: two universities; a number of conferences and workshops; and in conversation with colleagues and friends. I apologise, therefore, if I overlook any of those who played a part in the genesis of this work. Over the course of writing, Tarak Barkawi, Simon Caney, Howard Caygill, William Connolly, Marieke de Goede, Mick Dillon, Stefan Elbe, Stephen Graham, Louiza Odysseos, Andras Riedlmayer, Erna Rijsdijk, Michael Shapiro, Martin Shaw, Rob Walker and several anonymous referees have provided valuable comments and/or encouragement.

In addition to these valued sources of commentary several people have played a more sustained and central role in the production of this argument. David Campbell guided the initial formulation of the intellectual problematic and provided much-needed advice and encouragement at key junctures. Debbie Lisle's advice and comments have been important in shaping and sustaining this project from its inception in Keele. My parents, Ruth and Tim, have provided both the financial and emotional support necessary to complete this manuscript. They also provided the initial ethical and political groundwork out of which my contestation of forms of violence such as urbicide ultimately grew. Finally, this book is dedicated to my wife Alis and daughter Erin. Without their support, encouragement and, ultimately, patience this argument simply would have not been possible. I hope that you can accept this book as some compensation for the evenings and weekends I spent holed up in my office. As I have noted before, Foucault once stated that life 'is worthwhile insofar as we don't know what will be the end'. I look forward to the multiple possibilities life holds for us as a family.

Obviously, it remains to say that any error or opacity in this argument is entirely my own fault.

Introduction

The destruction of shared space

> Aida Mušanovic ... had visited the hospital in Sarajevo and had seen the carnage brought by the war. Yet the burning of the library struck her with a special horror. In the fire of the National Library, she realised that what she was experiencing was not only war but also something else. The centuries of culture that fell back in ash onto the besieged city revealed a secret.
>
> (Sells 1996, 4–5)

'There is no more Old Bridge'[1]

At around 10.15 a.m. on 9 November 1993, the Old Bridge, or *Stari Most*, at Mostar, Bosnia-Herzegovina, collapsed into the River Neretva. The bridge had spanned the Neretva for over 400 years linking East Mostar (and the Bosnian hinterlands) to West Mostar (and routes to the Adriatic Coast). Having survived natural disasters and wars, the bridge had finally been destroyed by Bosnian Croat forces intent on the ethnic division of the city of Mostar. Despite having previously worked to protect the *Stari Most* from Bosnian Serb shells, the Croatian Defence Council (HVO, the Bosnian Croat Army) subjected the bridge to a sustained bombardment. Beginning on 8 November, the HVO relentlessly shelled the bridge. Sarajevo newspapers reported that by the time the *Stari Most* actually collapsed it had been hit by over sixty shells (Traynor 1993, 10).

The *Stari Most* itself had already suffered attacks from the Bosnian Serb Army during the early stages of the Bosnian War. The Bosnian Serbs had both shelled the bridge and made it impassable due to sniper fire before they were forced into retreat in late 1992. However, it was the second phase of the war in Mostar, in which the Bosnian Croats turned on their former Bosnian Muslim/Bosniac allies, that was the most vicious.[2] According to a strategy sponsored by Croatian president Franjo Tudjman, the territory occupied by the Bosnian Croats would become the statelet of 'Herceg-Bosna'. Herceg-Bosna would be a 'homeland' for the Bosnian Croats, eventually joined to the 'homeland' of Croatia itself. Mostar was to be the capital of this entity. But in order for this to be possible, the future capital of Herceg-Bosna had to be cleansed of 'non-Croats'. Thus from May 1993 non-Croats were expelled from the western/right bank of Mostar. In effect, this meant that most Bosnian Muslims/Bosniacs fled West Mostar fearing for their lives, although a substantial number were murdered, sent to concentration camps, or simply disappeared (Beaumont 1996, 12; Eagar 1995, 19). This forcing of the town's Bosnian Muslims into the old part of the town effectively created a ghetto. For the next six months this ghetto was subjected to one of the most intense siege bombardments of the Bosnian War.

When the *Stari Most* itself became impassable due to sniper fire, the town was effectively divided: Bosnian Croats on the western/right bank, Bosnian Muslims/Bosniacs on the eastern/left bank.[3] A framework of wood and tyres had been erected by residents of Mostar around the *Stari Most* in order to try to save it from destruction. However, the *Stari Most* was the last structure bearing witness to a unified (and, therefore, 'ethnically mixed') Mostar. Hence, on 8 November 1993 the HVO began shelling the *Stari Most*. The shelling continued through to the next day, when the bridge finally collapsed (Traynor 1993, 10). In this way the HVO destroyed the last link that showed that the districts on the left and right banks of the Neretva comprised elements of a single, plural entity. That is, they destroyed the remaining testament to the ethnically mixed character of Mostar. The destruction of the bridge gave credence (at least in the eyes of its destroyers) to the notion of the existence of two homogeneous enclaves. As such, this destruction created the conditions under which the Bosnian Croats could claim an ethnic separateness from the Bosnian Muslims/Bosniacs.

The *Stari Most*

Mostar is a small town in western Herzegovina, the southern province of Bosnia-Herzegovina (Malcolm 1994, 3). It lies to the south-west of the capital Sarajevo, straddling the River Neretva (which runs from north to south) at a narrow point in the Neretva Canyon. The Neretva has acted historically as a barrier to movement from east to west across Bosnia. The river canyon thus divides off eastern Herzegovina, Montenegro, Serbia, Bulgaria and, ultimately Turkey, from western Herzegovina and the Adriatic Coast. Though there is a long history of settlement in the Neretva Valley, Mostar itself developed precisely because it was the site of a bridge across the river which provided a route by which traders, travellers and armies could pass from east to west and vice versa (Malcolm 1994, 3; Pasic 1995, 7).

According to historians, there has been a bridge at Mostar since medieval times. The earliest record of a bridge is in 1452 (Jezernik 1995, 472, 481). This medieval bridge was wooden, 'suspended from chains' and, according to the historian and geographer Katib Çelebi, 'swayed to such an extent that people feared for their lives in crossing it' (quoted in *Ibid.*, 472). The bridge was constructed to 'meet the needs of regional traffic'. Such traffic included 'Turkish troops [who] crossed it when conquering western Herzegovina and Dalmatia', and presumably traders taking goods to the Adriatic Coast to be shipped to ports around the Mediterranean (*Ibid.*, 481).

Božidar Jezernik contends that the precarious construction of the wooden bridge conditioned the early development of Mostar. Though settlement occurred on both banks of the river around the ends of the bridge, the town developed on the left/ eastern bank. The development of residential districts and markets on the left bank is attributed to the fact that only those who needed to cross the bridge actually did (Jezernik 1995, 481). The state of the bridge brought much of the flow of traffic to a halt at the eastern end of the bridge, resulting in the accumulation of settlers. This account would seem to indicate that the flow of traffic in the region was principally from east to west (which is indeed the direction in which the colonising forces of the Ottoman Empire flowed at that time). The bridge both enabled such a flow, and yet inhibited it in such a way as to lead to a concentration of settlement on the left/eastern bank.

Mostar came under Ottoman rule from the latter half of the fifteenth century.[4] By the middle of the sixteenth century the wooden bridge had become impassable and so the citizens of Mostar asked Sultan Suleiman the Magnificent (1520–1566) 'to authorise the building of a better, more substantial bridge across the Neretva' (Jezernik 1995, 472). This bridge was built according to the plans of Mimar (architect) Haireddin, and was completed in 1566. The bridge itself was a single span stone structure, measuring 28.7 metres wide (Pasic 1995, 14). The span stood some 19 metres above the river (Jezernik 1995, 470).[5] The bridge was referred to as the 'Great Bridge', and later, after the building of further bridges over the Neretva, became known as the 'Old Bridge' (*'Stari Most'*).

The bridge itself was built by a heterogeneous group of craftsmen. Michael Sells characterises the project to build the *Stari Most* as 'multireligious' (Sells 1996, 94). Although the project was overseen by the local representatives of the Ottoman Empire, it was executed by 'engineers and artisans' from a range of cultural backgrounds. According to Sells, the composition of the workforce is symbolic, a portent of the heterogeneity that characterised Mostar under Ottoman, and later Austro-Hungarian, rule.

The building of the *Stari Most* was fundamental to the town of Mostar in several ways. Firstly, as I have already noted, until the building of the stone bridge the crossing was dangerous, and, as the majority of traffic was from east to west, the settlement of Mostar was established on the left/eastern bank of the river so that only those needing to cross did so. The building of the *Stari Most* had a profound effect on the settlement on the eastern bank of the Neretva insofar as it made possible expansion onto the western bank. For the settlement to become a town, such expansion would need to occur. Moreover, if such expansion were to occur it would be because of the increasing importance of the settlement at Mostar. The bridge guaranteed this importance by providing a valuable river crossing over the Neretva. The *Stari Most* thus ensured the emergence of Mostar as a regional centre. Moreover, as the settlement expanded, the *Stari Most* made it possible to call this community – effectively divided into two by the Neretva Canyon – one, single town.

Secondly, the bridge gave a name to this growing community. Russian linguist Gil'ferding argues that the inhabitants of Mostar referred to themselves as 'Mostari', or 'bridge keepers' (Jezernik 1995, 483). Originally this term would have referred to the garrisons that protected and controlled this vital trade route. However, it appears that the use of this term was broadened out to include the inhabitants of the town. The Mostari, or inhabitants of Mostar, were thus collectively 'keepers of the bridge'.[6] This name was contracted to give the place name 'Mostar'. The use of 'Mostari' to refer to the inhabitants predicates the evolution of the town of Mostar upon the existence of the bridge across the Neretva. This naming thus established the centrality of the bridge over the Neretva in constituting the community of Mostar (Pasic 1994, 61).

Thirdly, it is also possible to note how the bridge became a focus for the everyday life of the town of Mostar. 'A number of customs and practices were … connected with the Old Bridge', most famously that of the young men of the town jumping from the top of the parapet into the river below (Pasic 1995, 19). This was a ritual which developed into a tourist attraction, with children earning money from visitors for their 'daring' jumps (Traynor 1993, 10). Other rituals also focused on this structure. One account of the centrality of the bridge to the life of Mostar suggests that it was traditional for the bridegroom to carry his bride over the bridge (Eagar 1995, 19). In addition, the bridge itself was originally guarded by a garrison stationed in its towers. This garrison had its own space for religious observance (a *mesjid*) in the tower on the left bank. Until the occupation of Bosnia by the Austro-Hungarian Empire in 1878, the garrison muezzin 'called worshippers to prayer while standing on the highest point of the bridge' (Pasic 1995, 19).

Finally, the *Stari Most* as a monumental, symbolic building that could be visited, seen, or conserved became synonymous with the town of Mostar. The bridge itself was taken to represent the essence of Mostar – a town composed of two parts divided by a river canyon, united by this spectacular bridge that in its very construction bore witness to the plural character of the community of Mostar. The bridge thus spoke to Mostaris, symbolising the tradition of plural co-existence that constituted the community in which they lived. Moreover, the Old Bridge was taken to represent a history and ethos that was characteristically 'Bosnian' – constituting a sign to 'the world' of Bosnia's rich cultural heritage. The *Stari Most* thus became a prolific sign, circulating in everyday representations of both Mostar and Bosnia-Herzegovina. As an image it appeared on Bosnian postage stamps and bank notes, tourist literature and book covers (Gunzburger Makas 2005, 60).[7]

The destruction of the *Stari Most* as exemplary event

The siege and destruction of the *Stari Most* became an exemplary event in the 1992–95 Bosnian War. The assault on, and destruction of this Ottoman bridge was taken to be representative of the larger violence that was consuming the former Yugoslav republic of Bosnia-Herzegovina. Pictures of the bridge prior to destruction, clad in rubber tyres and a makeshift wooden roof, served as a metaphor for 'ethnic division'. These images of the assault on a bridge literally linking east and west gave graphic representation to the notion that the former Yugoslavia was being forcibly 'unmade'.[8] The final collapse of the bridge into the river it had spanned for over 400 years was captured on video by local news media and broadcast around the world. The fleeting image of the end of this outstanding example of cultural heritage became an icon of the savagery and tragedy of the 1992–95 Bosnian War. The footage of crumbling stone represented in a concise and vivid manner the failure of both international and Bosnian attempts to contest nationalism and maintain a 'multi-ethnic' state. The collapsing/collapsed *Stari Most* was an image which immediately communicated to the world the finality with which Bosnia was being divided/partitioned. It was a superlative demonstration of the manner in which ethnic cleansing constituted an erasure of identity from territory. These images were thus burdened with the representation of both Bosnia and its war, taken to represent the destruction and division of a country with a rich and diverse cultural heritage.

The *Stari Most* was taken by many observers to symbolise the history and achievements of Bosnian society. The bridge's history condensed in one structure the hybridity of Bosnian society. Built by the Ottoman Empire, linking the territories east of the river to those west of the river, the bridge spanned and bound together supposedly heterogeneous cultural communities.[9] The *Stari Most* thus represented for many people not only the town of Mostar, but the nature of Bosnian society. Bosnia was seen as a bridge between the European West and the Ottoman East, where Orthodox, Catholic and Muslim communities co-existed: a meeting place in which plural cultures were interwoven (Sells 1996, 113). In being identified as that which captured the essence of Bosnian culture, the *Stari Most* was thus elevated to the status of cultural monument. It was taken to represent the common heritage of all Bosnians. As an example of such cultural heritage, it was taken to express the highest achievements of Bosnian culture. Moreover, it was acclaimed by many people as an exemplary achievement of human culture.[10] The *Stari Most* was thus a symbol of the heritage of humanity, an exemplar of the manner in which heterogeneous groups are bound into communities. This metaphor of bridging that found concrete form in the *Stari Most* exercised a strong grip upon the political imaginaries of those who observed, participated in and fell victim to the Bosnian conflict. It was hoped that the image of the bridge, spanning and thus binding separate groups, could serve as the guiding principle by which the heterogeneous communities of Bosnia could once again be assembled into a pluralist state.

The assault on the *Stari Most* placed such hopes in jeopardy. The images of the eventual destruction of the bridge were taken by observers to constitute a radical problematisation of all that the *Stari Most* had previously symbolised. As the arch collapsed, so too it seemed did all that the bridge had represented: a common Bosnian heritage; the possibility of the co-existence of heterogeneous identities; and ultimately, human achievement. For observers of the Bosnian War, the destruction of the *Stari Most* thus condensed, in a series of graphic images, the proof that Bosnia was, as the prevalent political imaginary held, a dark and primitive place in which it was no longer possible for supposedly separate ethnic groups to live together peacefully. Images of the siege and destruction of the *Stari Most* were thus taken to represent all that was at stake in Bosnia: plural society; continued co-existence; common humanity. In this way, images of the collapse of a 400-year-old bridge became exemplary, even iconic, of the Bosnian War.

The act of destruction itself seemed, for observers of the Bosnian War, to exemplify the logics of violence of the Bosnian War. Insofar as the bridge was recognised as an outstanding example of Bosnian cultural heritage, it represented the highest achievement of Bosnian society. Its history captured the complexity and heterogeneity of Bosnian society. Destruction of the *Stari Most* epitomised the manner in which the history of co-existence that characterised Bosnian society was being forcibly erased. Moreover, since the bridge was recognised as being part of the common heritage of humanity, the destruction brought about by the HVO gunners was deemed by many observers of the conflict to be an assault upon humanity itself. In destroying a building deemed to express the highest possible achievements of which human society is capable, the HVO were taken to be declaring that humanity and its achievements were no longer of any concern to them in their fight to create the mini-statelet of Herceg-Bosna.

The act of destruction was thus taken by many observers to demonstrate the supposed 'barbarity' of the Bosnian War. The very act of destruction itself appeared to resonate with 'savagery'. The destruction of a 400-year-old bridge that held little or no strategic value was taken to be excessive. This excess was confirmed in the manner in which the HVO shelled the bridge until it collapsed. The bridge itself had been impassable for some time (due to the damage inflicted by sporadic shells and the continual exposure to sniper fire of those attempting to cross the bridge). There was, therefore, no need to actually destroy it. The HVO action seemed vindictive and cruel and thus bore the hallmarks of savagery.

The destruction was also taken by observers of the conflict to be an exemplary instance of the emerging war on culture that was integral to the process of ethnic cleansing. Ethnic cleansing was not accomplished simply by the killing or displacement of those ethnic groups that threatened the homogeneity of a given ethnic territory. The destruction of cultural property was integral to the campaign to create homogeneous ethnic communities. Thus the seemingly savage and wanton destruction of symbolic buildings went hand in hand with massacres and displacement. This led to the destruction of buildings on a massive scale in Bosnia, well beyond what might be expected as collateral damage from a campaign to 'cleanse' a territory, or as acceptable damage from the targeting of strategically important structures.

The destruction of such symbolic buildings and other cultural artefacts can be understood, following Andras Riedlmayer, as a process of 'killing memory' (Riedlmayer 1995a). In destroying the *Stari Most*, Riedlmayer argues, the HVO were destroying the historical record, or collective memory, of the co-existence that had characterised Bosnian society for over 400 years. The destruction of the *Stari Most* is exemplary in this regard for the clarity with which it displays such destruction of the collective memory of co-existence. The bridge itself had united the town, enabling it to develop. All citizens had used the bridge in their daily lives and shared in rituals based around it. As such, the bridge held a rich symbolic position in all of their lives. To destroy the bridge is to deny this shared history. And this co-existence must be violently denied if one wants to build a new history based on the impossibility of co-existence and the demand for separate territories. Once the Neretva Canyon stood unbridged, the idea of separate communities possessing separate territories seemed much more natural. Nor could this separateness be contested, as the symbols that bore witness to the history of co-existence had disappeared.

A campaign of violence

Dwelling on the image – despite its iconic grip upon the imagination of those observing the conflict – of the besieged/destroyed *Stari Most*, however, reduces a complex conflict to the broad brushstrokes of metaphors for barbarity, division and the death of ideals such as co-existence and plurality. Furthermore, emphasising the symbolic dimension of this event – however iconic it might be – serves to mask the fact that the *Stari Most* is but one instance of a wider campaign of violence against the built environment in Bosnia. Indeed, the destruction of the *Stari Most* was embedded in a long campaign of deliberate destruction of Bosnia's urban environment by Bosnian Serb and HVO gunners which was not limited to such symbolic buildings alone.

Thus whilst the destruction the *Stari Most* offered a photogenic icon for a number of discourses circulating in the context of the Bosnian War, it should be seen as simply one instance in a wider campaign against the built environment that characterised the 1992–95 Bosnian War. In Mostar the old town, or *Stari Grad*, was shelled continuously following the beginning of ethnic cleansing by the HVO in summer 1992. Moreover, in Mostar the *Stari Most* was merely the most famous (and the last) of all the bridges to be destroyed. The bridges across the Neretva, as elsewhere, were not simply rendered impassable but razed to the ground.

In Sarajevo, the National Library and the Oriental Institute were destroyed by Bosnian Serb shells. The shells set the National Library alight and, as the collections burnt, the people of Sarajevo attempted to save the books by hand (Riedlmayer 2002). These events became landmarks in the siege of Sarajevo. Concerned observers, at a loss to understand the mentality of those who could, at the end of the twentieth century, burn books, mourned the loss of valuable collections of manuscripts. In both cases, the buildings were targeted deliberately and nearby buildings were left relatively untouched (Riedlmayer 1995b). This deliberate targeting of landmark buildings was confirmed even by those who were shelling Sarajevo:

> [I]n September 1992, BBC reporter Kate Adie interviewed Serbian gunners on the hillsides overlooking Sarajevo and asked them why they had been shelling the Holiday Inn, the hotel where all of the foreign correspondents were known to stay. The officer commanding the guns apologised profusely, explaining they had not meant to hit the hotel, but had been aiming at the roof of the National Museum behind it.
>
> (Riedlmayer 1995a)

The National Museum was badly damaged, though its collections survived. The apologies of the Bosnian Serb gunners highlighted the manner in which buildings themselves had become the targets of the ethnic cleansers.

Across Bosnia, mosques were destroyed by both Bosnian Serb and Bosnian Croat forces. Catholic and Orthodox churches were also attacked, though with less vigour. A pattern emerged in the destruction of mosques. Typically a mosque would be targeted for shelling, despite its lack of strategic significance. After occupation of a town, the mosque would be dynamited and, in some cases, the rubble removed. In this way, the urban environment was ethnically cleansed. The physical traces of a multi-ethnic history were removed, creating green fields, or car parks, in their wake (Riedlmayer 2002).

Such was the fate of the Ferhadija Mosque in Banja Luka. On 6 May 1993, the Ferhadija Mosque was destroyed by an explosion. Witnesses alleged that the Bosnian Serb Army was responsible: the streets around the mosque had been closed off and army trucks were seen in front of the mosque. After the initial explosion, the minaret remained standing. However, the Bosnian Serb authorities determined that the minaret would be demolished as it was unsafe. The minaret was demolished after midnight on 8 May. The remains of the mosque were removed by trucks to an unknown destination and the vacant lot turned into a car park (Gusic 1995; Husarska 1998; Peric 1999; Riedlmayer 2002).

However, it was not only symbolic buildings or significant elements of Bosnian cultural heritage that were targeted for destruction. The urban fabric of Bosnia came under a relentless assault. As Nicholas Adams notes, along with 'mosques, churches [and] synagogues', 'markets, museums, libraries, cafes, in short, the places where people gather to live out their collective life, have been the focus of ... attacks' (Adams 1993). In Sarajevo the list of target buildings included the central post office, apartment buildings, office buildings and markets (Association of Architects DAS – SABIH 1993). Whereas destruction of ancient bridges, museums and mosques can be understood as an assault upon the symbols of ethnic identity in Bosnia, the deliberate destruction of such mundane, profane buildings is more opaque. What is clear in such violence is that the buildings themselves were the target, and the violence was disproportionate to killing or displacing inhabitants.

The global destruction of built environments

The deliberate destruction of both symbolic and mundane elements of the built environment is not, however, confined to the 1992–95 Bosnian War. Such destruction can be seen in a number of other historical and contemporary instances. In *Axis Rule in Occupied Europe*, Raphael Lemkin notes that one of the earliest examples that could be considered to come under the concept of 'genocide' is the destruction of Carthage – during the course of which the city was razed to the ground and, supposedly, salt was then ploughed into the ground in order to prevent return to, or reconstruction of, the city (Lemkin 1994, 79). In the assault on Carthage, the city itself was a target, with the destruction exceeding that required in order to destroy or displace the inhabitants. Such destruction has been visited on a number of other cities throughout history, most notably Dresden, Hiroshima and Nagasaki. The destruction visited upon these cities was disproportionate to the objectives of the conflict in which they occurred, indicating that the city itself, rather than discrete installations relating to the pursuit of war, was the target (Markusen and Kopf 1995, 51–182).

Moreover, such targeting of built environments is not confined to situations of inter-state conflict. In the post-Cold War era, the deliberate destruction of the built environment in intra-state conflict has captured the attention of international observers. Russian tactics during the Chechen campaigns of 1994–96 and 1999–2000 and Israeli house destruction policies in the Occupied Territories have received particular attention in this regard. Russian assaults on the Chechen capital, Grozny, during the 1994–96 and 1999–2000 Chechen conflicts effectively reduced sections of the city to rubble.[11] Whilst Russian commanders argued that such actions were necessary in the face of stubborn urban guerrilla resistance, many argued that the destruction was out of all proportion to the military aims of the conflict. This destruction was not limited to the capital city alone and two Russian offensives between 1994 and 2000 left substantial damage to towns and villages across Chechnya. This assault on Chechnya's buildings could be said to be in keeping with the Russian tactic of 'rubbleisation' developed in the Afghan war (Goodson 2001, 60). Larry Goodson (2001, 94) notes that '[a]t one point or another ... virtually everything in Afghanistan has been a target. Cities, towns, villages, houses, mosques and minarets, schools, hospitals, industrial structures, other buildings, roads, bridges, orchards, and fields have all been damaged or destroyed during combat.' It should be noted that 'rubbleisation' is different to a scorched earth tactic, insofar as the former has as its goal the destruction of built environments and their infrastructure while the latter is deployed – often by a retreating force – to remove only those things of use to an opposing military force (food and materiel, largely). Whilst a scorched earth policy may destroy significant buildings, it is not designed for the purpose of destroying all buildings. Rubbleisation, as its name suggests, is intended to reduce the built environment to rubble.

Israeli house demolitions in the Occupied Territories have similarly been viewed as deliberate destruction of the built environment. According to the Israel Defence Force (IDF), one purpose of such destruction is to remove bases of operation from Palestinian organisations seeking to attack Israeli targets. Demolitions are carried out in order to destroy both places of concealment for weapons and/or places from which attacks might be, or have been, launched or planned. For example, in the last two years the IDF has demolished a significant number of homes (in excess of 400) in the Rafah Refugee Camp. These demolitions are part of a widening of the so-called 'Philadelphi route' which runs along the Gaza–Egypt border. The IDF asserts that this widening is necessary in order to combat the smuggling of weapons across the border through underground tunnels (Israel Defence Forces 2004a). Those living in the refugee camp have contested this, arguing that the destruction is indiscriminate (McGreal 2004).

A significant number of house demolitions constitute the destruction of the homes of suicide bombers or those accused or found guilty of planning terrorist activities. The IDF argues that '[t]he demolition of houses of terrorists sends a message to suicide bombers and their accomplices that anyone who participates in terrorist activity will pay a price for their actions' (Israel Defence Forces 2004b). Such demolition has a disproportionate effect upon families of terrorists and thus could be taken to comprise a form of reprisal or collective punishment where the message sent, and the destruction committed, do not affect the perpetrator of the crime but the wider community from which they came. As such, these house destructions have been criticised as violations of the tenets of international law (Amnesty International 2004).

However, destruction of Palestinian houses and businesses are not only perpetrated by the IDF. During its occupation of the West Bank, Gaza Strip and East Jerusalem, Israel has pursued a strict planning policy with regard to Palestinian homes. Whilst appropriating land in East Jerusalem and the West Bank for Israeli settlements, the Israeli authorities have made it exceptionally difficult for Palestinians to obtain planning permission to build homes. Palestinian homes that are deemed to have been built without planning permission are frequently demolished (B'Tselem 2007b, 2007c). Some observers have argued that this 'administrative' destruction of homes is part of a wider project of appropriation and settlement of the Occupied Territories (Lein and Weizman 2002; Segal and Weizman 2003). According to Rafi Segal and Eyal Weizman (2003, 19), for example, 'the lengthy bureaucratic mechanisms of planning are … a part of … territorial conflicts' such as those between Israelis and the Palestinians. Destruction through discriminatory application of planning measures serves, often, as either a mechanism of land appropriation or a precursor to the imposition of construction projects that indigenous populations regard as forms of occupation, settlement or displacement.

Moreover, such projects of 'administrative' destruction are not confined to situations of conflict. Indeed, writers such as Ada Louise Huxtable and Marshal Berman have noted that the development of New York City was responsible for the bureaucratic destruction of substantial sections of the built environment in order to clear space for projects such as Robert Moses' Cross Bronx Expressway or the World Trade Center (Huxtable 1972; Berman 1996, 172–192). Mike Davis catalogues similar forms of destruction in his *Dead Cities* (Davis 2002), while Porteous and Smith (2001) pursue this theme somewhat further, arguing that the contemporary era is witnessing the 'global destruction of home' through administrative projects such as dam building.

Understanding violence against built environments

Despite recognition that the built environment has been the target of widespread attacks, the nature of such violence remains largely unexplored. Indeed, the destruction of built environments remains an opaque aspect of political violence often regarded as either secondary to programs for killing and displacing individuals or the product of the wanton behaviour of specific soldiers. As such, this widespread phenomenon is not treated as a class of political violence in its own right, following its own logics with its own entailments. In an era seemingly defined by the spectacular suicide demolition of the World Trade Center, it would seem, however, that closer examination and deeper understanding of this phenomenon is an urgent intellectual demand. I want to respond to this demand by returning to a specific response to the loss of the *Stari Most* in Mostar; a response that I think opens up productive avenues for thinking about the global destruction of built environments.

Shortly after the destruction of Mostar's *Stari Most*, Croatian writer Slavenka Drakulic wrote an 'obituary' for *Stari Most* in the *New Republic* in which she attempted to understand the meaning of the violence against an element of the built environment (Drakulic 1993, 14–15). Drakulic's 'elegy' has exercised a strong grip on the imagination of those who have sought to understand the meaning of the destruction of the Old Bridge. Both the architect responsible for the post-war reconstruction of Mostar's historic core (including the *Stari Most*), Amir Pasic, and UNESCO have seen Drakulic's thoughts as an evocative enunciation of the fundamental issues that lie behind the destruction of a building.[12] The elegy is a broad meditation on the symbolism of the *Stari Most*, the nature of memory and the meaning of the destruction of buildings. It is this latter aspect which is of direct bearing upon any attempt to understand the nature of violence against, or destruction of, elements of the built environment.

Writing about the relation between a photograph of the space left between the two banks of the Neretva by the collapse of the *Stari Most* and a photograph of a Bosnian Muslim woman with her throat cut (after the massacre at Stupni Dol), Drakulic (1993, 15) asks, 'Why do I feel more pain looking at the image of the destroyed bridge than the image of the woman?' She goes on to reply:

> Perhaps it is because I see my own mortality in the collapse of the bridge, not in the death of the woman. We expect people to die. We count on our own lives to end. The destruction of a … [bridge] … is something else. The bridge … was built to outlive us … Because it was the product of both individual creativity and collective experience, it transcended our individual destiny. *A dead woman is one of us – but the bridge is all of us.*
>
> (Drakulic 1993, 15, my emphasis)

At first glance, this assertion appears counterintuitive: it seems to contradict our most deeply held values. Drakulic's assertion requires us to accept that it is possible for the destruction of a building to be more significant than the death of a human being. Indeed Drakulic's comments are a radical challenge to the anthropocentric perspective from which destruction in Bosnia has been viewed. Her remarks require an inversion of that understanding of the world which portrays subjects living out their lives centre-stage against an ephemeral background. Instead, Drakulic is suggesting that it is 'life' which is ephemeral and that the 'world' must be understood as being constituted by that which was previously thought to be the mere background for activity: buildings. Thus Drakulic is arguing that it is not sufficient to regard the bridge as a part of a material backdrop against which lives are played out, or as equipment instrumental to the pursuance of this 'life'.

For Drakulic, the *Stari Most* was more than a simple thing which satisfied a set of needs and calculations. It was more than a response to the logistical problem of how to traverse a canyon. To see the *Stari Most* as such is to misunderstand what it is. For Drakulic, the bridge must be understood as something which is *experienced collectively*. That which is experienced collectively offers the collective the possibility of *duration* as a community: in short, both a future and a past. Drakulic is arguing that, without the bridge as a collectively experienced structure, the community of Mostar does not have the possibility of being the particular, heterogeneous community that it had been prior to November 1993. When the *Stari Most* was destroyed, that particular community no longer had any durability and, hence, any future.

Drakulic should not be understood to be arguing that 'human life' is unimportant. However, she is arguing that existence is only possible as a community. The existence of the individual is *in* community and the possibility of this community is founded on the structures that give that community its future. Members of the community come and go within the frame of the durability, the possibility of the future, provided by this built structure. Drakulic sums this up in the assertion 'the bridge is all of us'. Only in this framework of 'us' am 'I' ('you'/'(s)he'/'it') possible. And, furthermore, the foundation of 'us' is not to be found in some form of explicit or implicit contract, but in that which gives this particular 'us' (in this case the 'us' that comprised Mostar pre-November 1993) durability: the *Stari Most* (amongst other structures).

Drakulic's 'elegy' thus offers a provocative understanding of the destruction of elements of the built environment. For Drakulic, such destruction comprises the negation of the conditions of possibility of the communities within which individuals have their existence. Destroying the Old Bridge radically contests the existence of individuals in Mostar as residents of specific, plural community. Such destruction brings into existence two separate communities and thus brings into being very different individuals – ones who are Croat or Muslim prior to being Bosnian or Mostari.

To destroy a building is, thus, to destroy that which comprises the condition of possibility of a community in the context of which individuated modes of existence are possible. This assault on community is one that is intended to reshape individual identity from one that exists in a state of plurality to one for whom homogeneity is the norm. In this sense Drakulic asks us to understand the destruction of the built environment as a fundamental aspect of the campaign to rewrite the ethnic-national geography of Bosnia. Destruction of buildings is thus not incidental to, but underlies, the campaign to homogenise populations. Such destruction destroys buildings that are constitutive of (provide conditions of possibility of durability of) plural communities in order to naturalise the emergent ethnic enclaves. The destruction of buildings is thus constitutive of communities, and individuals, for whom homogeneity – and hostility to difference – is the norm.

Contesting anthropocentric understandings of political violence

Drakulic's elegy requires, however, that we take the destruction of buildings to be at least as central to the program of ethnic-nationalist violence as the killing and displacement of people. Such understanding of the destruction of buildings represents, however, an inversion of the usual conceptual schema according to which political violence has been understood. Such conceptual schema are dominated by (a desire to mitigate) the harm suffered by individuals and are thus predicated upon images and events concerning the destruction of human life, the displacement of individuals/groups or the misery that human hatred can bring about. Thus news reports such as ITN's from the concentration camps of Omarska and Trnopolje, in which starved Bosniac men stare out from behind barbed wire, encapsulate conflict in iconic images of individual human suffering (Campbell 2002a). In short, such understandings refract political violence through an anthropocentric imaginary.

The rubble of conflicts such as the 1992–95 Bosnian War has been similarly seen through the lens of anthropocentrism. The destruction of the urban fabric of Bosnia has been interpreted as a phenomenon contingent to, and thus dependent upon, the violence perpetrated against the people of Bosnia. Thus the rubble of Bosnia is an element of genocide or war, rather than a phenomenon in its own right. And yet, as Kate Adie's interview with the Bosnian Serb gunners shows, we should be wary of 'thinking in terms of "collateral damage", incidental to the general mayhem of warfare' (Riedlmayer 1995a). The urban fabric of Bosnia was targeted deliberately, a fact attested to by the manner in which the violence against the architecture of Bosnia was disproportionate to the task of killing the people of Bosnia. This is the significance of the number of missiles used to destroy the *Stari Most*. In hitting a strategically insignificant, impassable, and effectively defaced bridge with such excessive force the HVO indicated that this violence was intended to destroy the building itself. The bridge was the target and nothing less than its collapse would satisfy the HVO.

'It is the expected thing to say that people come first', notes Nicholas Adams. 'And they do, but the survival of architecture and urban life are important to the survival of people' (Adams 1993, 390). The deliberate destruction of buildings poses questions equally as fundamental as those posed by the destruction of human life. Our political imaginaries are dominated by images of politics as the preserve of powerful elites and violent militias. We perceive the key to resolutions of conflicts to lie in the negotiations between the representatives of governments, in war crimes prosecutions and attempts to encourage multi-ethnic states. And yet such anthropocentric political imaginaries obscure the fact that the fundamental problematic at the heart of such conflicts is the construction of durable plural communities. If, following Drakulic, the destruction of urban fabric is the destruction of such a durable community, then understanding the core of such conflicts rests upon understanding the destruction of buildings. This is the logic of the destruction that is most dramatically highlighted in the collapse of the *Stari Most*, the 'secret' that Aida Mušanovic saw revealed in the ashes that fell from the burning National Library.

The political question

If we follow Drakulic, the deliberate destruction of elements of the built environment – such as the *Stari Most* – comprises an assault on the conditions of possibility (referred to by Drakulic under the rubric of 'durability') of community. Community represents an experience of plurality, of being with others who are distinguishable as such. Moreover, this being-with-others defines the core of that which we understand as political. That is to say, in defining a question, problem or event as political, it is asserted that, at its core, this question, problem or event concerns the negotiation of the problematic of being-with-others. The political is thus that which concerns the problematic of being-with-others. Political violence is the deployment of violence to influence the nature of being-with-others in a specific instance. The destruction of buildings thus comprises a fundamentally political form of violence. Scholarly argument responding to such violence will itself be fundamentally political theory: both in the sense that it relates to the core problematic of the political but also in the manner in which it seeks to understand this violence precisely to contest its particular, exclusionary assault on plural community.

In what follows I will, through an analysis of the destruction of built environments, look beyond the anthropocentric horizons of contemporary understandings of political violence in order to address this fundamental political question of being-with-others. I will show that it is only if we understand the manner in which the material, built environment is that which constitutes the possibility of community, or being-with-others, that we understand the reason for its destruction: to eradicate such being-with-others in favour of being in homogeneous enclaves. Moreover, understanding the manner in which destruction of the built environment comprises an assault on plural community enables us to discern the politics of such destruction. Such destruction serves as one of the central elements in exclusionary political forces, such as (though not restricted to) ethnic nationalism. Ethnic nationalism (and similar exclusionary forces) seeks to deny alterity and generate homogeneous enclaves hostile to all forms of difference. In an era of global interconnections, such campaigns of disavowal of alterity represent a reactionary force responsible for considerable levels of political violence. Understanding and contesting the dynamics that lie at the heart of their political imaginaries is thus an urgent task.

The argument

This book will be concerned, then, with the deliberate destruction of the built environment. I will contend that such destruction comprises a distinct form of violence that can best be understood through the concept of *urbicide*. Urbicide, I will contend, refers to the destruction of buildings as a condition of possibility of being-with-others. Chapter 1 will set the scene for the introduction of the concept of urbicide, with an examination of three common interpretations of the destruction of buildings: the military; the symbolic; and the metaphorical. These three interpretations will be shown to be lacking insofar as the destruction under examination exceeds the conceptual frameworks of each interpretation. A nascent literature has suggested that the concept of urbicide enables understanding of such violent campaigns against built environments.

Chapter 2 will comprise a detailed examination of the concept of urbicide. As a preliminary to a conceptual account of urbicide, the historical genesis of the concept will be detailed. The conceptual contours of urbicide will then be outlined. The relationship between urbicide and genocide will be examined. On the one hand, the deployment of a distinct concept of urbicide indicates that such urban destruction cannot be adequately explained as an instance of genocide. On the other hand, it will be argued that there are conceptual similarities between these two concepts that share the linguistic (and associated conceptual) element -*cide*. Just as genocide refers to the killing of individuals *qua* representatives of a particular group, so urbicide refers to the destruction of buildings *qua* representatives of urbanity. In other words, buildings are destroyed because they are constitutive of the existential condition known as 'urbanity'. 'Urbicide' thus refers to an assault on buildings in order to destroy urbanity. Through reference to urban studies scholars, urbanity will be defined as an existential condition of plurality or heterogeneity. Urbicide is thus an attack on buildings as the condition of possibility of a plurality or heterogeneity. The questions for the remainder of the argument will be twofold: how buildings constitute plurality/heterogeneity; and what the political and conceptual entailments of such destruction are.

Chapters 3 and 4 comprise a philosophical substantiation of the contentions made in Chapter 2. Specifically, these chapters offer a philosophical account of the way in which buildings could be said to be constitutive of a public or shared spatiality and, hence, of a plurality or heterogeneity. Such an interpretation is necessary if the contention that urbicide is an attack on buildings *qua* the condition of possibility of an existential heterogeneity (also referred to as 'urbanity') is to be given substance.

Chapter 3 unpacks the argument that buildings are constitutive of a shared, and hence plural, spatiality that we might say characterises urbanity. This argument will be advanced through a consideration of Martin Heidegger's understanding of the relationship between building and spatiality. Heidegger argues that, since buildings are fundamentally available to all, the spatiality constituted through buildings is fundamentally shared (or plural). Heidegger's explanation of the way in which buildings constitute a public spatiality thus substantiates the contention that buildings comprise the condition of possibility for an existential heterogeneity.

Chapter 4 comprises an examination of the nature of the heterogeneity, or being-with, implied in Heidegger's account of public spatiality. I will begin with an examination of Heidegger's proposition that being-with comprises an existential condition. Heidegger, however, does not fully develop the concept of co-existence (or heterogeneity). I will turn, therefore, to Jean-Luc Nancy's account of being-with, or community, in order to unpack the plurality/heterogeneity implicit in Heidegger's account of the public spatiality constituted by buildings. Community is, according to Nancy, a being-with-others and thus a being-with-difference (since others are always different, not the same). Nancy notes that such community comprises a heterogeneity which resists all attempts to impose singular political programs (since imposition of a singular political program would reduce difference to sameness). Urbicide thus comprises an attack on buildings as the condition of possibility of this community: an attempt to mask its irreducible difference and plurality and impose homogeneity.

Having outlined a philosophical understanding of the nature of urbicide – that is, how an assault on buildings can comprise a destruction of the plurality characteristic of urbanity – Chapters 5 and 6 will examine the political and conceptual stakes of such destruction. I will argue that there are two principal lessons to learn from urbicide. Firstly, politically, an analysis of urbicide demonstrates that violent regimes such as ethnic nationalism are characterised by the transformation of plurality into homogeneous enclaves: of agonism into antagonism. In other words, urbicidal political violence comprises a territorialisation of identity. This suggests that political violence in the city comprises not a displacement of population, but a carving out of enclaves. Secondly, conceptually, the phenomenon of urbicide entails a contestation of the anthropocentric perspective from which political violence has traditionally been understood. That is to say, urbicide entails a contestation of the traditional assumption that the subject of violence is the individual. An analysis of urbicide suggests that the buildings in and through which individuals live their lives are more than merely equipment for living. Indeed, they are constitutive of the nature of those lives. In this manner, I hope to be able to provide an account of the politics of urbicide that will cast new light upon the assumptions that political theorists and international relations scholars have made concerning what is at stake in instances of the destruction of the built environment.

After recapitulating and clarifying my argument, I will conclude by examining two key lessons that my analysis offers. Firstly, I will outline the endemic violence of the relationship between political programs seeking homogeneity and the city as a public, and thus heterogeneous, space. Secondly, I will look at the transformation of the nature of war in the post-Cold War era. As the world's population becomes increasingly urbanised it has been suggested that the dynamics of warfare will change to make the city and its residents its targets. As such, then, urbicide is a pressing problem for scholars of political violence in the twenty-first century.

1 Interpreting destruction of the built environment

In my Introduction, I noted that the deliberate destruction of the built environment – embodied in the destruction of Mostar's *Stari Most* – was both integral to the 1992–95 Bosnian War and widespread beyond the historico-geographical confines of that conflict. The destruction of the *Stari Most* itself became an iconic event that raised the destruction of the built environment onto the political agenda. And yet, perhaps paradoxically, the elevation of this event to iconic status served to deflect interest in the meaning of the widespread, deliberate destruction of the built environment towards the role that such destruction might play in the wider human tragedy of ethnic cleansing/genocide that was being played out across the Balkan Peninsula. That is, the destruction of the *Stari Most* was, by and large, interpreted as a symbol of the nature of the destruction of human lives and communities underway in Bosnia. In the Introduction I argued that such a reduction of the deliberate destruction of the built environment to a status ancillary to the killing of individuals was responsible for an avoidance of the question of understanding the destruction of the built environment as a form of violence in its own right. Such a failure to examine the widespread deliberate destruction of buildings as a distinct category of political violence might, I argued, be attributed to the anthropocentric lens through which conflict is customarily viewed.

I suggested, however, that Slavenka Drakulic's 'Mostar Bridge Elegy' offered an understanding of the destruction of elements of the built environment that treated such violence for its own sake rather than as an adjunct to human misery (Drakulic 1993). As such, it is a reversal of the anthropocentric lens that normally inflects enquiries into political violence. Drakulic understands the destruction of a building such as the *Stari Most* as the destruction of the possibility of duration of a specific community. When Drakulic (1993, 15) argues that the bridge is 'all of us', she is pointing to the role that the building has in constituting a given community. Community, according to Drakulic's argument, should be taken to be prior to individual identities. That is, it is only in and through belonging to a given community that a specific individual identity is constituted. For example, in destroying the bridge that constituted the possibility of duration for the plural community of pre-1993 Mostar, the Bosnian Croat Army (the HVO) was simultaneously destroying the conditions of possibility of individual identities that were Bosniac prior to being Bosnian-Croat or Bosnian-Muslim. That is, in attacking a plural community the conditions of possibility for individual identities that were not primarily determined by national affinity were also destroyed. Destroying such community and the identities it constitutes, by destroying its material foundations, is the precondition to establishing separate communities and identities.

Drakulic's understanding of the destruction of the built environment marks a radical inversion of the usual anthropocentric lens through which political violence is viewed. According to Drakulic, we must look not to the killing and displacement of individuals to understand the mechanisms of political violence at work in the 1992–95 Bosnian War, but rather to the way in which destruction of buildings comprised an eradication of the conditions of possibility for certain individual identities. Such an assertion indicates that we must treat destruction of the built environment as a form of political violence in its own right. I suggested that such a consideration is an urgent intellectual task, given the widespread destruction of the built environment across a range of historic-geographical contexts.

The principal flaw of Drakulic's commentary on the destruction of the *Stari Most* is the failure to treat the destruction of the bridge as an element of a wider deliberate assault on the built environment of Bosnia. As I noted in the Introduction, there is ample evidence for a number of campaigns of deliberate and widespread destruction of the built environment. Such campaigns are notable because it is not only historical and culturally significant buildings that are destroyed, but mundane, profane elements of the built environment as well.

Treating such violence as a deliberate assault on the built environment itself, rather than a by-product of an attack upon the inhabitants of a given built environment, requires us to recognise the widespread and deliberate nature of these attacks. I noted in my Introduction that a nascent literature has attempted such a treatment of destruction of the built environment under the rubric of 'urbicide'. In Chapter 2 I will examine this concept, its meanings and entailments. Elaborating the urbicidal nature of destruction of the built environment will sharpen the questions at the heart of an enquiry into understanding the destruction of the built environment. Through such a conceptual elaboration, I hope to indicate the principal issues that must be examined in order for an understanding of the meaning of such destruction to be explicated.

Before turning to the concept of urbicide, however, I want to demonstrate the necessity for such a concept. Whilst my Introduction may well have established a claim for consideration of the destruction of the built environment as an event in its own right, it is still necessary to demonstrate that 'urbicide' is the appropriate conceptual vehicle for such a consideration. It is possible to demonstrate this through the examination of three of the principal interpretations of the destruction of the built environment as an event in its own right. These three interpretations are not self-consciously defined as such. However, within the responses to the destruction of the built environment, I have identified three common interpretative themes. These three interpretations can be defined as (a) military, (b) symbolic, and (c) metaphorical. That is, these interpretations understand urban destruction through notions of (a) accepted norms/rationales of military action, (b) the destruction of buildings as elements of cultural heritage, and (c) the metaphor such destruction provides for political analysis.

Since I began my analysis of the destruction of the built environment with the case of the destruction of the *Stari Most*, I will concentrate largely on the manner in which these interpretations address the destruction of the built environment in the 1992–95 Bosnian War. However, I expect that these interpretations can be extrapolated to other examples in which the built environment comes under attack. This examination will show that these three interpretations fail to grasp the meaning of the destruction of the built environment in its entirety, leading me to conclude that only the concept of urbicide is fit for such a purpose.

Urban destruction as a product of military action

Perhaps the most conventional interpretation of assaults on the built environment conceives of the destruction as either collateral damage or the result of militarily necessary actions. 'Collateral damage', a term that came to prominence through its use by American commanders during the 1990–91 Gulf War, refers to 'incidental casualties and … property damage' (Rogers 1996, 15) that results from military action. On the whole, collateral damage is viewed as an undesirable, and yet possibly unavoidable, consequence of military action. The various laws of war relating to collateral damage can be interpreted as imposing two possible obligations on belligerents in a conflict. On the one hand, belligerents should restrict all collateral damage to accidental and unintended events. On the other hand, where damage is neither accidental nor unintended, it should be justifiable according to the rule of proportionality (i.e., that the risk of incidental civilian loss of life or damage to civilian property must be in proportion to the military gain expected from such an action). This rule will, of course, mean that some collateral damage is always both sustained and acceptable in military action. Collateral damage is thus either an unintended consequence of military action or the product of actions that satisfy the rule of proportionality. In the former case, where the destruction is an accident, the laws of war cannot be said to have been violated, and collateral damage is produced. In the latter case, the additional destruction may well have been foreseen and thus to an extent intentional. However, since the destruction is judged to be in proportion to (i.e., lesser than) the importance of the military goal achieved, the destruction is said to be 'collateral damage' attendant to legitimate war actions.

The destruction of buildings in Bosnia could thus be seen as collateral damage generated by the military action undertaken in the 1992–95 war. According to such an interpretation, the bridges, mosques and churches, houses, public buildings and so on, would have been destroyed either accidentally or in the course of legitimate military actions and be proportional to the goals aimed at or achieved. The simplest interpretation of the idea that urban destruction in Bosnia comprises collateral damage is that it is the consequence of munitions either missing their targets, or hitting other buildings on the way to their legitimate targets. A more complex interpretation might argue that the destruction of the urban environment was attendant (but proportional) to attempts to achieve certain military objectives. That is, given the nature of the combat in the Bosnian War (a large part of which was in urban environments), military action risked the destruction of buildings. Destruction of the built environment could then be explained as the consequence of such risks. This interpretation would depend upon the idea that the military actions in which such damage occurred were seeking legitimate military gains. Moreover, it would depend on the destruction being in an acceptable proportion to these legitimate military goals.

Such an idea introduces into the interpretation of urban destruction the idea of legitimate military action, or 'military necessity'. A narrow definition of 'military necessity' is found in the St Petersburg Declaration, which states that 'the only legitimate object which states should endeavour to accomplish during war is to weaken the military force of the enemy' (Friedman 1972, 192). A broader definition of military necessity might be 'those measures which are indispensable for securing the ends of the war, and which are lawful according to the modern laws and usages of war' (Lieber quoted in Rogers 1996, 4). Military necessity might then be said to be those actions indispensable for achieving the ends of a war. In respect of damage to the urban environment, it could be argued that certain buildings had to be destroyed in order to achieve certain military ends. The clearest case in which such an argument might apply is in relation to bridges.

Bridges are commonly taken to constitute military (as opposed to civilian) objects and thus are often destroyed in military conflict. A bridge, it is argued, comprises a link in communications, movement and logistics networks. In contemporary warfare, such networks are perceived to constitute a legitimate object of military action. That is, in order to weaken the enemy, or achieve the objectives of war, it is legitimate to attack the logistical structure that supports an opponent's war effort. The destruction of a building that might only seem to have incidental military use, can, therefore, be justified as militarily necessary.

Such an argument was prominent during the NATO bombardment of Serbia in 1999. In April 1999, at the beginning of its military action against Serbia, NATO destroyed a number of bridges, including road and rail bridges across the Danube in both Novi Sad and Belgrade. The logic behind the destruction of these key bridges could be questioned on the basis that these bridges constituted civilian objects designed for civilian infrastructural purposes (principally transport and trade) and were only incidentally used by the Serbian military. As such, these bridges would not comprise legitimate targets since the impact of their destruction would fall disproportionately upon the civilian population (i.e., their destruction would not be proportionate to the military goal achieved).

In reply to such questions at press briefings, Air Commodore Wilby justified the destruction as militarily necessary, noting that:

> the targets we go against are military-related facilities [such as] the highway bridges that we have been taking down recently. Of course they do inter-rupt the flow of civilian traffic and for that we are very sorry, but ... [w]e ... know that taking those bridges down, whilst it causes some inconvenience to

civilians … is causing immense inconvenience to the [Serbian military and special police] units that we are trying to stop resupplying their forces down in … Kosovo with the ammunition, the fuel, and the supplies to keep up their activities.

(North Atlantic Treaty Organization 1999a)

Later Wilby clarified this statement, saying:

every target we have struck has been one that has been considered to have great military significance to affect the Serbian military or the MUP [Serbian special police units] … bridges … have been selected because they are major lines of communication and … affect resupply of those troops … So, very firmly, I would say to you that all our targets have been justifiably military targets.

(North Atlantic Treaty Organization 1999b)

The destruction of bridges and other buildings in Bosnia could, similarly, be justified according to the logic of military necessity. That is, the argument could be used that these buildings represented elements in logistical networks, and, hence, militarily legitimate targets.

Interpreting the destruction of the built environment as either collateral damage or the product of militarily necessary actions does not, however, seem very satisfactory in the context of the 1992–95 Bosnian War (or indeed any of the other cases I have mentioned). Though it may offer superficial justification for the destruction of *certain* buildings, it does not adequately account for the widespread destruction of built environments.

The argument that this destruction comprises collateral damage sustained in the pursuit of legitimate military objectives can be easily refuted. For the destruction to comprise collateral damage it must be either accidental or a risk proportional to, and attendant on, the achievement of legitimate military goals. If the destruction is neither accidental nor attendant to achievement of another aim (i.e., that elements of the built environment were targets in their own right), then it cannot qualify as collateral damage. For example, we could recall the testimony of the Bosnian Serb gunner interviewed by Kate Adie quoted in the Introduction. In an interview, the officer commanding the artillery that was firing towards the Holiday Inn in Sarajevo (where the press were staying) explained to Adie that they had intended to hit the National Museum behind the hotel (Riedlmayer 1995a). Here we have a clear example of military personnel rejecting the idea that the destruction of civilian buildings such as the National Museum is either accidental or an acceptable risk proportional to the achievement of military objectives. The gunner made it clear that the National Museum constituted a target in its own right.

The idea that the destruction comprised collateral damage can be further problematised through the findings of the *Information Reports on War Damage to the Cultural Heritage in Croatia and Bosnia-Herzegovina* delivered to the Council of Europe Committee on Culture and Education by the Parliamentary Assembly Sub-Committee on the Architectural and Artistic Heritage of Europe. In respect of the destruction of the Oriental Institute in Sarajevo, the fourth *Information Report* notes

> In view of the location of the Oriental Institute and the force of flame produced, it is fair to presuppose that the shelling was carried out to plan: the Institute was directly targeted. This is even more believable in view of the fact that sources have provided details of how the invaders possessed remarkably precise military maps, and it is well-known that on the occasion of sorting through the Yugoslav Army material left in its building in Sarajevo after it withdrew, maps were found which had marked on them in precise detail all the targeted objectives in Sarajevo.
>
> (Council of Europe 1994)

In relation to the destruction of the minarets of mosques in Bosnia, the first *Information Report* notes that '[i]t may have been inevitable that mosques in a military "front" zone would be hit, but it is highly doubtful that a minaret can be brought down with a single large calibre shell, which implies a certain amount of deliberate targeting on these structures' (Council of Europe 1993). That the built environment of Bosnia was deliberately targeted is confirmed by the conclusion of the fourth *Information Report* that 'the small historic core of Mostar ... was clearly targeted by the heaviest guns available to the HVO [the Bosnian-Croat Army]' (Council of Europe 1994).

If the destruction of the buildings of Bosnia cannot be understood as collateral damage, can it be seen as militarily necessary? This argument is even easier to refute than that of collateral damage. For the destruction of all of these buildings to have been militarily necessary, they would have had to have played some form of role in the communications, transport and logistics networks of the various armies in Bosnia. There are instances in which such arguments may be credible. For example, the destruction of the central post office in Sarajevo or the modern road bridges over the Neretva in Mostar could be seen as attacks on legitimate military targets. The post office, for example, housed the central telephone exchange for Sarajevo, and thus comprised a vital element of Bosnian Army communications. In destroying it, the Bosnian Serb Army could claim it was attacking an object of significant military potential to its adversary. Similarly, some of the bridges in Mostar could be seen as supply or transport routes for military purposes and thus destruction could be legitimised.

However, the destruction of elements of the built environment is more widespread than these key buildings. In Sarajevo, for example, the Bosnian Serb Army shelled the city without any real regard for the military significance of buildings. Moreover, buildings of no military significance were regularly shelled deliberately. And the shelling covered a wide variety of buildings – housing, public institutions, cultural monuments, utility buildings – and open spaces. The National Museum, Oriental Institute, National Library and various mosques provide only a few, well-known, examples of such targeting. In *Just and Unjust Wars*, Waltzer describes strategy as 'a language of justification' (Waltzer 1992, 13). We could see military necessity in a similar light. Claims that the destruction of a target was militarily necessary are *post hoc* narratives that seek to justify the destruction. In cases such as Sarajevo's central post office or the Neretva road bridges, such narratives are convincing since they can align themselves with the commonly understood meanings of what constitutes a military object or a military objective. However, in the case of the widespread destruction of the built environment in which so much damage was done to buildings that could serve no such purposes, such narratives do not really serve to justify or explain the destruction of the urban fabric.

Understanding the widespread destruction of the built environment as an instance of collateral damage or a militarily necessary action is, therefore, deeply flawed for two reasons: 1) damage was neither accidental nor proportional to the goals of the conflict, and 2) though *certain* buildings could be said to comprise legitimate military targets, the deliberate widespread destruction of the built environment exceeds this smaller number of targets. Despite its flaws, however, this understanding is prevalent in cases of widespread destruction of the built environment. This understanding of the destruction of buildings seeks to draw a line that discriminates between legitimate and illegitimate forms of destruction. In this way a limited number of instances are seen as products of legitimate conduct of war. The remainder are written off as illegitimate consequences of the actions of barbarians or vandals. Understanding acts of destruction as vandalism or as the barbaric 'wanton destruction of cities, towns or villages' (Statute of the International Criminal Tribunal for the Former Yugoslavia cited in Roberts and Guelff 2000, 569) is thus the recto of the verso of concepts of collateral damage and military necessity.

Such notions of vandalism and/or 'wanton destruction' are unhelpful in an analysis of urban destruction for two significant reasons. Firstly, they rest on an idea of excess that is intimately linked to notions of military necessity. In other words, 'wanton destruction' circumscribes all those events that, by virtue of exceeding the bounds of necessity, escape being classified as legitimate military actions. Secondly, the notion that such destruction is 'wanton' implies a certain irrationality and bloodlust that suggests the destruction occurred for idiosyncratic reasons localisable to a person or group.

Thus, this understanding of the destruction of buildings fails in two regards. Firstly, the category of 'wanton destruction' becomes a conceptual dustbin to which all acts not in accordance with norms of legitimate military action are confined, unexamined. In this way, though such destruction is criminalised, it is not examined for its own patterns, consistencies and meanings. Secondly, insofar as the destruction is taken to be the wanton action of a person or group, it is seen as a deviation from a norm of behaviour implicit in the various codifications of Rules of War and Crimes Against Humanity. As such, 'wanton destruction' is reduced to the status of immorality, irrationality or evil. Thus, in seeing the destruction of built environments as instances of 'wanton destruction', the targeting of buildings is seen merely as a criminal deviation from the norm. In this way such accounts resist the urgent need to inquire into the meaning of such destruction, refusing to see such destruction as following a distinct rationale or logic. To put it another way (and to borrow from Hannah Arendt), whereas accounts that take the notion of 'wanton destruction' to satisfactorily explain instances of urban destruction take these events as exceptions to the norm, we should perhaps be considering them as instances in conformity with a norm (or logic) of their own.[1] What logic or rationale do such acts of 'wanton' destruction disclose? My argument would be that in order to pursue this question, 'wanton destruction' would be more productively understood as 'urbicide'.

Ethnic cleansing and the cultural dimension of genocide

The second of the three interpretations of the destruction of the built environment that I want to examine understands such destruction as the destruction of symbolic buildings. This understanding arises in relation to the destruction of cultural heritage. Cultural heritage is protected under the 1956 *Hague Convention for the Protection of Cultural Property in the Event of Armed Conflict*. This convention offers protection for 'movable or immovable property of great importance to the cultural heritage of every people' – a definition taken to include buildings such as museums, libraries and religious buildings, as well as monuments or public buildings that are of specific cultural significance (Roberts and Guelff 2000, 371–405).[2]

Accounts of the destruction of cultural heritage see it as an element of either ethnic cleansing or (cultural) genocide. Ethnic cleansing can be defined as the attempt to remake a given state 'as a series of small, pure ethnic states' (Council of Europe 1994): a violent erasure of ethnic heterogeneity and the imposition of homogeneity in a given territory. It is precisely through seeing this violent erasure as the overall war aim that the destruction of cultural heritage has been interpreted. Cultural heritage is destroyed because it represents what must be destroyed in order to achieve the aim of the erasure of, and thus purity of, ethnic identity on a particular territory.

According to Shaw (2007, 48–62), however, the concept of 'ethnic cleansing' obscures the genocidal nature of conflicts such as the 1992–95 Bosnian War. Accordingly, some observers of the destruction of cultural heritage have sought to argue that the targeting of cultural heritage is better understood according to the rubric of genocide. There is, however, disagreement as to whether such destruction is distinct from, or an element of, genocide. Orentlicher (1999) notes that cultural genocide was left out of the 1948 Genocide Convention, adding weight to the view that the extensive destruction of buildings, monuments and cultural artefacts should be interpreted as a distinct form of violence: 'cultural genocide'. These acts of destruction, it is argued, whilst part of a program to intentionally destroy the cultural artefacts of Bosnia-Herzegovina, are to be regarded as separate from genocide itself (see, for example, Bevan 2006, 210). This separation of 'cultural' genocide from 'human' genocide is intended to distinguish between the value of human life and the value of the artefacts humans produce. Destruction of mosques, churches, museums, bridges and so on may well be part of an organised program, but this program is separate to (though not necessarily unrelated to) the program of killing and displacement carried out by forces such as the Bosnian Serbs or Bosnian Croats.

Despite this case for consideration of destruction of cultural heritage as a distinct form of violence, both Sells (1996) and Shaw (2007, 66) contend that the destruction of buildings should rightly be seen as an integral component of a program of genocide. Insofar as the 1948 Genocide Convention is used to define the act of genocide, the destruction of symbolic buildings and cultural artefacts can be construed to be circumscribed by the 'intent to destroy, in whole or in part, a national, ethnical, racial or religious group'.[3] Even though such groups consist of the individual persons that comprise it, the sense of being a member of such a group is provided by a shared culture. To destroy the shared culture is a de facto destruction of the national group: it deprives individuals of the shared culture that provides the condition of possibility of there being a sense of belonging to a group. As such, this destruction should be seen to be integral to, rather than distinct from, genocide. The destruction of a building such as the *Stari Most* is, therefore, understood by Sells to be an exemplary event in the genocide against the Bosnian Muslims. When taken together with the destruction of mosques in Mostar, Sarajevo, Banja Luka and elsewhere, the destruction of buildings such as the *Stari Most* can be held to be an organised attempt to destroy in whole or in part that which makes it possible to speak of Bosnian Muslims: their shared culture.

Common to both interpretations of the destruction of cultural heritage – either as ethnic cleansing or (cultural) genocide – is the understanding that this destruction is a means to achieve the objective of ethnic/cultural homogeneity. These interpretations argue that certain buildings are destroyed because they represent ethnic/cultural heterogeneity. Andras Riedlmayer's work to draw attention to the destruction of the cultural heritage of Bosnia-Herzegovina provides a particularly cogent example of such an interpretation. Riedlmayer (1994, 16) argues that although our attention focuses on the people of Bosnia, 'we should also take a look at the rubble'. This rubble, he argues, 'signifies more than the ordinary atrocities of war … Rubble in Bosnia and Hercegovina signifies nationalist extremists hard at work to eliminate not only the human beings and living cities, but also the memory of the past' (*Ibid.*). Furthermore, Riedlmayer (*Ibid.*) argues that although '[w]e are … told that "ancient hatreds" are what fuel the destruction … this is not true'. That this is not the case is precisely what the buildings that are destroyed attest to. The museums, libraries, mosques, churches and monuments 'speak eloquently of centuries of pluralism … in Bosnia. It is this evidence of a successfully shared past that the nationalists seek to destroy' (*Ibid.*). It is the nature of the nationalist project that drives this destruction.

The nationalism that drove the destruction during the 1992–95 Bosnian War was characterised by a project to naturalise the idea that the so-called 'ethnic' groups in Bosnia are fated to live separate existences. The myth of 'ancient hatreds' installs the idea that ethnic groups were always distinct and in antagonistic relationships. Nationalist ideas of separation and ethnic purity are the logical outcome of the acceptance of this idea. However, such ideas are simply the myths on which the nationalist edifice is built. Indeed, Bosnia has a long history of pluralism which exhibits a high degree of indistinction (such as inter-marriage) and co-existence between these supposedly distinct and incompatible ethnic groups (Hayden 1996, 788–790; Botev and Wagner 1993; Bringa 1993; Bringa 1995). It is precisely the built environment that represents this pluralism. The built environment in cities such as Sarajevo and Mostar are testament to the pluralist character of Bosnia. The co-existence of Ottoman, Austro-Hungarian and vernacular buildings is a constant reminder that the nationalist project of ethnic separateness is a present-day fiction belied by the past. Thus, to paraphrase Riedlmayer, nationalists sought to destroy evidence of a successfully shared past in order to legitimise a contemporary goal of ethnic separateness. The nationalists sought to naturalise the idea of ethnic sepa- rateness by propagating the myth of historical antagonism and difference between ethnic groups. However, 'before inventing a new past [characterised by the fictional "ethnic hatreds"] the old must be erased' (Riedlmayer 1994, 16).

The destruction of the buildings that comprise the cultural heritage of Bosnia is thus understood as an integral element of the logic of nationalism: a means to achieve the war aim of ethnic separateness. In one sense, this account gets closer to the theme of the destruction of the shared spaces of Bosnia-Herzegovina than the previous account of destruction as the result of either collateral damage or military necessity. Indeed this account understands the destruction of certain buildings as part of the logic of nationalism that has at its heart the destruction of the conditions of possibility of pluralism, key among which is the evidence of co-existence provided by the built environment of Bosnia.

However, this account suffers from its focus upon the symbolic buildings, or the cultural heritage of Bosnia. In other words, it focuses upon the buildings whose loss is judged to be a cultural loss. Analysing the destruction of urban environments on the basis of such examples is, therefore, problematic precisely because the destruction of buildings that are not regarded as being part of the heritage of a distinctive culture is overlooked. Indeed, it is partly the concern that analyses which focus on the destruction of cultural heritage are exclusionary in this manner that motivates the definition of the destruction of the built environment as 'urbicide'.

Analyses that focus on the destruction of cultural heritage fail to recognise that the act of designating buildings/urban environments as worthy of cultural heritage status is necessarily exclusionary. There exist two understandings on the basis of which such designation can be made, one more narrow and formal than the other. Firstly, buildings or built environments can be designated as comprising the physical heritage of a particular culture (be that a national/ethnic culture or the more generic culture of humanity) by national governments and/or international governmental organisations such as the United Nations Educational, Scientific and Cultural Organisation (UNESCO). These procedures produce the so-called 'heritage lists' that comprise a canonical designation of the cultural heritage of both nations and, in the case of UNESCO, humanity.[4]

Secondly, there is a more generic understanding of what comprises cultural heritage that might extend, in principle, to buildings beyond the narrow scope of the 'heritage lists' such as UNESCO's. This more generic understanding of which buildings comprise the heritage of a particular culture can be seen in the work of the Kosovo Cultural Heritage Survey, which has documented the widespread destruction of cultural heritage in Kosovo between 1998 and 2000. This survey provides a clear example of the exercise of a generic notion of what comprises cultural heritage, since it is focused on those buildings whose loss it is thought in some way impoverishes both the culture to which they belong and humanity in general (Herscher and Riedlmayer 2000). It is precisely this generic understanding of what constitutes cultural heritage that was deployed in respect of the destruction of urban fabric during the 1992–95 Bosnian War. Indeed most of the buildings that were destroyed were not listed by official organs of either national governments or international governmental organisations. Further, it should be noted that UNESCO's World Heritage List contains no sites in Bosnia-Herzegovina.

It was thus according to a generic notion of what comprised cultural heritage that observers and participants in the 1992–95 war appealed for the protection of buildings taken to represent the cultural heritage of Bosnia from the widespread destruction that was occurring. These appeals were intended to point out the violations of the extant laws of war that were occurring in Bosnia and draw attention to the assault on culturally significant buildings that may otherwise have been overlooked, given that most observers of, and participants in, the conflict were, at the time, predominantly concerned with the widespread human rights abuses that were taking place. This generic understanding comprises a more general concept in which buildings are understood to be representative of the achievements or character of a culture.

However, the status of 'cultural heritage' is bestowed only upon those buildings/ monuments that are taken to either exemplify the achievements of, or typify the development and existence of, a given culture (usually restricted to religious buildings, monuments, cultural institutions and striking examples of indigenous architecture). Moreover, in endorsing either (inter)governmental, or generic, understandings of what constitutes the heritage of a distinctive culture, analyses that concentrate on the destruction of cultural heritage imply that those buildings not defined as such are in some way dispensable for that culture. Thus the destruction of houses, office blocks, multi-storey carparks, and supermarkets is excluded from analyses of urban destruction that are focused on the violation of the laws protecting cultural property. Indeed, the destruction of buildings not designated as cultural heritage is deemed to be the result of either poor targeting, military expediency, or excessive force.[5] Either way, this destruction is not of analytical consequence for understandings of the destruction of the built environment focused on the assault on cultural heritage (it comprises merely the general rubble of war and can be explained as the result of either expediency or excess).[6]

On the whole, this means that the buildings for which concern is shown are those that were striking examples of a particular cultural influence upon the pluralist history of Bosnia. Ancient mosques, grand National Library buildings, and 400-year-old bridges are thus the subject of this account, as it is these that are the symbolic reminders of the pluralist culture of Bosnia. There is, however, a two-fold problem with this interpretation of the destruction of buildings as an attack on cultural heritage. In the first place, it restricts itself to the analysis of specific, high-profile cases of destruction of culture. This gives the impression that other buildings are not culturally significant. This is clearly not the case, and buildings of indistinct cultural provenance (such as the bland modernism of the 'Unis Co.' tower blocks in Sarajevo) do play a role in the cultural life of cities and nations.[7] Secondly, and more importantly, culture is taken to be something that belongs to national and/or ethnic groups and thus this interpretation must accept the political landscape of ethnic nationalism as its starting point. Insofar as a building cannot be said to be part of a distinct ethnic or national culture, its destruction cannot be said to be the destruction of cultural heritage. It is in this manner that buildings of indistinct cultural provenance escape this interpretation. After all, these buildings are part of the cultural landscape of all Bosnians, and not any specific national, ethnic or religious group.

Thus the interpretation of urban destruction as an attack on cultural heritage provides only a partial (though striking) account of the destruction of the built environment in Bosnia. Urbicide, however, comprises a more widespread phenomenon than the destruction of the cultural heritage concentrated upon by those who interpret the destruction of buildings through the lens of the 1956 Hague Convention. Hence, understandings of the destruction of the urban fabric of Bosnia will need to substantially elaborate upon this interpretation and extend its narrow focus upon examples of cultural heritage.

Balkanisation, Balkanism, ethnicity and despair

I have referred to the third and final interpretation of the destruction of buildings that I want to examine as a 'metaphoric' understanding. The metaphoric interpretation (which understands the destruction as a sign of the concepts at stake in the war) does not treat the ruins in themselves as the material fabric of a culture but, rather, as signs evocative of ideas and values (concepts). This interpretation is, therefore, a *semiotic* understanding that treats buildings as a sign that refers to a concept.[8]

The destruction of the *Stari Most* provides an exemplary instance of such a semiotic understanding of the destruction of the urban environment in Bosnia. As a sign, the collapsing bridge embedded itself in the political imaginaries of those who observed, participated in, or fell victim to the 1992–95 war. This sign gave graphic representation to the concepts and values that were taken to be at stake in the Bosnian War.[9] Insofar as this event became a sign that provided a convenient shorthand that summarised the tortuous complexities of the conflict, it had profound effects upon understandings of, participation and intervention in, and attempts to negotiate a conclusion to, the war. On the one hand, the rubble of the *Stari Most* was a sign with an assumed connotation that could be substituted for a comprehensive understanding of the conflict. On the other hand, this sign precipitated, solidified, or gave expression to, certain conceptual formations that framed the horizons of the political imaginaries of both participants and observers. As such then, this sign, and its interpretation, influenced courses of action taken by those whose political imaginaries it both shaped and expressed.

As a sign, the ruined *Stari Most* (and the rubble of Bosnia in general) is associated with two specific concepts. Firstly, for observers of the conflict, the destruction of the *Stari Most* signified in graphic fashion the *Balkanisation* of Bosnia. According to James Der Derian (1992, 146–150), '[b]alkanisation is generally understood to be the break up of larger political units into smaller, mutually hostile states which are exploited or manipulated by more powerful neighbours'. The destruction of the *Stari Most* by the HVO gave such an idea exemplary form. That is, the destruction of the last remaining bridge between the two halves of Mostar was performed by a group manipulated by Croatian President Franjo Tudjman and effectively sealed the creation of two mutually hostile entities (East and West Mostar). Through such signs, the concept of 'Balkanisation' framed the political imaginaries of those who observed, or intervened in, the Bosnian War.

However, Balkanisation is not simply a technical term for the creation of mutually hostile states, but a more general concept that refers to the violent fragmentation of territory into ever-smaller, exclusive communities. This concept found its exemplary signifier in the rubble of Bosnia, the ever-proliferating signs of fault lines in a hitherto pluralist community. This elevation of the notion of Balkanisation to the position of horizon of understanding required the concept to be 'transvalued' from a simple term referring to geopolitical machination to a motif capturing the concept of an inexorable, violent fragmentation of political landscapes.[10] Mike Davis, for example, emphasises precisely this motif of violent fragmentation that dominates the concept of 'Balkanisation'. In his discussion of the 'power lines' that shape the urban environment in Los Angeles, Davis refers to 'Balkanised' cities such as Chicago or Boston (Davis 1992, 102). In this manner, the specificity of 'Balkanisation' to a correlate cartographic/geographic entity (i.e., the 'Balkan' Peninsula) has evaporated. Rather, the term connotes simply violent political and social fragmentation.

The division of Bosnia into ever-smaller, homogeneous ethnic territories was clearly represented in the gulf opened up between the two banks of the Neretva by the destruction of the *Stari Most*. However, the Balkanisation that this sign represented had an additional stratum of meaning. The destruction of the elegant Ottoman bridge not only signified the violent social and political fragmentation of Bosnia-Herzegovina, but also the truly 'Balkan' character of the violence by which this fragmentation was being achieved. That is, this destruction confirmed the stereotypes that observers held of those who were executing this Balkanisation. These stereotypes are best referred to, in keeping with the conceptual terrain of Balkanisation, as expressions of *Balkanism*.

'Balkanism' is a 'variation on orientalism'.[11] 'Orientalism', as Bakic-Hayden and Hayden (1992, 1) note, 'refers to pervasive patterns of representation of cultures and societies that privilege a self-confidently "progressive", "modern" and "rational" Europe over the putatively "stagnant", "backward", "traditional" and "mystical" societies of the Orient'. Bakic-Hayden and Hayden (1992, 2) demonstrate 'an orientalist framework of analysis, primarily by Yugoslavs from the north and west parts of the country [Slovenia and Croatia], and by some foreign observers'. That is, Slovenes, Croats and foreign observers operated with a 'political vision of reality whose structure promoted the difference between the

familiar (Europe, the West, "us") and the strange (the Orient, the East, "them")'
(Said 1991, 43). Slovene, Croat and foreign political imaginaries assume their
naturally progressive, modern and European nature, whilst also assuming the
backward nature of those in the eastern and southern parts of the former Yugoslavia.
This orientalism manifests itself in, for example, the hierarchical division of the
country according to religion. Croats and Slovenes regard Catholicism as naturally
more rational and modern than Orthodox Christianity or Islam. As such, this leads
to the ascription of further characteristics on the basis of this hierarchy: Serbs are
more warlike, Albanians are more traditional (backward), whilst Croats are more
deserving of European recognition since they are, after all, Catholics.

In *Imagining the Balkans*, Maria Todorova (1997, 3–20) develops this 'variation
on orientalism' into the fully fledged concept of 'Balkanism'. Todorova notes that
'orientalism', as originally defined by Said, refers to a representational regime
that is intimately connected to colonial structures of domination. Orientalism
is a discourse that attempts to define, as an element of colonial domination, a
geographical region that does not exist as a naturally pre-given entity. In contrast
to this idea, Todorova notes that the Balkan Peninsula is both a fairly well-defined
geographic location and, though the subject of imperialism, never a truly colonised
region. As such then, the representational regime concerning the Balkans is not,
according to Todorova, an orientalist discourse that circumscribes and classifies
a colonial other, but rather a discourse that essentialises the characteristics of a
region that forms the ambiguous edge of occidental Europe.

Balkanism views the Balkans as a transitional bridge between Occident and
Orient. The transition that can be observed in the Balkans is not only spatial but
evolutionary: the inhabitants of the Balkans are taken to be in the process of evolving into occidental Europeans. The Balkans are thus taken to be a reversion to a
pre-modern stage of civility. Furthermore, Balkanist stereotypes view the Balkans
as a zone of flux (since all transition involves instability). Balkanism attributes an
essential character to the Balkan Peninsula that is the logical correlate of Balkanisation. The reversion of civility to medieval standards, coupled with the state
of instability given by the transitional nature of the region, entails perpetual and
violent struggle, even conditions of mutual hostility and barbarity. Moreover, it is
not only Western observers who deploy Balkanist stereotypes. Balkanism is rife
within the Balkans, as each community attempts to characterise its neighbour as
being in some way less civilised, and themselves as in some sense more European
(or Slavic) than Balkan. Thus, as Balkanisation proceeds to fragment states into
ever-smaller entities, so Balkanism fragments the cultural landscape into ever more
mutually hostile groups who draw conceptual distinctions between themselves.

The fragmentation of the political landscape thus proceeds according to ideas
of civility (Todorova 1997, 130–133). Wherever the difference between groups is
promoted, it is on the basis of being more or less civilised. The interpretation of the
destruction of the *Stari Most* by some observers of the conflict comprises a classic
example of Balkanism. The *Stari Most* was taken to be an exemplary instance of
cultural heritage: a striking example of Bosnian culture and part of the universal
heritage of humankind. The elevation of this bridge to the status of a monumental

exemplar of the cultural heritage of, variously, Yugoslavia, Bosnia, the Ottoman Empire, Europe and humanity, served to suggest that visiting, seeing and conserving this bridge was the duty of those who held the value of human cultural endeavours in high regard. And so the destruction of this exemplar of cultural heritage was invariably decried as an act of barbarity, savagery or philistinism. Those who destroyed this bridge, it was argued, could not hold human cultural achievement in very high regard. Of course, cultural achievement is only attained over time, as is regard for the artefacts this achievement leaves behind. One has to develop a cultural sensibility; it is the mark of a culture that has attained a degree of sophistication, a culture that has left behind its immature and barbaric past. What the HVO had done was therefore taken to reveal a total lack of comprehension of the value of the artefacts produced by a culture, a comprehension that can only come through a sort of human maturity. The HVO, thus, could only be immature savages.

Despite being meant as a harsh condemnation of the action of the HVO, a reprimand meant to make the HVO stop and see the value of what was being destroyed, the image of the fallen bridge came to represent the savagery and barbarity of the Bosnian War: the failure of (European) civilisation to extend into the Balkans. This idea framed the political imagination of those observing the conflict. Talk of 'ancient animosities' was given new life by this supposed sign of ferocious barbarity. Leaders of Western, 'civilised' nations threw their hands up in despair: 'How can we help when these people don't share even the basic values of civilisation?', they reasoned. 'We should leave them to fight this conflict out amongst themselves.'[12] The *Stari Most*, as a signifier of the barbarism of the Bosnian Croats (and by extension all Croats and even all Bosnians), thus gave the Balkanism of Western observers a form with which to associate such concepts.

The second concept which the destruction of the *Stari Most* is taken to signify is that of the 'bridging' of supposedly distinct ethnic groups. The idea that Bosnia was 'a bridge', spanning and linking otherwise foreign cultures, captured the political imagination of observers of, and participants in, the conflict (Sells 1996, 113). Indeed, the gulf that the collapse of the *Stari Most* opened up between the left and right banks of the Neretva was for many observers the ideal metaphor to express the prevalent understanding of the Bosnian War as an 'ethnic' conflict. The collapse of the bridge neatly summed up the widespread idea that Yugoslavia had been an artificial creation that had forced pre-existent national groups to live side by side. Without the firm hand of Tito, it was assumed that these national groups would naturally separate out and, in places where this was not possible, there would be conflict. The crumbling bridge symbolised the death of Tito's ideal, the collapse of the remnants of a forced co-existence between the three naturally separate ethnic groups that occupied the territory of Bosnia-Herzegovina: 'Serbs', 'Croats' and 'Muslims'. The rubble left in the river between the banks captured the sense that nothing but destruction would come out of attempts to create a so-called 'multi-ethnic' Bosnia.

This motif of bridging, signified by the ruined *Stari Most* before, during and after its destruction, thus framed the political imaginaries of both participants and observers in the conflict. For the HVO, the link to Muslim East Mostar provided by the *Stari Most* threatened their attempt to establish the 'ethnically pure' Bosnian Croat statelet of 'Herceg-Bosna'. With their political horizon framed by the notion that ethnic national identities were the natural order of things – a natural order which was artificially suppressed by the bridging accomplished under Tito's program of 'brotherhood and unity' – it was logical for the HVO to destroy that which represented such bridging. The bridge was the link that had artificially bound together the otherwise separate ethnic groups in Mostar. To destroy the bridge was to re-establish the natural separateness of Croatian, Catholic western Bosnia from Muslim, Turkic eastern Bosnia.[13] With their political horizons shaped by the logic of natural primordial ethnicities that was the logical underside of the metaphor provided by the image of the bridge, the HVO set about destroying that which threatened the purity of their 'homeland'.

In contradistinction to the vision of the HVO, the bridge provided a sign of hope for those who worked to resolve the conflict or to re-build Bosnia in the wake of Dayton. The destruction of the bridge, however, turned this sign of hope into one of despair. Bridge-building has been a common theme in the rhetoric of diplomacy for a considerable time. References to the bridging of differences, or to building bridges that cross divides that separate cultures, nations or ideologies, litter the history of attempts to reconcile both global and local divisions. For example, on the occasion of being awarded the 1996 International Democracy Award, chair of the presidency of Bosnia-Herzegovina, Alija Izetbegovic, remarked that 'Bosnia and Herzegovina is a country – *a bridge* – in which two worlds meet three cultures and four religions. That is why the issue of Bosnia is, here and now, the paramount question of democracy' (Izetbegovic 1997, my emphasis).

Ironically (or perhaps tragically), the logic by which the bridge was elevated to this mythical status in the rhetoric of post-Dayton multi-ethnic democracy had common roots with, and shared the same political imaginary as, the HVO.[14] This seemingly conciliatory metaphor rests on the assumption that there are indeed naturally existing and distinct ethnic groups such as 'Croat' and 'Muslim', who would naturally occupy distinct territories, the gaps between which would, of course, need bridging. This logic can also be seen to frame the political imaginaries of many of the agencies charged with the task of rebuilding Bosnia after the signing of the Dayton Agreement. The idea that the creation of a multi-ethnic polity required establishing links between distinct ethnic groups was prevalent in the rhetoric of bridge-building employed by, amongst others, the European Administration of Mostar (Yarwood 1999, 13). The end result is that the rubble of Bosnia became a sign of the despair that these agencies expressed regarding the possibility of creating a multi-ethnic community. Of course, part of the problem is that the sign itself, in the way that it constitutes the idea that ethnic communities are naturally occurring separate entities that need artificial linking, leads to the pessimistic conclusion that such artifice is impossible (a conclusion that the HVO would heartily endorse).

The problem with either interpretation of the rubble of Bosnia is that the destruction itself is not treated as an event worthy of attention in its own right. Rather the rubble is taken, appropriated we might say, as a sign connotative of a more general concept. I am not trying to revive a spurious distinction between the real and the sign at this point. Indeed, insofar as the sign of Balkanisation, Balkanism and bridging established the conceptual horizon for many who intervened in the 1992–95 Bosnian War, it was constitutive of certain political realities. I am trying, rather, to note that whilst the destruction of certain buildings may serve as the sign for several concepts, this does not get us any closer to understanding the meaning of the destruction of the built environment. To take an analogy, genocide can be taken as a sign of barbarity, and yet this obscures the question of what is occurring in the event of genocide. Which is to say, the concept drains the sign of its own specificity. If one sees the Holocaust as a sign of German barbarity, the destruction of the Jews is not taken as something important in its own right, but rather the signifier of something else. This is, I believe, precisely the point that Bauman makes when he notes that:

> the exercise in focusing on the *Germanness* [i.e., the purported special barbarity of the Germans] of the crime [the Holocaust] ... is simultaneously an exercise in exonerating everyone else, and particularly everything else ... [and] results not only in the moral comfort of self-exculpation, but also in the dire threat of moral and political disarmament.
>
> (Bauman 1991, xii)

In a similar manner, by accepting the idea that the destruction of the built environment is simply the sign of some sort of barbarism, or the working-out of the linkages between naturally separate ethnic communities, the specificity of the destruction itself is ignored. This results in 'moral and political disarmament', since it means that the question is not 'What does the destruction of the built environment disclose about a fundamentally political form of violence?', but rather 'How can these aberrant concepts, signified by this destruction, be reversed?'.

It is thus my argument, following Bauman's, that this interpretation of the destruction of the urban fabric of Bosnia comprises a valuation of the event that is substituted for the far more urgent task of the analysis of the structure and meaning of the event itself. Which is to say that the destruction of built environment may become the sign that frames certain political imaginaries. However, we deny ourselves crucial political possibilities if we simply accept those significatory stories, since we accept that this destruction is interesting only insofar as it connotes concepts such as savagery or attempts to stitch communities back together. We must ask instead what is destroyed when the built environment is destroyed, and what this reveals about the political and conceptual entailments of such destruction. In rather unfashionable terms, one could say that the question is not what the destruction signifies, but what the urban fabric *is* and what its destruction discloses.

Conclusion

The three interpretations of the destruction of the built environment discussed in this chapter all fail, therefore, to get to the heart of the problem raised by such violence: namely what that violence comprises in its own right. Each interpretation treats such violence as, respectively, subsidiary to military violence, an element of wider patterns of violence, or a sign of deeper, metaphorical concepts. As such, these accounts cannot address urban destruction as a form of violence in its own right. That such an approach is necessary is indicated by the critical flaws exhibited by each account. In other words, the fact that each of these interpretations fails to provide an adequate account of the destruction of the built environment should lead us to investigate another direction of enquiry – one that treats this violence as a phenomenon in its own right. It is precisely to such a task that I will now turn. The next chapter will thus comprise an elaboration of the outlines of a novel concept which addresses the destruction of the built environment as a distinctive form of violence: *urbicide*.

2 The logic of urbicide

New conceptions require new terms.

(Lemkin 1994, 79)

In his analysis of the occupation policies of the Axis powers in World War II, Raphael Lemkin notes that all existing interpretations of political violence fail to adequately capture the systematic and exterminatory nature of the violence that characterised the Holocaust. Lemkin argues that concepts such as 'mass murder' only partially address the program enacted to destroy existing populations and impose the Nazi political program. Insofar as this is the case, he argues, it is necessary to conceive of a new concept in order to grasp the specific nature of the violence that marked Axis occupation and led, ultimately, to the final solution. Likewise, I want to argue that if we use existing understandings of the destruction of buildings, we fail to address the specific nature of this destruction. A number of writers have noted that a new concept is required in order to grasp the nature of widespread and deliberate destruction of the built environment: *urbicide*. It is, thus, to this concept that I want to turn. As Lemkin did with 'genocide', I want to elaborate the conceptual entailments of 'urbicide' and note the distinct form of political violence that it describes.

'Urbicide': historical genesis of a concept

In 1992 the issue of the widespread destruction of buildings in Bosnia was thematised by a group of architects from Mostar in a publication entitled *Mostar '92 – Urbicid* (Ribarevic-Nikolic and Juric 1992).[1] The authors of *Mostar '92– Urbicid* presented the destruction of buildings in Mostar as a central aspect of the ongoing war. This collection of pictures and text attempted to demonstrate that the devastation of the built environment manifest in (though not limited to) the destruction of bridges, mosques and churches, department stores, blocks of apartments, public buildings, hotels and public spaces (such as parks), was more than collateral damage. As such, *Mostar '92 – Urbicid* was intended to bring attention to the plight of architecture in the former Yugoslavia. Despite the clear advocacy agenda of this publication, it drew attention to the need to consider the phenomenon of the destruction of the built environment under a distinct conceptual category: urbicide. Central to this publication, therefore, is the claim that the destruction of the built environment has a meaning of its own, rather than being incidental to, or a secondary feature of, the genocidal violence (or 'ethnic cleansing') that characterised the Bosnian War.

Such consideration of the destruction of buildings as both a distinctive phenomenon and one falling under a separate conceptual category is not, however, novel. The term 'urbicide' has been invoked by a number of commentators in order to draw attention to the need for a consideration of destruction of the built environment as a form of violence in its own right. Originating in discussions of urban renewal programs in America, the concept of urbicide was intended to indicate the manner in which the city, both as architectural form and socio-political experience, was under attack in twentieth-century urban planning and development. The term is used by Pulitzer Prize-winner Ada Louise Huxtable for the subtitle of her compendium of *New York Times* articles. In *Will They Ever Finish Bruckner Boulevard? A Primer on Urbicide*, Huxtable considers a number of cases of urban planning and development in New York that she regards as marking a definitive decline in – indeed a sustained assault upon – the urban experience (Huxtable 1972). The new buildings of the Columbia University Gym and the World Trade Center are taken to represent disruptions of an urban ideal. Along with road-building projects such as the Lower Manhattan Expressway, these developments are taken to comprise a wholesale assault on an ideal notion of urbanity. Whilst it is not clear exactly what this ideal might be (after all, this is a collection of essays, not a sustained argument), it is clear that the manner in which development in New York fails to integrate into the built environment, thus fracturing what was previously taken to be an integrated public space, is the central issue of concern for Huxtable.

Such urbicide by development is also taken up by Marshall Berman in his 'Falling Towers: City Life After Urbicide' (Berman 1996).[2] For Berman, considering the fate of his childhood home as one of the many buildings destroyed in Robert Moses' redevelopment of New York City, the destruction of buildings is to be understood as a destruction of the city. The city, for Berman, comprises a substrate upon which identity can take root. In destroying the city, such a substrate is lost and identity can no longer take root. In destroying neighbourhoods to make way for the Cross Bronx Expressway, therefore, such a substrate of identity was also destroyed and, along with it the very fabric of the city, characterised as it is by the co-existence of identities. For Berman, however, urbicide is a widespread, ubiquitous phenomenon, permeating the history of human development. Ancient urbicides such as that visited on Sodom and Gomorrah in the book of Genesis and the destruction of cities in the Peloponnesian War demonstrate, according to Berman, that '[a]s long as people have lived in cities they have been haunted by fears of urban ruin' (Berman 1996, 175).

Despite offering powerful indictments of the destruction of the material substrate upon which urban ways of life are predicated, these accounts of the manner in which the city has been targeted were largely marginal to the discourse of twentieth-century urban development. However, the notion of urbicide returned as an analytic category in the post-Cold War era. The various intra-state conflicts in the former Yugoslavia, the former Soviet Union, and the Middle East, seemed to represent a new, particularly vicious, form of warfare that had novel distinguishing features. One of these features was the destruction of cities. Although Allied area bombing in World War II (Markusen and Kopf 1995, 151–182; Hewitt 1983) and Russian tactics of 'rubbleisation' in Afghanistan (Goodson 2001, 60–66) had shown that inter-state war could unleash furious hostility upon cities, it appeared that these post-Cold War conflicts targeted the city not as a mechanism for the reduction of the capacity of an enemy to fight, but for its own sake.

In the context of the conflicts in the former Yugoslavia from 1991 to 1999, observers noted the manner in which the built environment was targeted in its own right. Writing about the destruction of the Croatian town of Vukovar by the Yugoslav National Army, Bogdan Bogdanovic introduced the notion that such destruction was urbicidal because it constituted the targeting of the urban by 'city haters' (Bogdanovic 1993, 20; Bogdanovic 1994, 37–74). This was a popular motif in commentary upon the disintegration of the former Yugoslavia (Bougarel 1999). The violence was commonly interpreted as an assault by the forces of reactionary rural tradition upon the cosmopolitan urbanity of the cities. Carl Grodach (2002, 77), for example, notes the way in which Donia and Fine (1994, 28) blamed 'much of the violence [in the 1992–95 Bosnian War]' on 'uneducated armed hillsmen, with a hostility toward urban culture and the state institutions'. This interpretation of the violence visited upon Bosnia, Croatia and Kosovo rests upon an assumed distinction between rural and urban life and a positing of mutual antagonism between the two. Urbicide is thus the destruction of the city in order to eradicate urbanity itself. I will return to the theme of the distinction between the urban and the rural later in this chapter, but it is wise at this point to note Grodach's (2002, 77) caution that such notions of urbicide 'risk perpetuating surface differences and stereotypes' such as 'the traditional versus the modern and the cultured versus the ignorant' and thus valorising an urban existence over a supposedly 'rural' one. As such, the notion of urbicide conceived as the destruction of the city by the countryside fails to get to grips with the meaning of the destruction itself, acting rather as a denunciation of the 'backwardness' of the rural way of life and thus as a mechanism for stigmatising the forces of ethnic-nationalism as foreign to the civilised space of the city (for a similar charge, see Herscher 2007). Whilst there is much to condemn within ethnic nationalism, concentrating on supposed barbarity or backwardness distracts us from a considered analysis of the role the destruction of the built environment plays in such political programs.

The use of the term 'urbicide' to identify a specific form of destruction is not, of course, without its own political entailments. Thus in examinations of destruction in Bosnia, Israeli house demolitions in the West Bank and the destruction of the World Trade Center in New York City, 'urbicide' has been deployed in order to indicate that a pattern of deliberate destruction of elements of the built environment was a form of political violence in its own right, integral to specific political programs. Stephen Graham argues that the urbicidal destruction of the Jenin refugee camp by bulldozer is part of a wider program to erase Palestinian identity from certain areas of the Occupied Territories (Graham 2002; Graham 2003). Similarly, in his considerations of the significance of the World Trade Center attack on 11 September 2001, Michael Safier regards the destruction of these buildings as a deliberate attempt to erase a structure that acts as a substrate for a certain kind of identity or way of life (Safier 2001).

'Urbicide' is thus discursively deployed to indicate that the destruction of the urban environment is an event worthy of attention in its own right. That is, 'urbicide' is deployed to ensure that such destruction is not seen as secondary, or incidental, to other political dynamics. However, in addition 'urbicide' represents a discursive attempt to indicate both the systematic nature of attacks on the built environment and the politically deleterious effect of such violence. In other words, 'urbicide' represents an attempt to show that a variety of cases of urban destruction comprise a single phenomenon, rather than isolated cases. In outlining such a phenomenon, 'urbicide' also represents an attempt to contest the politics underlying such violence. Identification of the phenomenon of urbicide is thus not a neutral or disinterested academic enquiry, but rather comprises an ethico-political act that illuminates a distinctive violence whilst also contesting the political logics underlying it. In this sense, 'urbicide' shares much with other discursive terms (e.g., 'genocide') used to address political violence, which similarly identify violences in order to contest their underlying logics. Despite commonalities in discursive deployment, however, usages of the concept of urbicide have not been systematic. Accordingly, urbicide has not received a sustained elaboration regarding both its meaning and entailments. It is worth, therefore, outlining the conceptual contours of urbicide in more detail.

'Urbicide': a conceptual definition

A systematic enquiry into the meaning of the concept of urbicide must begin with an inquiry into the meaning of the term. 'Urbicide' derives its meaning from the joining of 'urban' and '-cide'. Taken literally, 'urbicide' refers to the 'killing, slaughter' or 'slaying' of that which is subsumed under the term 'urban' (Oxford English Dictionary 1989, Vol. III, 213–214). At stake in the meaning of 'urbicide', therefore, is what is to be understood in the concept of 'the urban', what it is that is destroyed in this act of literally 'killing the urban'.

'Urban', derived from the Latin *urbanus*, refers to that which is 'characteristic of, occurring or taking place, in a city or town' (Oxford English Dictionary 1989, Vol. XIX, 331). Importantly, the term has a dual meaning. Insofar as 'urban' refers to the characteristics that identify towns or cities (originally in opposition to rural villages or estates), it refers both to the material conditions that constitute the town or city as such, and the way of life specific to such material conditions. That is, 'urban' refers to both the specific building patterns (in particular, to the density and size of these patterns) that identify the city as well as to the particular experience of life in such an environment. 'Urbicide', therefore, refers both to the destruction of the built environment that comprises the fabric of the urban as well as to the destruction of the way of life specific to such material conditions. Indeed urbicide is the destruction of a specific existential quality through the destruction of the built environment. This 'existential quality' is a common characteristic of all those ways of life that are considered 'urban' by virtue of occurring in the spaces constituted by the built environment. The question, therefore, is, 'What specific characteristic is common to all those ways of life that could be said to be "urban"?'. Once we have identified this characteristic, it will be possible to address the manner in which destruction of buildings comprises a destruction of this existential quality.

In his classic essay 'Urbanism as a Way of Life', Louis Wirth argues that it is the size, density and heterogeneity of the populations of cities that constitute 'those elements of urbanism which mark it as a distinctive mode of life' (Wirth 1996, 190). Despite naming three factors that characterise urbanity, it is heterogeneity that is its principal aspect according to Wirth. Indeed, the size of an urban population is pertinent only insofar as it leads to a greater number of different identities and associations and thus heterogeneity of tradition and belief. Similarly, density of the urban population is important insofar as it gives rise to a greater frequency of encounters between these heterogeneous traditions and beliefs. *Heterogeneity*, then, can be said to be the defining characteristic of, or existential quality that defines, 'the urban'.[3]

If we identify urbanity as entailing, principally, heterogeneous existence, we can say that the destruction of urban life is the destruction of heterogeneity. The destruction of the built environment that constitutes the material substrate of urban existence is, therefore, the destruction of the conditions of possibility of heterogeneity. What is at stake in urbicide is thus the conditions of possibility of heterogeneity. Urbicide, then, is the destruction of buildings not for what they individually represent (military target, cultural heritage, conceptual metaphor) but as that which is the condition of possibility of heterogeneous existence.

Such a definition of urbicide is, however, merely a lexical clarification of what might have been an unfamiliar term. This clarification tells us little about urbicide in any of the contexts in which we find it. Moreover, it tells us little about the manner in which destroying buildings can be understood as the destruction of the conditions of possibility of heterogeneity. In order to proceed with an examination of these twin themes, I want to turn to the conceptual kinship between 'urbicide' and 'genocide'. By looking at the systematic nature of destruction implied in both concepts, it is possible to identify the manner in which a 'logic' of destruction inheres to urbicide.

Urbicide and genocide: distinct yet interrelated concepts

The term 'urbicide' discursively implies both a similarity and a distinction between violence brought to bear on the built environment and genocide: the 'practice of extermination of nations and ethnic groups' (Lemkin 1994, xi). On the one hand, 'urbicide' draws upon a lexical-conceptual similarity with 'genocide' in order to emphasise the scale and importance of the destruction that occurs, whilst on the other, 'urbicide' stresses that the destruction of the built environment is an event that, whilst interrelated with 'genocide', is nonetheless lexically (and thus conceptually) distinctive and, therefore, deserving of treatment in its own right.

When defining 'genocide' in 1944, Raphael Lemkin found that it was necessary to coin a new word for the violence perpetrated by the Nazis (Huttenbach 2005, 443). Though there had been various acts of violence throughout history with which one might draw parallels in order to understand Nazi violence (Lemkin cites, amongst others, the example of the destruction of Carthage in 146 BC), it was necessary, argued Lemkin, to coin a new term that took account of the systematic character of the Holocaust. 'Genocide', argued Lemkin, signified a 'coordinated plan of different actions aiming at the destruction of essential foundations of national groups, with the aim of annihilating the groups themselves' (Lemkin 1994, 79).

And yet in using a separate term, the authors of *Mostar '92 – Urbicid* were indicating that it was not sufficient to understand the destruction of the built environment as an aspect of the 'destruction of essential foundations of national groups' (Lemkin 1994, xi). To subsume it in such a manner would essentially limit us to two possible ways of understanding the destruction of buildings: as either acts of symbolic destruction (destruction of the cultural symbols that underpin a national group); or acts of collateral damage attendant to the overall project of the elimination of a national group (things that were hit whilst driving out or killing a particular ethnic group).

'Urbicide', therefore, was intended to signify that there was a 'coordinated plan of different actions aiming at the destruction' of the built environment: buildings, infrastructure, and monuments in particular. The use of 'urbicide' noted, however, that this coordinated plan, and the violence attendant to it, had a logic that was not subsidiary to genocide. As such, *Mostar '92 – Urbicid* was a plea to observers of the Bosnian War to recognise the distinct nature of the violence against the built environment.

It is important to note the manner in which these distinctions and interrelations are drawn. On the one hand, those deploying the concept of urbicide intend to note that the target of this violence and, hence, the political entailments, are substantially different to those of genocide. And, hence, they argue, the destruction of the built environment should be regarded as a distinct form of political violence. On the other hand, however, those deploying the notion of urbicide intended to demonstrate that it shared crucial distinguishing features with the concept of genocide. Genocide, it is argued, is a concept that indicates a *systematic* form of political violence. It is this systematicity that those using the concept of urbicide intended to draw upon in order to show that, whilst *targets and political entailments* may differ between genocide and urbicide, the *nature of the execution of these forms of violence* did not. Put simply, the analogy with genocide was intended to show that, despite different targets and entailments, there was a *logic* of urbicide that could be said to be similar to that of genocide.

The 'logic' of urbicide

In referring to a 'logic' of urbicide I am not arguing that urbicide is 'logical' in the sense of the necessary outcome of a particular set of circumstances or decisions. The notion that urbicide has a 'logic' that is not identical or subsidiary to that of genocide is intended to indicate that urbicide is a conceptual term for a set of events that, *taken together*, amount to a 'coordinated plan of different actions' (Lemkin 1994, 79). 'Logic', therefore, refers to the articulation of contingent events or elements in a consistent pattern, thus giving rise to a specific overall phenomenon. Logic is not a mathematical function or algorithm (which would have a logical outcome), but rather a grammar into which different meaningful, and yet contingent, elements can be put. The separation of 'logic' and 'logical' allows the identification of the coordinated combination of a set of elements in order to produce a given phenomenon whilst also recognising the contingency of such a coordination. That is, it recognises that this combination was neither inevitable, nor the product of a single will or intent.

We might say that the 'logic' of a political formation such as genocide or urbicide is akin to Deleuze and Guattari's notion of *the concept*. 'Concepts', as Deleuze and Guattari (1994, 16) note, 'are connected to problems without which they would have no meaning and which can themselves only be isolated or understood as their solution emerges … [thus] concepts are … created as a function of problems which are thought to be badly understood or badly posed'. Genocide exists as a concept to name the 'coordinated plan' for the destruction of national groups. The Holocaust (or Shoah) exists as a concept to name the destruction of European Jews. In both cases, these concepts name the consistent and yet contingent articulation of certain elements into a specific political formation. In both cases, these events comprise problems that are thought to be badly understood or badly posed under the concept of, for example, the destruction of civil populations in war time.

'Concepts', argue Deleuze and Guattari, have a certain 'consistency' or 'endo-consistency'. That is, concepts represent the specific conjunction of components in such a manner that they are rendered inseparable insofar as the concept is concerned. The *concept* of genocide requires a certain set of interlocking components in order to be recognised as such. When a certain consistent combination of elements occurs, as it was argued to have done in the case of the violence against Bosnian Muslims or Rwandan Tutsis, the concept of genocide is recognised to be manifest. What is important here is the notion that '[c]omponents remain distinct, but something passes from one to the other' (Deleuze and Guattari 1994, 20). It is in this sense that a 'concept' (in Deleuze and Guattari's sense) could also be said to be a 'logic'. *Logic* captures a sense of articulation in which something from one element passes to another, giving rise to an interlocking set of elements that must be seen, *in toto* as one event.

Thus, when

> radical … anti-Semitism of the Nazi type; transformation of that anti-Semitism into the practical policy of a powerful, centralised state; that state being in command of a huge, efficient bureaucratic apparatus; states of emergency … which allowed the government and the bureaucracy it controlled to get away with things which could, possibly, face more serious obstacles in time of peace; and the non-interference, the passive acceptance of those things by the population at large

> (Bauman 1991, 94)

come together, one has what can be recognised as 'genocide'. In this combination, anti-Semitism is not simply an isolated event, but rather gives something to bureaucracy which, in turn, takes something from the powerful state in order to become radical (that is, exterminatory).[4] We could say that these elements give rise to a political formation which would only be properly understood by using the *concept* of genocide. We could say that the manner in which these elements are articulated together, the way in which one gives something to another, comprises the *logic* of genocide.

Those who argue that urbicide is deserving of attention in its own right argue along similar lines. Urbicide, according to this perspective, is the name of a problem that is inadequately understood as part of the logic, or concept, of genocide. Urbicide is the consistent, though contingent, combination of a number of elements such that, together, these elements generate a specific phenomenon with its own conceptual logic. The destruction of buildings happens in many contexts. However, it is argued that in the case of the destruction of buildings in a conflict such as the 1992–95 Bosnian War, a contingent set of events were articulated together in a consistent manner that cannot be understood under previously extant conceptual logics. That is, the widespread destruction of the urban fabric is distinct from the destruction of either strategically important or symbolic buildings or the collateral damage attendant to war or genocide. The destruction of the urban fabric of Bosnia suggests a consistent articulation of a number of elements: the destruction of all types of buildings; the concomitant destruction of the basis of urbanity; and, importantly, the creation of new, homogeneous, communities as a consequence of this destruction.

However, noting a conceptual logic in the destruction of built environments is at best an analytic tool. The concept of urbicide and the logic of destruction entailed in this concept is an analytic device to demonstrate that destruction of elements of the built environment are not isolated instances or cases of violations of the extant laws of war, but rather part of a wider formation of political violence. Identifying the logic itself, however, tells us little about the meaning of the particular conjunction of elements that the concept represents. And it is here that the kinship between urbicide and genocide is particularly productive.

The meaning of the logic of genocide, the specific phenomenon that emerges out of the contingent articulation of a number of elements into a form recognisable under the concept of genocide, can be illuminated by reference to Lemkin's original attempt to understand Nazi occupation techniques. According to Lemkin, Nazi occupation techniques comprised a coordinated practice to destroy the occupied nations. Lemkin argues that this 'practice of extermination of national and ethnic groups' can be understood as consisting of two distinct phases. Firstly, the 'destruction of the national pattern of the oppressed group' and secondly, 'imposition of the national pattern of the oppressor', an imposition that may be upon either 'the oppressed population that is allowed to remain, or upon the territory alone' (Lemkin 1994, 79).

It is these two phases that provide the key to the meaning of the contingent articulation of elements that are recognisable as genocide. The events that comprise genocide entail both the destruction of a particular national or ethnic culture (this need not be achieved through extermination, since destruction of the conditions under which a culture can exist will be sufficient) and the imposition of another national or ethnic culture. It is precisely the manner in which genocide is directed at the destruction of a national group that defines the concept of genocide. Without this defining feature, manifest in the two phases of genocide, the various elements that combine to give the concept of genocide would be seen merely as a forced relocation or a bloody massacre. This defining feature led Lemkin to conclude that in genocide, violence 'is directed against the national group as an entity, and the actions involved are directed against individuals, not in their individual capacity, but as members of the national group' (Lemkin 1994, 79).

The concept of genocide entails *an understanding of destruction in relation to that which is destroyed.* It is implicit in our understanding of killing as part of the logic of genocide that we do not simply see the killing of *each* individual as a *means* to the end of extermination. In fact, it is not *extermination* – however (in) complete this may be – which defines genocide.[5] Rather, what we understand to be the meaning of genocide is played out in *each and every death, each and every time.* Since genocide is enacted in each and every death, it expresses a relation between what is destroyed and the meaning of destruction that is other than the simple death of the individual – that is why each death is an instance of genocide and not simple homicide. It is integral, therefore, to our understanding of the conceptual logic/consistency of genocide that we recognise what 'it' is that is destroyed, and the meaning of the destruction. In genocide, 'it' is a member of a national or ethnic group and the destruction has the meaning of the eradication of this group.

It is precisely here that the simultaneous kinship and difference between urbicide and genocide can be noted. In drawing an analogy between the destruction of urban fabric and the destruction of ethnic groups, the authors of *Mostar '92 – Urbicid* noted that the destruction of urban fabric derived its meaning from the relationship between the destruction and what 'it' is that is destroyed. At the same time, they noted that what 'it' is that is destroyed is distinct from that destroyed in genocide. If we draw on the previous lexical definition of urbicide, it is possible to outline the relationship of destruction to that which is destroyed that gives urbicide its specific conceptual logic. Put simply, urbicide entails the destruction of buildings as the constitutive elements of urbanity. Buildings are destroyed because they are the condition of possibility of urbanity. Urbicide is, therefore, the destruction of urbanity for its own sake. The logic of urbicide then is the destruction of the conditions of possibility of heterogeneity.

This destruction is, like genocide, a two-phase affair. Firstly, the conditions of possibility of heterogeneity are destroyed, followed by the imposition of homogeneity. The destruction of the conditions of heterogeneity is, as I have noted before, the destruction of the condition of possibility of the being-with others that constitutes the political. Urbicide, then, is a fundamentally political matter since it represents the violent foreclosure of the possibility of the political. Such foreclosure is the exemplary totalitarian moment, a violent foreclosure of the heterogeneous political arena that precedes the determination of society according to one single political program.[6] What an understanding of the meaning of urbicide yields, therefore, is an opening onto an inquiry into precisely how the built environment constitutes this condition of possibility of heterogeneity that I have argued is at the heart of what we understand as political existence.

Intent

Referring to the 'logic' of urbicide or genocide, however, raises one of the abiding problematics in the definition of genocide: the concept of 'intent'. I have suggested that urbicide draws upon a similarity with genocide insofar as both could be said to have (though not share) 'a logic'. That is, in both genocide and urbicide a number of acts or events are articulated together to constitute a specific type of political violence. Urbicide and genocide are distinct insofar as a) the acts and events that comprise each are different, and b) each represents a distinctive form of political violence. Nevertheless both have a distinct logic: each is identifiable as a distinct concept insofar as a certain set of acts or events are combined in a consistent manner to constitute a specific type of political violence. Moreover this type of political violence will have a certain endoconsistency: each act/event will confer something on the others in such a way that, taken as a whole, none of the acts or events is separable from each other.

The question arises, then, whether there is a single factor that binds together these acts/events into an endoconsistent form of political violence. For many scholars and commentators, the acts/events that comprise genocide are bound together by the *intent* of the genocidal party. Given that genocide and urbicide could be said to both be logics of destruction, it could be argued that both logics are bound together by the same factor. It is worth, then, examining both the manner in which intent has been understood as the underlying articulatory force behind genocide and whether it could serve a similar function with respect to urbicide.

In the codification of the United Nations Genocide Convention (UNGC), genocide was defined as 'intent to destroy in whole or in part a national, racial, or religious group as such' (Andreopoulos 1994, 229). This formula represents the legal codification of Lemkin's 'coordinated plan of different actions aiming at the destruction of essential foundations of national groups, with the aim of annihilating the groups themselves' (Lemkin 1994, 79). 'Intent' is thus the codification of 'coordination'. Historically this has led to a distinctive problem with the prevention and punishment of genocide. Intent has been notoriously difficult to establish and, hence, 'coordinated plans' for the destruction of a national, ethnic, racial or religious group have, in the absence of proof of intent, been seen as acts other than genocide.

Central to the problem of intent is the manner in which interpreters of the UNGC have supposed that proof of intent requires either establishing a chain of command through which an authority was able to execute a plan for genocidal destruction or unlocking the psychological motives of those perpetrating violence. However, these represent very particular, problematic interpretations of Lemkin's original notion of 'coordination' (Shaw 2007, 81–92). Establishing chains of command assumes that the force committing genocide is formally organised in a manner akin to the modern European state. Insofar as the Holocaust represents the model on the basis of which the UNGC was developed, such an assumption is understandable. However, in less formalised circumstances, where genocide may be committed by paramilitary or informal forces, such a chain of command is difficult to establish.

Furthermore, suggesting that 'coordination' comprises a chain of command represents an attribution of blame that tends to shift the focus of enquiry away from the manner in which otherwise everyday acts/events became articulated into a specific type of political violence. To reiterate Bauman's (1991, xii) argument, if we focus upon the manner in which the final solution was planned and orchestrated by the Nazi command structures, we lose sight of the manner in which anti-Semitism, bureaucracy, transport, technology and nationalism combine to create a specific type of political violence. This is not to suggest that those who bear greatest responsibility for the destruction of the Holocaust should not be held responsible and punished accordingly. It is, however, to say that the articulation of such acts and events into the logic of genocide is not achieved by those in power alone. Indeed, as Bauman notes, to stop our efforts to understand genocide at those who bear greatest responsibility would result in our failing to delineate the intimate connections between modernity and genocidal violence.

Establishing the psychological motives of individuals, or the collective ensembles they form, is even more problematic. Indeed, sociologists would argue that such endeavours are, by virtue of their psychologism, contrary to most of the accepted methodologies for the study of social phenomena. In her survey of the nature of genocide as a sociological concept, Helen Fein notes that the understanding of intent as psychological motive represents a basic confusion of the two categories (Fein 1993, 19). Intent, Fein argues, consists of 'purposeful action': 'deliberate or repeated acts with foreseeable results' (*Ibid.*, 20). We could say that such purposeful action is equivalent to a deliberate act of destruction. The concept of purposeful action, then, is intended to rule out cases in which destruction is committed on an accidental basis. However, the concept is also intended to remove the need for speculation regarding psychological motives. Indeed, if we say that destruction is intentional insofar as it is deliberate and its results were foreseeable, it is not necessary to speculate about the 'perpetrators' construction of an account or motive' (*Ibid.*). For Fein, purposeful action is a sociological 'bridge' between the problem of legal guilt and psychological motive. Where the former does not explain the wider mechanisms at work in a particular type of political violence, the latter is largely a matter of speculation and thus is difficult to hold up to any scholarly scrutiny.

Understanding intent as purposeful action removes from discussions of the logic of destruction in genocide the idea that there is a single point from which the various acts and events that comprise this type of political violence are coordinated. Intent, then, only refers to the way in which destruction was carried out purposefully: that the destruction was deliberate and its results foreseeable. Coordination, on the other hand, must be taken to refer to the manner in which the various acts and events are articulated together such that they become interlocking and, thus, consistently identifiable as a specific type of political violence. Intent, then, gets us no closer to understanding what the 'logic' of violence such as genocide or urbicide entails. Intent merely sets us off on a distracting path to attribute guilt and/or ascribe narratives of psychological motive. It is not integral to the *logic* of urbicide or genocide then to demonstrate intent. *Logic* simply implies that the various acts or events that make up such political violence are articulated into a wider program of destruction. What is at stake then for scholars of such political violence is not the proof of intent, but rather understanding both how various acts and events are articulated together and the consequence of such a combination.

Excursus: on 'definitionalism'

Writing about accounts of the conceptual logic of genocide, Israel Charny comments on the 'ills of definitionalism' (Charny 1994, 90). Charny argues that there is a tendency within genocide studies towards 'a perverse, fetishistic involvement with definitions to the point at which the reality of the subject under discussion is "lost"' (*Ibid.*, 91). Charny's argument lies with those who would craft narrow definitions of genocide that reserve the concept for one type of mass killing alone, thus diminishing the importance of others. Paradoxically, however, Charny's understanding of genocide becomes so broad as to be unable to distinguish between different types of political violence. Furthermore, in arguing against definitionalism, Charny verges on a repudiation of the formulation and refinement of concepts to understand various types of political violence. As Shaw (2007, 33) notes, Charny's indictment of definitionalism thus has the counterproductive effect of becoming a 'justification for adopting loose definitions that [make] it difficult to distinguish types of violence in a coherent way'.

Whilst I cannot, therefore, support Charny's notion that we do not need precise and refined concepts for understanding the multiple forms of political violence, I want to take his warning as a provocation to explore two of the 'ills of definitionalism' that might be said to affect anyone attempting to outline and understand the logic of urbicide. In the first place, accounts of urbicide themselves face an accusation of definitionalism in the form of an argument that the distinction between urbicide and genocide is falsely drawn. This critique argues that the politics of exclusion at work in distinguishing urbicide from genocide distracts from the 'real' work of recognising the mass killing that comprises genocide. I will examine this argument in relation to comments made by Martin Shaw regarding the relationship between urbicide, genocide and war.

Secondly, it is possible to find a perverse logic of definitionalism at work in another criticism of the term 'urbicide'. This critique begins by noting the manner in which 'urbicide' relies on a definition of 'urbanity' that conflates 'the urban' and 'the city' unproblematically. Moreover, this argument contends that accounts of 'urbicide' arrive at an understanding of urbanity through a contrast between 'the urban' and 'the rural' (or city and countryside). Such a contrast, it is argued, is problematic due to the fictive nature of the distinction between urban and rural ways of life. Ultimately, the critique argues, there is nothing that could be said, unproblematically, to comprise the urban, and thus 'urbicide' is an empty conceptual term. I will argue that this definitionalism, whilst worth examining, ultimately distracts us from the rubble of destroyed buildings that comprises the proper object of enquiry for accounts of the logic of urbicide. Finally we should note that, whilst both types of definitionalism are, ultimately, a distraction, these arguments represent an opportunity to sharpen the focus of my inquiry into the nature and entailments of urbicide.

Is urbicide really distinct from genocide?

In his essay 'New Wars of the City: Relationships of "Urbicide" and "Genocide"', Martin Shaw argues that urbicide cannot be seen as distinct from genocide (Shaw 2004).[7] Shaw's argument is intended to show, ultimately, that urbicide is an element of genocide and that the latter must be seen as an illegitimate form of war. Shaw begins by noting that the city has been a target for military attack throughout history. Shaw argues that the rise of the modern nation-state has led to a de-fortification of the city and, hence, an increasing vulnerability of urban life to military attack. Shaw then argues that, whilst attacks upon the city may well be an attack on urbanity, such violence comprises a means to the end of genocide. That is to say, targeting the city is a means to target the population within the city as part of genocide. Moreover, Shaw argues that there are multiple instances of destruction outside the city that would be ignored were one to focus upon urbicide. Having demonstrated that urbicide is an element of genocide, Shaw then argues that genocide itself must be understood as an illegitimate form of warfare in which an aggressor attacks a defined group regardless of their surrender or capacity to defend themselves. As such, then, urbicide is merely an element of genocidal war.

Shaw's argument is a critique of a perceived definitionalism in accounts of the logic of urbicide. For Shaw, treating urbicide as a distinct category risks failing 'to grasp the unities of the relationships and processes of violence and destruction' by counterposing 'different dimensions of these actions/experiences as categorical opposites' (Shaw 2004, 149). It is worth responding to this critique as it will help both to clarify the nature of what is targeted in urbicide and to specify the proper relation of urbicide and genocide.

In the first place, it should be stated that urbicide is not counterposed to genocide. In the account of the logic of urbicide above, I draw upon the kinship between urbicide and genocide in order to sketch out the former's logic through analogy with the latter. Despite the conceptual similarities, I argue that urbicide is distinct from genocide. I do not, however, argue that the two are mutually exclusive when it comes to describing instances of political violence. Identifying the destruction of the built environment as urbicide does not preclude identification of the simultaneous occurrence of genocide. Insofar as instances of political violence are, as Shaw rightly notes, complex, many forms of violence (not to mention other forms of social relation) might co-exist together.

The question, then, is whether we should discriminate between such forms of violence, or roll them into one, encompassing category. It is, of course, possible to argue that proliferation of terms for forms of violence constitutes the creation of a set of euphemisms that elide the true horror of mass killing. Indeed, this is the argument levelled against the use of 'ethnic cleansing': that this term, devised by the (Bosnian) Serb aggressors, masks the genocidal nature of the killing and displacement in the 1992–95 Bosnian War (Sells 1996, 10; Shaw 2007, 48–62). As such, this is a political critique aimed at demonstrating the way in which categorisation might be used to diminish the criminality or tragedy of mass killing. However, the concept of urbicide is deployed not to mask, but to reveal hitherto unnoticed forms of violence. Indeed, urbicide is neither mutually exclusive of genocide nor does it mask the destruction of the built environment by eliding this with the destruction of the population of such environments. On the contrary, the concept of urbicide illuminates that which has been masked by the anthropocentric bias of much analysis of political violence: the deliberate destruction of the built environment. Thus this critique seems somewhat redundant.

Shaw, however, argues against the deployment of urbicide as distinct category for another reason. Whilst agreeing that the urban way of life is one of plurality, Shaw argues that it is not the buildings (as condition of possibility of such plurality) that are at stake in assaults on the built environment, but rather the population of the towns and cities under attack. Seen in this way, of course, urbicide is an aspect of genocide. However, this repositioning of urbicide as an element of genocide relies on a confusion of the target of urbicide with that of genocide. Clarifying this confusion offers a chance to sharpen the focus of the concept of urbicide.

The concept of 'urbicide' can be seen as invoking two possible meanings. On the one hand, urbicide can be taken to comprise an attack on the city in order to destroy the specific way of life that is found in the city (as opposed to the countryside). On the other hand, urbicide could be said to comprise the destruction of buildings *qua* the condition of possibility of a certain type of space (in principle, public space) that is itself productive of a variety of identities. As such, then, the space established by buildings would be the crucible of politics, the place in which a plurality of identities negotiate the multiple boundaries of self and other. Urbicidal political programs attack buildings, therefore, because they want to destroy the political possibilities that inhere to the public space generated by buildings. Whilst the former sense of urbicide might be that invoked by Huxtable (1972), the latter is the one I wish to concentrate on in this argument.

According to this use of 'urbicide', it is the manner in which buildings comprise the substrate for a plurality of identities that is at stake in such violence. This is crucial to understanding the logic of such urbicide: it is the buildings themselves (as a condition of possibility for plurality or heterogeneity in general) that are targeted for destruction. In this sense, buildings are not targeted as a means to an end, where the end is the destruction of a specific way of life (or population) that may be heterogeneous to that of an aggressor. Rather, buildings are destroyed as the material substrate that is the condition of possibility of plurality or heterogeneity in general. In other words, it is the conditions of possibility of urbanity (public space constituted through and around buildings), rather than a specific urban existence (i.e., a given population), that are at stake in urbicide. Shaw has correctly asserted that destruction of specific forms of urbanity is indeed best understood as an instance of genocide. However, destruction of buildings as the condition of possibility of all the possible identities that might (at any time) comprise a particular urban population should be seen as distinct from genocide.

Of course, it is possible to redefine genocide as the destruction of heterogeneity in general. However, at that stage genocide includes not only war, but also town planning, colonialism and many other – undeniably violent, yet distinct – forms of violence. This is not Shaw's intention, and I would concur that this is an undesirable route for scholars of political violence. Overall, then, Shaw's argument provides an opportunity to sharpen my account of the logics of urbicide insofar as it affords the opportunity to restate the target of urbicide. Moreover, it affords the opportunity to restate that at no point should the logics of urbicide be taken to preclude the simultaneous operation of the logics of genocide.

Urban/rural

In my account of the logics of urbicide above, I argued that buildings are targeted in order to destroy an 'existential quality': urbanity. I identified the distinctive feature of urbanity to be 'heterogeneity'. I argued, therefore, that the built environment was targeted as that which constituted the conditions of possibility of heterogeneity. Identifying that quality which is common to all experiences which might be called 'urban' is, however, a more problematic venture than this spare definition indicates. Indeed, in urban sociology there have been various attempts to divine the defining characteristics of 'the urban' which have yielded mixed results (for surveys of these attempts, see: Saunders 1986; Savage and Warde 1993; Dewey 1960). This difficulty in defining 'the urban' gives rise to a particular, definitionalist critique of the concept of urbicide.

This critique is predicated upon the argument that accounts of the qualities that inhere in 'the urban' posit a fictive distinction between the city and the countryside. It is thus argued that 'the urban' taken to be at stake in urbicide is a fictive entity defined in relation to a fictive 'rural' life. On close inspection, it is argued, this fictive urbanity is found to have no basis other than its opposition to an invented rurality. Thus it is not possible to find a substantive quality that can be referred to as 'urbanity', and although buildings may be destroyed in a variety of contexts, it is not possible to say that they share a single common characteristic.

This critique gives rise to two further, interrelated criticisms of the concept of urbicide. Firstly, it is argued that, in the absence of being able to identify an unambiguous quality that defines urbanity, the concept of urbicide elides 'the urban' and 'the city', thus defining urbicide as that which threatens the city (cf. Herscher 2007). Secondly, it is argued that the definition of 'the urban' in contrast to 'the rural' comprises a normative privileging of the former over the latter. Moreover, insofar as 'the urban' and 'the city' are elided, urbicide comprises the normative elevation of the city over the countryside. Thus it is argued that accounts of the logic of urbicide comprise a valorisation of metro- and cosmopolitan life and a covert attack upon the supposed barbarism and backwardness of the countryside. Such an understanding fails to see the violences that occur outside the confines of the city. As such, then, the concept of urbicide is said to perpetuate crude stereotypes. It is worth examining these arguments in turn as responses to both will help, once again, to sharpen my account of the logics of urbicide.

In his survey of urban sociology, Peter Saunders argues that Louis Wirth and George Simmel represent the principal attempts to define 'the urban' as an experience or phenomenon (Saunders 1986, 85–105). Both thinkers base their definitions on a perceived distinction between the urban and the rural. For Wirth, the urban comprises an experience of heterogeneity (by virtue of the density, size and plurality of cities) that is absent in a rural existence. Simmel, on the other hand, takes the urban to mark a temporal distinction between the modernity of the city and the pre-modernity of the countryside. Neither conception of the urban is possible without a corresponding conception of the rural. In *The Country and The City*, Raymond Williams examines this opposition between urban and rural (Williams 1973). Williams demonstrates not only the mutually constitutive nature of this conceptual pairing, but also the problematic nature of any assumption regarding the clarity of a dividing line between either concept. It is not possible, argues Williams, to see the countryside as a reservoir of tradition and homogeneity: indeed, it is agrarian capitalism that provides the engine of progress, and the country estate which forms a point around which a number of heterogeneous social forces and modes of production are established.

In surveying the perceived difference between urban and rural, Richard Dewey came to the conclusion that it is a continuum rather than a binary dualism (Dewey 1960). Moreover, as Savage and Warde (1993, 109) note, urban and rural do not exist separately, but in admixture. Features that are supposedly characteristic of the urban can be found in contexts that are classified as rural and vice versa: progress on the farm, homogeneity in city enclaves. It is precisely this impossibility of separating urban from rural that led Dewey to conclude that the rural–urban continuum is 'real but unimportant' (1960, 66).

Such a conclusion supports the definitionalist critique of the concept of urbicide. In support of such a critique it is possible to assert that destruction of buildings is not confined to supposedly 'urban' contexts. For example, villages and farms are destroyed in conflicts such as the 1992–95 Bosnian War. Such destruction of buildings cannot be said to comprise the destruction of 'the urban' lest that concept lose all specificity. Thus urbicide could be said to be needlessly restrictive in the range of phenomena it covers and hence somewhat arbitrary in its formation. In addition, it is possible to argue that whilst cities such as Sarajevo can be seen to be instances of plurality or heterogeneity, other instances of destruction of the built environment could be said to comprise destruction of homogeneous enclaves. Such an observation is intended to demonstrate that the concept of 'urbicide' is based on an idealised, fictive notion of the plurality of the city.

To this critique must be added that of the normative connotations of the urban–rural distinction. Urbanity, or '[f]ollowing the pursuits [and] having the ideas or sentiments ... characteristic of town or city life' (Oxford English Dictionary 1989,

Vol. XIX, 332) is, according to Anton Zijderveld, 'usually seen as a synonym of suavity: a refined politeness or courtesy … It comes close to civility, derived from the Latin *civilitas*' (Zijderveld 1998, 21). Just as being humane, or displaying humanity, is taken to comprise the exercise of those virtues (such as compassion or mercy) that express the qualities that distinguish humans from animals, so urbanity is taken to refer to the characteristics that distinguish city-dwellers from those who live in the country. Moreover, given urbanity's association with notions of civility, 'urban' is taken to indicate the progressive nature of city living versus the traditional nature of country dwelling.

This normative connotation is clear in the various commentaries on the 1992–95 Bosnian War which portray this conflict as a 'revenge of the countryside' (Bougarel 1999, 157). As I have noted, it was common to portray the dissolution of Yugoslavia as a conflict driven by a nationalism which was rural in origin. Such a portrayal, drawing on the work of early twentieth-century ethnographers such as Dinko Tomasic, posited that the rural population of former Yugoslavia was characterised by its cult of heroism and opposition to the urban culture of the towns and cities of the region (Bougarel 1999, 158–159). Ramet describes this rural backwardness as the '"idiocy" of the countryside', drawing on the ancient Greek root of the concept of idiocy, *idios*, meaning private (Ramet 1996, 70–87). According to Ramet, the 'idiocy' of the countryside lies in the manner in which rural communities could be said to be inward looking, whilst the urban is characterised by the public nature of its political life. Rural life is thus traditional, homogeneous and, ultimately, a populist refusal of the heterogeneity and plurality of the city (*Ibid.*, 71–73).

Such characterisation of the violence against cities can easily slide into a stereo-typing of such violence as a revenge upon the urbane forces of progress by those who are backward-looking and isolated. Such a characterisation tends to portray rural populations as inherently opposed to the city, and to normatively code the urban experience as progressive. Such characterisations lead to a mythologisation of the distinction between countryside and city in which urbicide is no longer a concept that reveals a logic of destruction, but a condemnation of the manner in which barbaric rural forces have destroyed a progressive cosmopolitan future (Grodach 2002, 76–77). That this is problematic can be seen in the manner in which paramilitary militias were drawn from depressed industrial towns in Serbia, and in which many rural villages were just as much a target of violence as cities such as Sarajevo.[8]

It is important to respond to these critiques in order to sharpen the focus of my outline of the logics of urbicide. With respect to the crude stereotyping of the violence against cities such as Mostar and Sarajevo as a 'revenge of the countryside', it is important to note my comments with regard to Shaw's confusion of the target of urbicide. In my account of the logics of urbicide, it is the built environment that is the target, not any specific form of urban life. Thus if urbicide is a condemnation of anything, it is a condemnation of the destruction of buildings. As such, I have held in suspension the question of whether city life is normatively superior to rural life. I doubt, however, that such a question is even worth pursuing. Insofar as rural and urban exist in admixture and the heterogeneity of urbanity admits of all forms of existence, it seems logical that there will be both progress and its lack in both rural and urban (insofar as these are identifiable).

However, this leaves the question of whether the difficulty of identifying the quality that defines 'the urban' leaves the concept of urbicide with little purchase. This critique seems to me to require a more complex response, but one that represents an important clarification of the logic of urbicide nonetheless. It is important to note that despite arguing that the rural–urban continuum is sociologically unimportant, Dewey nevertheless regards this continuum as real (Dewey 1960, 66). This suggests that, whilst it may be difficult to offer a concept of 'the urban' that is useful for sociological analysis, the notion of 'the urban' has some purchase in naming a certain type of experience (or existential quality). I would contend that the core of such an experience is the heterogeneity whose condition of possibility is constituted by buildings. 'Urbanity', then, is a plurality or heterogeneity constituted by buildings. It is possible, therefore, to speak of an experience or existential quality identifiable as 'urban' and yet not locatable in a geographico-demographic manner. That is to say, 'urbanity' cannot necessarily be confined to a specific type of settlement on the basis of either its size, density or modernity (as either Wirth or Simmel might have liked to have posited). The built environment is fundamental to such a definition and thus urbicide is, at its core, the destruction of buildings in order to destroy a certain existential quality constituted by those buildings.

Such a definition, of course, broadens urbicide beyond the destruction of the city. This is not a problem unless we cling to the stereotypical definition of the rural–urban continuum that defines one as residing within the city limits and the other as falling outside such a boundary. Indeed, such a broadening of the possibilities of the urban resonates with commentaries on the urbanisation of life under globalisation. As Richard Skeates (1997) notes, the urban experience in the era of globalisation cannot be easily identified with the city as it has traditionally been conceived. This problem arises due to the disappearance of easily recognisable boundaries for the city. Indeed, the globalised sprawl of the twenty-first century, with its multiple networks of production and circulation, seems to defy any such easy categorisation. And yet it is possible to speak of the 'urban' experience that such sprawl entails.

Despite making it difficult to talk of urbicide as destruction of the city alone, responding to the definitionalist critiques of urbicide allows a sharpening of focus. After all, why should the destruction of villages across Bosnia and Chechnya, or West Bank and Gaza refugee camps, be excluded from the concept of urbicide by virtue of falling outside some narrow notion of the correspondence of the urban and the city? Thus the logic of urbicide should not be taken to be restricted to the destruction of the city alone. In response, it might be objected that this broadening of the scope of 'urbanity' beyond a simple equivalence with the city constitutes the removal of the 'urban' from urbicide. However, such problems arise in the specification of all concepts: why, for example, should the *genos* that (along with the epithet *-cide*) is the lexico-conceptual constituent of 'genocide' be restricted to 'race, nationality, ethnicity or religion'? I would prefer to argue, rather, that it is necessary to note that the understanding of urban implied in my account of the logics of urbicide is very specific. So long as 'urban' is taken to refer to a specific existential quality constituted by buildings, then urbicide is a viable concept for identifying a distinct form of political violence (destruction of heterogeneity through destruction of the buildings that comprise its condition of possibility), regardless of whether such violence occurs in a city, town, village or farm.

Conclusion

Thus we arrive at a delineation of the conceptual logic of urbicide. Urbicide is the deliberate destruction of buildings *qua* the conditions of possibility of a specific 'urban' existential quality: heterogeneity. The logic of urbicide is one in which a number of events coalesce into a distinct pattern of destruction, the meaning of which is the destruction of heterogeneity in and through the destruction of buildings. Urbicide is not restricted to, nor does it comprise a valorisation of, 'the urban' conceived of as coterminous with 'the city'. Additionally, urbicide is distinct from, though intertwined with, genocide. Urbicide and genocide thus have separate targets whilst sharing a logic of destruction. This logic is a two-phase affair in which heterogeneity is first destroyed, following which homogeneity is installed. Nothing in the relation of genocide and urbicide prevents them from co-existing in specific conflict situations.

A precise delineation of the conceptual contours of urbicide and its logic is, however, something of a preliminary exercise. This delineation leaves us with little more than an heuristic tool for identifying urbicide. A number of questions still remain, chief among which is how buildings constitute heterogeneity. Only if we can show how buildings constitute heterogeneity can we show what is lost and/or achieved in such destruction. The remainder of this book will, thus, comprise an enquiry into both the manner in which buildings are constitutive of heterogeneity and what is lost and/or achieved in urbicidal destruction. I will begin with the examination of the manner in which buildings (the target of urbicide) are constitutive of the heterogeneity that characterises urbicide. I will contend that this examination necessitates an enquiry into the spatialities constituted by buildings. Having outlined the manner in which buildings are constitutive of heterogeneity, I will elaborate upon what I will refer to as the 'stakes of urbicide': what is lost and what is accomplished in the destruction of buildings.

3   The built environment and shared spatiality

The outline of the logic of urbicide provided in the previous chapter represents a lexico-conceptual account of this particular form of violence. According to this account, urbicide comprises a logic of destruction in which buildings are targeted in a coordinated manner as the conditions of possibility of a heterogeneity that is the existential quality which defines urbanity. Urbicide is thus the killing of urbanity. Such an account provides a powerful argument for considering the destruction of the built environment as a form of violence in its own right, distinct from other forms of violence such as genocide.

However, this lexico-conceptual account of the logic of urbicide leaves its central substantive core unexplained. Specifically, neither the manner in which buildings might be constitutive of heterogeneity nor the nature of such heterogeneity are explicated. As such then, the definition of urbicide provided in the previous chapter raises a number of unanswered questions. Responding to such questions is important for two reasons. Firstly, the lexico-conceptual account of urbicide provided in the previous chapter does not demonstrate the basis for contending that heterogeneity is at stake in the destruction of buildings. It thus has the appearance of an unsupported assertion. Secondly, if we are to understand what is at stake in urbicide, it is first necessary to understand the mechanism that constitutes the heterogeneity that it is argued is lost in such violence. The manner in which such heterogeneity is constituted will colour our interpretation of its loss.

Responding to these questions will thus provide the basis for the remainder of this book. In Chapter 4, I will examine the nature of that heterogeneity, while Chapters 5 and 6 will outline what is at stake in urbicide. However, prior to this it will first of all be necessary to examine the basis for the contention that buildings are constitutive of heterogeneity. Only if I can provide a satisfactory argument for accepting this contention will the examination of the nature of heterogeneity or what is at stake in its loss be of consequence.

According to the account given in the previous chapter, urbicide comprises an attack on buildings *qua* that which is constitutive of urbanity: heterogeneity. This account thus rests on the contention that buildings constitute heterogeneity. How are buildings constitutive of such heterogeneity? I will argue that buildings are constitutive of heterogeneity insofar as they are constitutive of a fundamentally public spatiality. That is to say, buildings constitute a spatiality that is always already shared. As such, this spatiality always already holds the possibility of the existence of an other within it (indeed, publicness implies sharing, which in turn implies an ever-present possibility of alterity). Whether the presence of this other is actual or not, its always present possibility means that the spatiality constituted by buildings can never be rid of the trace of alterity. This spatiality is thus experienced as always already heterogeneous. The existential quality that pertains to being in the built environment is thus heterogeneity. Urbicide (a coordinated assault on the built environment) represents a coordinated assault on the conditions of possibility of such heterogeneity.

Substantiating the contention that the built environment is constitutive of heterogeneity therefore rests on similarly substantiating the contention that buildings are constitutive of a fundamentally public, and thus shared, spatiality. It is to this contention that I will turn in this chapter. In order to demonstrate the manner in which buildings constitute shared spatiality, I will turn to Martin Heidegger's understanding of existential spatiality. Heidegger's account of the spatiality of Being-in-the-world (*Dasein*) stresses that existence, rather than occurring *in* space, is fundamentally *spatial* (cf. Norberg-Schultz 1971). Moreover, for Heidegger, the spatiality of such existence is constituted in the encounter with objects such as buildings. Furthermore, insofar as such objects can, in principle, be encountered by all, they constitute fundamentally public spatiality. Heidegger's account of the manner in which such spatiality is constituted thus provides a powerful tool for sketching out the manner in which the built environment is constitutive of shared spaces that are the condition of possibility of heterogeneity. By setting out Heidegger's arguments concerning being, dwelling and spatiality, it is possible to illuminate the manner in which urbicide comprises the destruction of the shared spaces that constitute existence as heterogeneous.

Being-in-the-world as em-placement

An exegesis of Heidegger's thinking concerning spatiality must start with his account in *Being and Time* of the essentially spatial character of Being-in-the-world. Central to this account is the concept of '*Dasein*'. The concatenation of *da* (there) and *sein* (to be) forms *Dasein*, meaning 'to be there, present, available, to exist' (Inwood 1999, 42). *Dasein*, however, is more than a term for identifying individual human beings as things that exist in the world. As Heidegger notes, 'with the term "*Dasein*", we are expressing not its "what" (as if it were a table, house, or tree) but its Being' (Heidegger 1962, 67). That is, *Dasein* does not tell us *what* individual human existence is (as if 'it is Being-there' would suffice as an explanation of what a human being is), but indicates *the way in which human beings exist*. *Dasein* thus refers to both 'a way of being that is characteristic of all people' and the way of being of individual human beings (Dreyfus 1991, 14). However, Heidegger does not want *Dasein* to be reduced to the subjective individual consciousness that is the central character of traditional metaphysical ontology. *Dasein* is, as we shall see, certainly not the Cartesian *cogito*. And it is precisely for this reason that it is not so much *what Dasein* is (the individual beings that *Dasein* can possibly be), but the *way in which it is* (the essential structures that are the condition of possibility of human existence) that is the central concern of *Being and Time*.

Division 1 of *Being and Time* comprises an analysis of this existential structure of *Dasein*. Heidegger notes that such an analysis must start with the 'average everydayness' of *Dasein*'s existence (Heidegger 1962, 37–38; Mullhall 1996, 18–20). Heidegger argues that *Dasein* is always already in-the-world. Being-in-the-world, then, is the average everyday state of *Dasein*. The way in which *Dasein* comprises Being-in-the-world is thus the starting point for Heidegger's existential analytic of *Dasein*. It is precisely in relation to *Dasein*'s Being-in-the-world that Heidegger notes the essentially spatial character of such existence.

A clue to this spatial character lies in the fact that *Dasein* is literally Being-*there*. However, this 'Being-there' is not the simple fact of taking up a particular position in the world. Rather, as Heidegger notes, '[the] "There" [*das 'Da'*] is not a place [...] in contrast to an "over there" [*'dort'*]; *Dasein* means not being here instead of over there, nor here and over there, but is the possibility, the condition of oriented being here and being over there' (Inwood 1999, 42; Inwood is referring to, and translating, Heidegger 1996, 136). If Being-there were simply the designation of the *location* of the place of an individual *Dasein* in a three-dimensional space, this would refer only to *what Dasein* is: a *thing* in a specific location ('that thing there as opposed to this thing here'). But, since *Dasein* refers to a *way* of Being, Being-there must be understood as an em-placement. The 'there-being' of *Dasein* is thus not a thing in a location but rather that which is the condition of speaking about various places (of being in a place as opposed to another place). That is, to be in-the-world is to be *placed* in that world and in being so placed to be that in relation to which here, there and so on make sense. It is this em-placement that Heidegger refers to as 'the condition of oriented being' that comprises Being-there (or *Dasein*).

'Place' refers to a 'particular ... [or] definite ... situation ... with reference to other bodies' (Oxford English Dictionary 1989, Vol. XI, 937–942). A place is a particular locus of a specific set of references to other bodies/things. To be 'in a place', then, is to be the locus of a set of references to other bodies/things. Place, then, consists of the references a specific locus makes to other bodies/things: a relational network unfolding from a specific location. The 'place' opened by the em-placement of Being-there is thus the constitution of a set of references to other bodies and things. That is, *Dasein* is in 'a place' by understanding itself to be in a network of relations with the various entities it encounters in the world. It is precisely this referentiality that comprises 'oriented being'. Orientation is to be understood as a positioning that allows a network of references to be constituted. This positioning is thus ascertained precisely in relation to other bodies/things. To be oriented is, therefore, to be placed or em-placed in relation to other bodies/things.

It is to this em-placement in relational networks of places, in contrast to the understanding of objects as taking up positions in space, that Heidegger is referring when he draws a distinction between 'Being in' and 'Being-in'. Though this distinction might appear to be an exercise in philosophical hair-splitting, it is indicative of the always already em-placed character of *Dasein*. Division 1 of *Being and Time* comprises a fundamental critique of the tradition of metaphysical ontology that Heidegger sees embodied in Descartes and Newton. For both of these thinkers, Being takes place *within* a universal, objective, three-dimensional *space* that pre-exists any beings. For these thinkers, the concept of 'Being in' is to be understood as the placing of an object into a region of space rather in the same way that we put water into a container. The space pre-exists the thing put into it and is unaffected (although it is occupied) by that thing.

For Heidegger, this account is somewhat back-to-front. Heidegger argues that a conception of the world as a uniform space into which discrete objects are placed at certain positions is a theoretical construct made possible by the fact that *Dasein* is always already em-placed, or oriented towards a worldly context. That is, *Dasein* constitutes a network of places and then abstracts from this to create the idea of a space in which this network exists. 'Being-in' thus refers to the way in which *Dasein* always already exists in relation to those things that it finds around itself in its everyday life. Those things that *Dasein* primarily encounters in its everydayness are those things which come in handy for practical tasks. For example, Heidegger argues that I do not see a chair, writing desk, pen and paper as discrete entities in a particular container-like space. Rather, I see them as an 'equipmental whole': things that do a particular task, or a context for accomplishing the task.

'Being-in', then, is not simply being in a particular position in space, but is, rather, Being as a location in a relational network of everyday things – or being em-placed. Moreover, if Being-in is *Dasein*'s basic state, it means that *Dasein* is essentially worldly. Any other understanding of itself that *Dasein* may have – for example, as taking up a position in space – is derived from theoretical reflection upon its worldliness. Thus, notions of space as medium are derived, or abstracted, from the place-networks of existence through theoretical reflection. Such reflection is predicated upon, and obscures through theoretical abstraction, a more essential state of Being: *Dasein*'s worldliness.

Despite offering a provocative contestation of metaphysical notions of space as a neutral, universal medium external to Being and yet constituting the necessary backdrop for existence, Heidegger's understanding of *Dasein*'s existential em-placement requires extension if it is to provide an explication of the constitution of a fundamentally public (and thus shared) spatiality. Starting from a notion of Being-in-the-world as an em-placement, rather than occupation of pre-existing space, however, gives an entirely different understanding of spatiality. Spatiality must be understood not as a medium, but rather as a way of Being. Spatiality is thus not something into which either *Dasein* or the objects it encounters are placed, but rather a way in which such entities exist. It is to an explication of this way of existing, predicated upon the em-placed nature of *Dasein*, that I will now turn.

The essentially spatial character of existence

Heidegger derives the spatiality of Being-in-the-world from the 'equipmental wholes' in which *Dasein* is always already oriented. Equipmental wholes could be said to be the various related bodies and things that accomplish a specific task, or fulfil a particular role. Any task or role requires a number of bodies and things to be related in particular ways such that in the completion of the task or performance of the role these various entities could be said to constitute a whole. For example, writer, pen, desk and paper could be said to comprise an equipmental whole constituted in and through the writing of a letter.

'Equipment', notes Heidegger, 'has its *place*, or else it "lies around"; this must be distinguished in principle from just occurring at random in some spatial position' (Heidegger 1962, 136). It is this fact that things have a *place* that is the basis of Heidegger's account of spatiality. Em-placement is determined by two dimensions: 'closeness' and 'direction'. Closeness is achieved through what most English translators of *Being and Time* call 'de-severance'. De-severance refers to the way in which *Dasein* engages with different elements of the world in different ways (what Heidegger refers to as the 'circumspective concern' that *Dasein* exhibits towards the world). As Heidegger notes, '[w]hen, for instance, a man wears a pair of spectacles which are so close to him distantially that they are "sitting on his nose", they are environmentally more remote from him than a picture on the opposite wall' (Heidegger 1962, 141). The picture on the wall is what the man is engaging with, and is thus de-severed, whilst the spectacles are not an item with which *Dasein* is concerned, and, hence, are not de-severed. Closeness in this sense does not refer to a proximity measured in terms of a distance between two points. A given piece of equipment can thus be closer than another despite the relative proximity of either to *Dasein*.

'Direction' consists of the relation between the various pieces of equipment in the equipmental whole. These various bits of equipment are not only close, but they are also in particular positions vis-à-vis each other. Thus in the example referred to above, both picture and spectacles are 'in front of' the man. It is precisely this directionality that is the source of the essential orientation that characterises Being-in-the-world. Insofar as it is always already in-the-world, *Dasein* has a pre-theoretical understanding of directionality through its engagement with equipmental wholes. However, it is not the closeness and directionality of equipment alone that gives *Dasein* its spatiality.

Heidegger's understanding of the spatiality of existence is completed by the concept of the 'region'. The region is that which 'makes possible the belonging-somewhere of an equipmental totality as something that can be placed': what Heidegger calls the 'whither' of a place (Heidegger 1962, 136). Were things only to have place because of their closeness to *Dasein* and relation to each other, there would be no account of the place one given equipmental whole had in relation to another. Or, rather, the account would revolve around the constitutive power of *Dasein*, and we would have effectively arrived at a Husserlian phenomenological position in which separate worlds are constituted by and for individual subjects. Instead, the concept of region offers a horizon of intelligibility that is external to each *Dasein*, but accessible by all *Dasein*s. This horizon allows the placing of all the various equipmental wholes in relation to each other. *Dasein* engages in the world in terms of closeness and direction of ready-to-hand items and yet understands its overall position in this world in relation to the regional horizon. Thus whilst the directionality of the entities in the equipmental whole gives *Dasein* an understanding of how one entity relates to another, the region allows all *Dasein*s to understand where one equipmental whole stands in relation to others. Thus Heidegger makes clear both the importance of *Dasein*, in terms of the way in which it interprets its own existence relative to the closeness or readiness-to-hand of certain items, depending on its everyday needs, and at the same time a certain public horizon that means that *Dasein* is not a solipsistic constructor of its own world.

It should be possible to glean from this account that spatiality is not a question of distance in space and, hence, is something that is *constituted*, not *discovered*. The spatiality of Being-in-the-world is constituted jointly by items of equipment, the regions that orient the entirety of places that such equipment can occupy, and *Dasein*. This constitution occurs in what is best described as a 'from-back to' movement (Casey 1998, 258). *Dasein* constitutes items of equipment as ready-to-hand through 'circumspective concern'. *Dasein* establishes relationships by being engaged (and thus close to, or de-severed) with certain things and unconcerned with others. However, that an item is close to *Dasein* is not sufficient; this item must have a place within the equipmental totality. This place can only be constituted if the item has a directionality that indicates its location in relation to other items. This directionality belongs to the items themselves. However, in order for the various equipmental wholes to have a location vis-à-vis each other, a horizon of intelligibility must be established according to which all places can be located. This is 'the region'. It is regionality that makes it possible to say one thing is above another, or behind it, or beyond it. Thus the constitution of spatiality passes from *Dasein*, to the items constitutive of the possibility of spatiality, to the region that orients all the places that these items can occupy and back again to *Dasein*, whose concernful Being-in-the-world is oriented in terms of its place in the region.

Space, distance and public, shared spatiality

It should thus be clear that the spatiality with which Heidegger is concerned is very different from the absolute space with which thinkers such as Newton or Euclid are concerned. For Newton, for example, space is an absolute, metaphysical entity, separate from Being, in which beings can be located. This absolute space is a homogeneous, universal entity that is neutral towards Being and merely plays the part of (necessary) backdrop to existence. Moreover, this space has no places (understood as a nexus in a network of relations), merely locations that any object can occupy, including beings. In this way, Newtonian space is indifferent to the kind of relationships that Heidegger is positing as the constitutive features of *Dasein*'s spatiality (Casey 1998, 142–150).

Heidegger sees such space – space that could be understood as the volume inside an empty container – as being derived from a more fundamental existential spatiality. More specifically, this space is derived by reification of the relations that characterise Being-in-the-world into measured/quantified *distance*. Distance

– understood as measurement/quantification of a given relation – does not exist prior to *Dasein*'s circumspective concern with the world. It is only because of *Dasein*'s pre-theoretical understanding of closeness, directionality and regionality that it is possible to derive a system of measuring and, hence, a sense of distance. Distance (and the space it describes) is thus a product of reducing a relationship between two items to a measurement according to a common/standardised, but nonetheless arbitrary, unit.

Heidegger, however, is referring not to the space described by distance, but, rather, to a spatiality constituted through the interrelationship of *Dasein*, equip-mental wholes and regions. Such spatiality is not a matter of extension, but rather of relation. It is a matter of the constitution of places that comprise a nexus in a network of relationships. Moreover, this spatiality is not something that simply unfolds from, and for, a single *Dasein*. Rather, insofar as the region that gives each place overall intelligibility vis-à-vis other places is public, it is a spatiality in which many *Dasein*s co-appear and co-exist. It is thus a shared spatiality constituted in *Dasein*'s everyday encounter with things.

It is important to emphasise the fundamentally public nature of the existential spatiality (and the spaces that can be derived from it) that Heidegger outlines. Whilst *Dasein*'s de-severance is central to Heidegger's account of spatiality, it is only part of the story. The place orientation effected by regions, and the directionality inherent to equipment, make this spatiality an essentially public one. Both regions and equipmental wholes are in principle available to the circumspective concern of any *Dasein*. No singular de-severance of equipment by a particular *Dasein* can thus foreclose the possibility that there might be others who have similarly taken a circumspective concern with these items. *Dasein*'s world is therefore a shared world. And this shared character is established by the fact that the places constituted by the things with which it is concerned are essentially public.

To this point, I have traced out the manner in which Heidegger demonstrates that it is the things with which Being-in-the-world is concerned that constitute that world as a multitude of essentially public, and thus shared, places (and, by derivation, spaces). It is my argument that it is precisely this essentially public, and thus shared, spatiality that is constituted by the buildings that comprise the urban environment. Later in this chapter, I will demonstrate this argument by utilising the preceding conceptual schema to interpret the existential spatiality of an urban environment. Firstly, however, it is necessary to extend the exegesis I have given of Heidegger's account of the spatiality of existence to say something about its implications in relation to the built environment.

The spatiality of the built environment

A built environment can be seen as both a region and an equipmental whole. On the one hand, as a region the buildings comprise the environment that orients all the possible places or things within it: a public horizon that gives intelligibility to a variety of equipmental wholes. The ensemble of buildings that comprises, for example, a town is a horizon of intelligibility that orients all the possible places that items may occupy within the urban environment. The town orients *Dasein*'s immediate sense of here and there, before and beyond, above and below. It is within this built environment that *Dasein* finds its orientation and is able to understand where the place of one item is in relation to another.

On the other hand, as an equipmental whole the built environment is an ensemble of buildings that refer to each other in various ways, an ensemble that enables the accomplishment of certain tasks – shelter, commerce, production and so on. *Dasein* thus has a pre-theoretical understanding of the directionality that makes a built environment into an equipmental whole. *Dasein* does not understand the role of individual buildings and then, as it were by a process of addition or straightforward connection, compose them into an holistic ensemble. Rather, *Dasein* understands the relationship between, say, the house s/he lives in and the places of worship s/he or others may use, the public buildings that may be places of work or of business, and the other spaces (such as parks and cemeteries) that are also part of the urban environment. It is precisely this pre-theoretical understanding of the directionality in a built environment that means that *Dasein* understands this environment as a whole rather than a random collection of buildings.

The built environment thus constitutes a basis for *Dasein*'s existential spatiality. However, two points should be borne in mind. Firstly, the ensemble of buildings that comprises the built environment as both equipmental whole and region is fundamentally public. Whilst individual *Dasein*s may experience the built environment in different ways (by engaging with, or de-severing, elements of that environment differently), the buildings constitute an environment that is fundamentally available to all. The town is not a private map, but a public horizon that makes the locations of all the places within it (and the equipmental wholes that occupy these places) available to all.

Secondly, since the spatiality that *Dasein* experiences is constituted by a fundamentally public directionality and regionality, the space that is derived from the various places within the built environment is *always already a shared space*. That is, the space that is derived by measuring and quantifying the distances between buildings in a street is not a purely subjective phenomenon (the mental imagining of an individual *Dasein*). Rather, this space is derived from the fundamentally public directionality of the ensemble of buildings that *Dasein* experiences. The relationship between buildings is public and pre-theoretically understood by every *Dasein*. And this means that each and every *Dasein* can perceive the same spaces because they can perceive the same points of reference between which measuring will occur. Moreover, when *Dasein* calculates the space that exists in a certain region of the built environment, s/he knows that the buildings that constitute the possibility of measuring are always already available to other *Dasein*s and, hence, there is a pre-theoretical alterity inherent in this spatiality. The built environment is thus ineluctably heterogeneous.

And it is precisely this *possibility of heterogeneity* that is at stake in urbicide. Urbicide comprises the destruction of that which constitutes the fundamentally public character of the built environment. If buildings and their directionality in relation to one another are available to all *Dasein*s, they are thus publicly available shared objects. Such buildings exist as points of reference, places to be enjoyed, by any *Dasein*. They are thus ever-present indicators of the possibility of others existing in the spaces abstracted from their spatiality. Destroying such buildings comprises an attempt to erase such public objects and, with them, the possibility of others sharing the spaces of the built environment. If the building is destroyed, so the logic goes, then it cannot be a point of reference for another and, hence, the possibility of alterity that it offered is foreclosed.

It is in this manner that the ethnic nationalist politics of the Bosnian Croat destroyers of Mostar's *Stari Most*, the HVO, can be understood. The buildings of the built environment in Mostar formed an equipmental whole. It was in the context of all of these buildings taken as a town, rather than an aggregate of individual buildings, that existence was accomplished by the inhabitants of Mostar. This built environment was the region that oriented all the possible places in which they lived their daily lives. Moreover, the buildings gave directionality to the individual experience of the town. The bridge, for example, referred to both sides of the river, and thus constituted the relational designation of 'east' Mostar as on the opposite bank of the Neretva to 'west' Mostar. This directional reference was a property of the bridge, not of individual experiences of the bridge. Moreover, since the bridge and the directional relationship it entailed were in principle available to all, it was a public, shared place.

It is precisely the fact that the bridge was a fundamentally public place that sealed its fate. To leave the bridge standing is to leave intact the possibility of sharing Mostar. And it is this possibility of sharing the built environment with heterogeneous others, and the alterity attendant to such sharing, that comprises the principal target of ethnic nationalist politics. Urbicide thus destroys the fundamental possibility of heterogeneity, the always already present alterity that the public character of the spaces constituted by buildings comprises. It is not only that east and West Mostar should be separated, but that any possibility of otherness within West Mostar should be eradicated. This must start with the condition of possibility of such difference, that which intimates in its public character an ineluctable alterity: buildings.

In this way we can demonstrate the manner in which buildings (as that which, in being public, constitute a shared space) are the condition of possibility of heterogeneity that is at stake in urbicide. My account above, however, treats buildings as simple objects. Whilst our principal, everyday experience of buildings is as objects, this neglects the fact that building also refers to a constitutive activity. Heidegger, however, pays no attention in *Being and Time* to building as an activity constitutive of the spatiality of existence. However, it is with precisely such an activity – namely the destruction or 'unbuilding' of the built environment – that the study of urbicide is concerned. Thus an examination of buildings simply as objects is not, to my mind, sufficient. We must supplement such an examination with an account of building as a constitutive activity. In other words, we cannot just say 'what' is destroyed in urbicide. We must also say 'how' it is destroyed. If destruction is an 'unbuilding', then an examination of building will shed some light on its characteristics; at least it will show the characteristics of that which urbicide works against. Heidegger examines the nature of building as an activity in his writing on dwelling. It is thus to the question of dwelling that I will now turn.

Thinking in the context of the destruction of buildings

In 1951 Heidegger delivered the lecture 'Building Dwelling Thinking', to the Darmstadt symposium on *Man and Space* (Krell 1993, 344). The lecture marks a major revision of Heidegger's thinking regarding the relation between building, spatiality and existence. World War II left in ruins many built environments in Germany. Allied bombing had reduced towns and cities to rubble. In *Being and Time*, Heidegger notes that one of the principal ways in which questions concerning the nature of Being-in-the-world are raised is when a particular everyday item malfunctions, is lost or destroyed (Dreyfus 1991, 99–100; Mullhall 1996, 48–50). In this situation, *Dasein* must reflect on the manner in which the lost/destroyed item was part of the worldliness of *Dasein*'s world and what its loss means.

It is precisely in the context of such disturbance that Heidegger's lecture should be understood.[1] Heidegger himself never explicitly thematises the disturbance (or destruction) of the built environment during World War II. This is, of course, in keeping with the reprehensible silence concerning the Nazi period that characterises his entire thought. That it is reasonable to assume that the destruction of the built environment that comprises the context of Heidegger's essay can, however, be found in the brief mention he makes to 'today's housing shortages' (Heidegger 1993a, 348).

It is precisely because Heidegger moves directly to pose ontological questions concerning building and dwelling that we should see the radical disturbance of *Dasein*'s everyday world as the context for the essay. Heidegger notes that his 'thinking concerning building does not presume to discover architectural ideas, let alone give rules for building' (*Ibid.*, 347). The radical loss of the built elements of *Dasein*'s world cannot be understood simply by offering guidelines for the reconstruction of the lost elements. Rather, this loss must, necessarily, lead us to ask the following questions: '1. What is it to dwell?; 2. How does building belong to dwelling?' (*Ibid.*, 347). In other words, the loss of the buildings that comprised the worldliness of *Dasein*'s everyday Being-in-the-world, leads us to ask what it is to live in such a world, and in what way building contributes to the experience of living in that world.

Dwelling, gathering and locales

Heidegger begins his enquiry by questioning the priority that exists in our everyday understanding of the relationship between building and dwelling. Heidegger notes that dwelling has been traditionally understood as a human activity that 'man performs alongside many other activities. We work here and dwell there' (Heidegger 1993a, 349). Buildings play a key role in this understanding of dwelling. Indeed, Heidegger notes that our traditional understanding of the relationship between building and dwelling has been in terms of a means–end relationship whereby dwelling is an activity performed in and around certain buildings. For example, we dwell in our houses, not in our places of work. According to this understanding, we build certain buildings in order to dwell in them. However, this understanding separates building and dwelling into two activities and subordinates the latter to the former. As long as this separation is maintained, argues Heidegger, we remain unable to see the 'essential relations' between building and dwelling. Indeed, we will be confined to asking technical questions concerning whether a particular architectural design is a good or bad means towards the end of dwelling. In being confined to such technical questions, we will overlook the ontological questions that the destruction of built environments poses.

It is precisely in order to investigate the essential relations between building and dwelling that Heidegger reverses the priority that exists in the traditional understandings of the terms. Thus Heidegger argues, contrary to the traditional understanding that views building as a means towards the end of dwelling, that we build precisely because we always already dwell. Building is thus that which embodies the fact that we are dwellers. Or in Heidegger's owns words: 'we do not dwell because we have built, but we build and have built because we dwell, that is, because we are *dwellers*' (Heidegger 1993a, 350).

In order to demonstrate that we build because we are dwellers, Heidegger turns to the etymology of building, arguing that '[i]t is language that tells us about the essence of a thing, provided that we respect language's own essence' (1993a, 348). With this in mind, Heidegger asks 'what does *bauen*, to build, mean?' (*Ibid.*). Heidegger traces the contemporary German *bauen*, to the Old High German *buan*. *Buan*, Heidegger argues, means 'to dwell'. Because we think of building as an activity that is a means to the end of dwelling, we forget that it is etymologically rooted in the concept of dwelling itself. In this manner, Heidegger proposes that within our everyday language there is a covert etymological trace of the fact that building is always already a dwelling and that 'to build is really to dwell' (*Ibid.*, 349).

However, this minimal etymological clue does not tell us anything about what the dwelling signified in building actually is. Heidegger notes that when we think about dwelling, we usually think of it as an activity that 'man performs alongside many other activities' (1993a, 349). No one merely dwells, to do so would be to exist in a state of 'virtual inactivity' (*Ibid.*). What kind of activity, then, is dwelling? Again Heidegger turns to the etymology of *bauen*, arguing that the Old High German words '*bauen, buan, bhu, beo* are [the contemporary German] word *bin* in the versions: *ich bin*, I am, *du bist*, you are' and so on (*Ibid.*). *Ich bin*, I am, is thus signified by the notion of dwelling. It is Being that is invoked in the concepts of dwelling and building. In some ways this is not surprising, since both building and dwelling are ways in which *Dasein* is in-the-world: modes of Being. However, the direct linkage between *bauen* – to build as a dweller – and Being, suggests to Heidegger a fundamental relationship between dwelling and Being that is not the case for other modes of Being (such as working, or travelling, for example). Dwelling is thus said by Heidegger to be 'the manner in which we humans are on the earth' (*Ibid.*). Dwelling is thus precisely Heidegger's term for Being-in-the-world in his later work.

The derivation of such a central concept through etymology may attract a certain amount of criticism. Indeed the value of etymology and other such linguistic devices is called into question by Heidegger elsewhere in his work. As Elden notes in relation to Heidegger's translations of certain Greek terms, 'we get our knowledge of words in a foreign language from a dictionary, which is based on a preceding interpretation of linguistic concepts. A dictionary can give us pointers as to how to understand a word, but it is never an absolute authority to which we are bound. All translating must be an interpreting' (Elden 2000, 412). Thus what is important in Heidegger's etymology of *bauen* is precisely the way in which he interprets the significations of the term. Heidegger interprets dwelling to be the existential condition of *Dasein*. That is, dwelling is the way in which *Dasein* is in-the-world (or on-the-earth). And since dwelling is inextricably linked to building (indeed all building is a dwelling), it is building that will exemplify the manner in which we are on-the-earth (since we are never merely on the earth in an inactive state).

Prior to considering the way in which building belongs to dwelling, Heidegger sketches out the way in which dwelling, as the way humans are on the earth, should be understood. Heidegger thus provides an outline of the concept with which he will replace Being-in-the-world in his later work. Through another etymological interpretation, Heidegger argues that the 'old word *bauen*' is related to the Old Saxon *wuon* and the Gothic *wunian*. According to Heidegger (1993a, 350), these words all mean 'to remain, to stay in a place'. But more significantly, these words all signify a specific way of remaining: '*Wunian* means to be at peace, to be brought to peace, to remain in peace' (*Ibid.*, 351). Again tracing a web of meaning through etymological association, Heidegger (*Ibid.*, 351) argues that peace, or *Friede*, actually means 'free ... preserved from harm and danger, preserved from something, safeguarded. To free, actually means to spare.' Dwelling, argues Heidegger, is thus a 'sparing'. This sparing has a positive connotation, however. It does not merely signify allowing something to exist. Rather it means to 'leave something beforehand in its essence', or to 'return it specifically to its essential being' (*Ibid.*).

As in much of Heidegger's work, this central concept has a somewhat ambiguous definition. How are we to understand this 'sparing' of which dwelling consists? Heidegger indicates that what is spared, or returned to its essential Being in and through dwelling, is the way in which humans are on the earth. Specifically, human beings are on the earth as mortals. It is this mortal existence that is returned to its essential Being by dwelling. Dwelling, or the 'stay of mortals on the earth', consists of a four-fold relationship between earth and sky, man and gods (Heidegger 1993a, 351). It is this four-fold relationship, in which the four terms are distinct and yet inseparable, that is spared by dwelling (returned to its essential Being). Man is on the earth and below the sky, which is to say that earth and sky form the horizons of man's worldly existence. Throughout his work, Heidegger differentiates between world – or that in and through which *Dasein* has existence – and earth, the natural realm that is the origin of the items that comprise worldliness. Earth is revealed by world insofar as the objects created by *Dasein* refer to their earthly components or basis. In 'The Origin of the Work of Art', for example, Heidegger (1993d, 167–168; Inwood 1999, 50) notes that a 'temple reveals the rock on which it rests, the storm that buffets it, and the stone from which it is made … Earth is [thus] revealed as earth by the world.' The sky similarly features throughout Heidegger's work as a point of orientation for human existence.[2]

The pairing of mortals and divinities is harder to fathom, referring not to the physical surroundings in which *Dasein* exists, but to the existential horizons of human Being. *Dasein* is, literally, mortal. Existence, or Being-in-the-world, is characterised by the finitude of *Dasein* (represented most clearly in the fact that *Dasein* will die). It is precisely the finitude of *Dasein* that leads to the relationship between man and gods. As a concept, gods remains ambiguous throughout 'Building Dwelling Thinking'. This is not a theistic appeal for piety, nor a reference to specific gods. Rather, it should be seen as a reference to the various social and cultural attempts that are made by mortals to comprehend and overcome their finitude.

The four-fold itself is both enigmatic and unclear as a figure of thought. Perhaps it is best to interpret the four-fold as a drawing together of the poles, or horizons, according to which human existence is understood. The world of mortals is constituted on the earth (as that which provides the material out of which a world is built) and under the sky (as that which orients existence, both directionally and temporally, especially in terms of the division of our lives into night and day). And mortals comprehend their existence on the earth as finite only in and through attempts to overcome that finitude in appeals for communion with the divine. If dwelling consists of returning *Dasein* to its essential state of Being, it is a gathering together of the horizons that make *Dasein*'s existence intelligible as Being-in-the-world (or on-the-earth). Dwelling is thus a making-intelligible of the stay of mortals on-the-earth as Being-in-the-world. Dwelling should thus be understood as the gathering together of the horizons that constitute worldliness. Rather than refer to the four-fold, therefore, I will refer to the *world* that is gathered in dwelling.

While it is clear that in Heidegger's later work dwelling is the basic existential state of human beings, the manner in which this dwelling occurs has not yet been discussed. Heidegger (1993a, 353) notes that dwelling is 'always a staying with things'. In this way, Heidegger reintroduces the role of things into the argument. Indeed, Heidegger argues that it is things that gather the world together. In other words, it is things that constitute the world in which mortal existence occurs. It is in the things which *Dasein* encounters, then, that dwelling, or the gathering together of a world, is accomplished. And this is precisely how building – as the constitution of things – belongs to dwelling.

The bridge

In order to demonstrate the way in which building belongs to dwelling, Heidegger examines a specific built thing: a bridge. The bridge, according to Heidegger, exemplifies the way in which built things gather the world together. If we see the bridge as a means to an end, the fundamental character of the built thing is obscured insofar as we presume that it was the answer to an already existing set of questions and circumstances. That is, it is presumed that the landscape preceded the bridge, which was built as a means to solve the problem of the disruption of movement by a river.

However, for Heidegger this obscures the essential character of the bridge. The built thing – the bridge, in this case – is not just another object in the world, but is constitutive of that world in the way that it gathers the world together. Thus the bridge 'does not just connect banks [of the river] that are already there. The banks emerge *as banks* only as the bridge crosses the stream' (Heidegger 1993a, 354, my emphasis). Similarly, '[t]he bridge gathers the earth as landscape around the stream' (*Ibid.*). That is, our world exists only after it has been gathered together in various ways by built things. The banks of the river exist as opposing banks only after they have been joined together. The river is only an obstacle to transport or movement after the bridge has created ease of movement. The hinterlands behind each bank are connected together and thus brought into the same world by the bridge. And, if we follow Slavenka Drakulic (1993, 14–15), the bridge brings mortals together by expressing a durability that transcends individual finitude.

Building thus constitutes the existential world by constituting a nodal point around which a gathering occurs. And this is precisely how the directionality that was central to Heidegger's early account of the spatiality of existence is constituted. The bridge refers to either bank, and to the various towns that it joins by creating a route for goods and labour. When *Dasein* encounters the bridge, it is this gathering that is implicitly understood as directionality. The built thing is thus a *locale*, a place in which gathering occurs and from which directionality is constituted. The locale, or place, consists of a number of signifying relations constituted by the building. It is precisely these significations, established by the built thing, that are the directionality which creates the world in which human beings exist.

As a place, a locale could be said to be spatial insofar as the significations constituted by the building are directional, implying a here and there, right and left and so on. Moreover, the locale could be said to function in much the same way as Heidegger's earlier concept of region. The building is precisely that in relation to which all the other possible places in the world can be understood. In this sense the building functions as a horizon of intelligibility. 'Horizon' should be understood in the Greek sense of *horismos*, not as something at which an entity ends but, rather, as a point from which something *unfolds* (Heidegger 1993a, 356). It is from the building that the world, as a series of significations and relations, unfolds.

The space within this spatial world is a secondary and derived feature. Heidegger again argues that the places in which human beings exist are not simply arranged in a pre-existent space, but, rather, that space is derived from the spatiality constituted by the things that make up our everyday world. Space is derived by measuring the relationship between different elements of the world. These elements are of interest to us precisely because they are signified by the buildings that constitute the world. Thus it is that we measure the distance between home and work, or one home and another. This measurement takes the form of establishing a common unit of distance to which all measurements can be reduced. Thus spatiality, which may refer to the relationship between two elements of the world in colloquial terms (i.e., over yonder), is reduced to space (i.e., sixty kilometres, or an hour's drive).[3]

Heidegger thus makes building central to his account of the manner in which humans dwell on the earth. In the context of Darmstadt, Heidegger is noting that the destruction caused by Allied bombing was more than the destruction of a means to the end of living. Rather, this destruction was an existential blow, destroying the world in which the existence of the citizens of the town had been possible.[4] Moreover, this destruction altered the spatialities of the built environment, destroyed spaces (since it destroyed those things between which distances had emerged through measurement), and ungathered the world. In order to expand upon this argument, I want to briefly re-view the question of the destruction of the urban environment in Mostar during the 1992–95 Bosnian War in terms of the conceptual schema Heidegger provides in his account of dwelling.

The locale as a shared/public place

Mostar's *Stari Most* provides an exemplary illustration of the manner in which a building constitutes a locale that gathers together the world, and thus comprises dwelling. Moreover, this example also returns us to the question with which this particular chapter is concerned: the heterogeneity proper to the spaces constituted by buildings. As a building, the *Stari Most* constitutes a locale. There are, of course, many possible locations along the Neretva River where a bridge could have been built. However, the construction of the bridge at that particular position constituted a specific place. This place is defined by the manner in which the locale gathers together the world. The *Stari Most* gathers the two sides of the Neretva Canyon as opposing banks. In this way, the bridge gathers together the hinterlands and routes to distant regions on each side of the Neretva. This gathering together of the landscape around the bridge constitutes an unfolding of a certain directionality from the bridge itself. The settlements on either side of the river are brought near to each other (indeed made into a single town). The old quarter of the town at the foot of the bridge on the eastern side is oriented by the bridge in relation to the newer buildings built both beyond it on the same, eastern bank of the Neretva, and beyond the bridge on the western bank. The hinterlands to which access is now available via the road over the bridge are also directionally and proximally oriented.

As a locale, the place established by the bridge can be understood as a complex relational network. This complex relational network unfolds from the bridge as the *horismos* against which orientation can be understood. Moreover, since every building constitutes a locale in this manner, the town consists of an infinitely complex intertwining of networks of relationality. The everyday experience of the town is precisely of such networks of relationality. Any place can be oriented a number of ways according to which locale forms the locus, or *horismos*, in relation to which one is oriented.

Furthermore, the space in which we think the town is located and which comprises the medium in which the buildings are distributed, is actually a derivative of our everyday understanding of these complex relational networks. Indeed, the space of, for example, the road over the *Stari Most*, is derived from the reduction of the relationship between the two parapets to a quantifiable distance. The spaces of the town are simply distances, quantified according to an arbitrary but common measure, between nodes in the relational networks. The impression of objectivity that such distance achieves in the modern era can be attributed to the manner in which cartography no longer measures the distance from one locus to another as if it were embedded in the world, but attempts to give the impression that it is possible to measure the distances in the world as if one were not actually in that world.[5] However, all distances are, in the end, simply the quantification of a relationship established by locales.

Finally, the locale is a fundamentally public horizon. The gathering that a building such as the *Stari Most* constitutes is, in principle, available to each and every human being. The world gathered together by the bridge is not, therefore, a subjective one, but a public one. And it is precisely in this respect that heterogeneity is ineluctably present in each and every locale. The *Stari Most* gathers together a set of elements into a relational network. This relational network is, in principle, available to everyone who encounters the *Stari Most*. Individual experiences of the *Stari Most* may comprise an emphasis on certain elements of the relational network and an ignorance of others. Indeed, the bridge may be many things to many different people: a cultural object; an imperial remnant; a transport link between markets; a place to display one's diving prowess devoid of all cultural or historical significance. And yet no one experience of the bridge can exclude the other possible experiences. Human experience of locales, of dwelling even, is thus always already a shared experience. That is, the relational network in which our existence is oriented, the spaces that are given to us, always admit of other possible experiences, other possible uses, other possible users. Locales are never mine alone, rather they are public places at which our shared world is gathered together.

It is precisely this public gathering that is at stake in urbicide. The HVO's destruction of the *Stari Most* represents an assault on the public gathering that the bridge constitutes. Ethnic nationalist politics are predicated on what Jacques Derrida refers to as 'ontopological' assumptions.[6] 'Ontopology', according to Derrida, refers to an 'axiomatics linking indissociably the ontological value of present-being [*on*] to its *situation*, to the stable and presentable determination of a locality, the *topos* of territory, native soil, city' (Derrida 1994, 82, emphasis and parentheses in original).[7] Ethnic nationalism thus seeks to link indissociably Being and the locale as that which is constitutive of *topos* (spatiality, territory). Ethnic nationalist politics must, moreover, contest any suggestion that a locale on which its identity is predicated admits of heterogeneity. Since ethnic nationalism is founded upon the notion of distinctness of identity being drawn from a relationship with a locale, heterogeneity would challenge the distinctness of any identity. This is the motor of urbicide. Ethnic nationalist groups attempt to secure their identity through the destruction of the traces of alterity inherent to the locales constituted by buildings. Urbicide is, thus, an attempt to ungather the world. This is especially evident in Mostar, where the destruction of the *Stari Most* was the dissolution of the final relational network that gathered the settlements on both banks of the Neretva into the same world: Mostar. The destruction of the *Stari Most* is, effectively, the destruction of one world to create two: the destruction of Mostar to create east and West Mostar. The gathering that constituted multi-ethnic Mostar is dissolved thus creating two, ethnically distinct Mostars.

Towards co-ontology

It is thus possible, through a Heideggerian interpretation of the nature of the spatiality constituted in and through buildings, to demonstrate the conceptual proposition that underlies my definition of the logic of urbicide: that urbicide is the destruction of buildings *qua* that which constitutes space as fundamentally public and thus shared by others. Furthermore, it is possible to assert that since the spaces constituted by building(s) are always already public and shared, the urban environment is a site of ineluctable heterogeneity.

The Heideggerian analysis of Being-in-the-world is thus particularly productive for the analysis of urbicide. Heidegger accounts for the way in which buildings are constitutive of an ineluctably heterogeneous, or shared, existential spatiality. This account is distinctive insofar as it treats spatiality as a network of relations constituted through a worldly engagement with (built) things. In this way the Heideggerian understanding, in contradistinction to those understandings that treat space as an absolute medium, can account for the manner in which buildings are constitutive of, and do not simply occupy, the spaces in which we exist. This account enables us to say something about what is lost in urbicide. If space is treated as an absolute medium in which buildings are located, the destruction of buildings will have no effect upon that space. Indeed, the space will remain after the destruction of the buildings. If spatiality is constituted by buildings, however, it is possible to say that this spatiality is lost when the buildings are destroyed.

Moreover, Heidegger's account stresses the ineluctable presence of others in the spaces constituted by buildings. Heidegger argues that the buildings constitutive of these spaces are fundamentally public things, available for others. Moreover, it is clear from Heidegger's account that this public character of the things that constitute *Dasein*'s world should be taken to imply not merely the possibility of alterity, but the real and ineluctable sharing of these things with others. Heidegger's account is thus distinctive insofar as it stresses the way in which Being-in-the-world is, precisely because of its constitution through an engagement with public/shared things, always already a being-with-others.

Insofar, then, as the destruction of buildings is the destruction of public/shared spaces, it is being-with-others that is at stake in urbicide. The very conditions of such being-with-others are destroyed by those who raze towns and cities. And it is precisely to this being-with-others that I want to turn in the next chapter. So far I have shown that buildings are constitutive of shared spatialities and, hence, disclose the ever-present possibility of alterity that is sufficient to argue that the existence constituted by dwelling is fundamentally heterogeneous. However, I have said nothing about the nature of this heterogeneity (or being-with-others) that Heidegger's account shows to be a fundamental characteristic of the built environment. It is this heterogeneity that constitutes the target of urbicide. This question of being-with-others – or the fundamentally heterogeneous nature of existence – is taken up by Heidegger in his work on the concept of '*Mitsein*'. *Mitsein* represents the being-with-others that necessarily follows from the public spatiality that characterises the existence of *Dasein*. However, as Jean-Luc Nancy notes, in his response to the questions posed by the concept of *Mitsein*, Heidegger's analysis falls short of providing a coherent account of the heterogeneous nature of existence. It is thus to Nancy's notion of a co-existential analytic, and its reformulation of the Heideggerian understanding of Being-with as a sharing or community, that I will have to turn to provide a complete account of the heterogeneity targeted for destruction in urbicide.

4   The nature of heterogeneity: from *Mitsein* to *the inoperative community*

The world of *Dasein* is a *with-world*. Being-in is *Being-with* others. Their Being-in-themselves within-the-world is *Dasein-with*.

(Heidegger 1962, 155)

The analytic of *Mitsein* that appears within the existential analytic [of *Being and Time*] remains nothing more than a sketch; that is, even though *Mitsein* is coessential with *Dasein*, it remains in a subordinate position. As such, the whole existential analytic still harbours some principle by which what it opens up is immediately closed off.

(Nancy 2000, 93)

From the analysis of urbicide to the question of heterogeneity

In the previous chapter, I argued that Being-in-the-world (or dwelling, according to Heidegger's later re-formulation) is spatial in character. This spatiality is constituted in and through that which expresses the fact that we are dwellers: building. Buildings, as that which expresses our Being-in-the-world as dwellers (rather than being a means towards the end of that dwelling), constitute our world as a series of locales that comprise spatial networks of reference and directionality. Moreover, according to Heidegger, the buildings that constitute such locales are inherently public. That is to say, the world does not appear subjectively for a single *Dasein*. Rather, the world in which we dwell is constituted through things that are, in principle, available to all those that have the character of *Dasein*. Thus the spatiality established in locales is, in principle, open to sharing with others that have the character of *Dasein*.

It was on this basis that I argued that I had demonstrated that, insofar as they constitute the world as a shared/public, spatial experience, buildings are the condition of possibility of an essential heterogeneity. My assertion that 'urbicide' is the correct term for the destruction of built environments in conflicts such as the 1992–95 Bosnian War rests on this basic proposition. Urbicide refers to the 'killing' (by destroying its conditions of possibility) of that which characterises urbanity (broadly construed): heterogeneity. Since buildings constitute the spatiality of existence as fundamentally shared/public, I argued that I had demonstrated that destroying buildings is essentially a destruction of the conditions of possibility of heterogeneity. Where that destruction has occurred, or is occurring, it is thus possible to say that heterogeneity itself is under assault.

This demonstration of the link between dwelling, building and heterogeneity rests on the assumption that heterogeneity is a self-evident matter (i.e., that the heterogeneity referred to – and the difference it implies – requires no further clarification). It is this assumption that I want to address in this chapter. In order to do so, I will turn first to Heidegger's examination of the essentially heterogeneous nature of Being-in-the-world before turning to Jean-Luc Nancy's more recent reinvigoration of this conceptual terrain.

Mitsein

In Division 1, Chapter 4, of *Being and Time*, Heidegger recognises that his initial demonstration of *Dasein*'s worldliness (Division 1, Chapters 2 & 3) has been primarily concerned with establishing the manner in which Being-in-the-world is constituted in and through *Dasein*'s involvement with ready-to-hand things. Indeed, he notes that '[i]n our previous analysis, the range of what is encountered within-the-world [by *Dasein*] was ... narrowed down to equipment ready-to-hand or Nature present-at-hand, and thus to entities with a character other than that of *Dasein*' (Heidegger 1962, 154).[1] This concentration on *Dasein*'s involvement with the world of things privileges one of *Dasein*'s 'structures of Being', with the consequence that not all of the 'constitutive items' that comprise Being-in-the-world stand out 'with the same phenomenal distinctiveness as the phenomenon of the world itself' (*Ibid.*, 149).

The initial account of worldliness in *Being and Time* thus fails to give priority to an exposition of the structure of Being that accounts for an individual *Dasein*'s relation to other beings with the same character as *Dasein*. The structure of Being elaborated in the early sections of *Being and Time* could thus give the impression that *Dasein* is to be conceived of in a similar manner to the *ego-cogito* of Cartesian-Husserlian philosophy. That is, in giving an account of how Being-in-the-world is constituted by *Dasein*'s situatedness in respect of the things it finds ready-to-hand (or present-at-hand) in the world, Heidegger could be taken to be conforming to an account of Being that asserts the priority of an individual's encounter with its world. Heidegger's account of Being-in-the-world thus appears open to the Cartesian-Husserlian idea that the individual self (and its consciousness, or experience of the world) is to be accorded an ontological priority.

Heidegger, however, has already shown the fundamentally shared, or public, nature of the things, and thus the world, in relation to which Being-in-the-world is constituted. This means that 'the world is always the one I share with others' (Heidegger 1962, 155). More importantly, however, '[t]hese entities [the others with whom I share the world] are neither present-at-hand nor ready-to-hand; on the contrary, they are like ... *Dasein*' (*Ibid.*, 154). Which is to say that, although the individual *Dasein* has been the focus of attention in Heidegger's preliminary account of the worldhood of the world, *Dasein* co-exists with others who have the same ontological characteristics of *Dasein*. The subject implied by *Dasein* is thus a situated Being which is always already a being-with-others which cannot thus have the kind of subjectivity that has traditionally been attributed to it by the Cartesian tradition of modern philosophy: namely, a sovereign individuality accorded ontological priority over alterity.

Heidegger (1962, 149) seeks to address the nature of *Dasein*'s subjectivity 'by asking *who* it is that *Dasein* is in its everydayness'. The obvious answer to this question, according to Heidegger (*Ibid.*, 150), is that '*Dasein* is an entity which is in each case I myself: its Being is in each case mine'. However, Heidegger (*Ibid.*) contests this obvious answer, arguing that '[i]t could be that the "who" of everyday *Dasein* just is not the "I myself".' Rather, the notion that *Dasein* is the 'I' (the 'me' of the 'mine' that *Dasein* is in each case) is in fact not the average everyday existence of *Dasein*, but a mode of Being that covers over the everyday 'who' of *Dasein*. That is, the assumption that the 'I' (or 'self') comprises the subject of Being actually covers over a more fundamental, everyday subject.

The relation of the 'I' (or self) to *Dasein*'s everyday mode of being is analogous to the relationship between a thing reduced to its physical or chemical components and the thing understood as something which one uses, on an everyday basis, to accomplish an aspect of living. Nature considered as a present-at-hand, quantifiable ensemble of minerals and substances is a deficient mode of understanding the ready-to-hand equipmental wholes with which *Dasein* has an everyday familiarity. According to Heidegger, understanding a thing as a present-at-hand substance is the product of theoretical reflection. Similarly, conceiving of *Dasein* as a substantial 'I', abstracted from its everyday circumspective concern for the world, is a product of theoretical reflection. Moreover, such an understanding commits one to seeing *Dasein* as a present-at-hand thing, in the same way that theoretical reflection commits us to seeing the things around us as present-to-hand, rather than ready-to-hand, elements of equipmental wholes that accomplish tasks. And, as Heidegger (1962, 150) has already noted, this is simply inconsistent with his previous argument that 'presence-at-hand is the kind of Being which belongs to entities whose character is not that of *Dasein*'.

Heidegger is, of course, arguing here against an imagined interlocutor identifiable, as I have noted, as a Cartesian-Husserlian hybrid (Dreyfus 1991, 146). This imagined interlocutor represents the transcendental (metaphysical) tradition that has dominated the history of philosophical thought concerning ontology (or the question of Being). This tradition is founded on, and propagates, the assumption that the subject of everyday Being (the 'who' of *Dasein*) is the 'I'/self. The problem, according to Heidegger (1962, 154), is that the history of philosophy has framed the question of the 'who' of *Dasein* as one in which it is necessary to 'start by marking out and isolating the "I" so that one must then seek some way of getting over to the others from this isolated subject'. Of course if one starts from such an assumption, one is easily led into the 'pitfall' of seeing *Dasein* as the 'I'.

This is not to suggest that conceiving of *Dasein* as an 'I' or self must simply be abandoned. After all, it is as an I/self that *Dasein* often proceeds in its activities in the world (which is to say that the history of philosophy has not simply been a flight of fancy, or a grave mistake). Rather, this way of answering the question of the 'who' of *Dasein* so beloved of the philosophical tradition (and exemplified by Cartesian-Husserlian thought) represents an account of a deficient mode of Being. This is a mode of Being in which *Dasein* misrecognises its 'self' as something (literally some-thing) that has a character quite other than that already ascribed to *Dasein* by Heidegger in his explication of Being-in-the-world.

Insofar as it is correct to speak of *Dasein* being 'an entity which is in each case I myself' (Heidegger 1962, 150), this is an *ontical*, not an *ontological* statement. Whilst ontology is concerned with the meaning of Being, the ontic refers to 'the distinctive nature of particular types of [existent] entity' (Mulhall 1996, 4). The ontic thus denotes the actual ways in which beings exist. Ontic statements, therefore, concern 'beings, not their [B]eing' (King 2001, 46). Heidegger (1962, 151) notes that '[I]t may well be that it is always ontically correct to say of this entity [*Dasein*] that "I" am it.' However, an 'ontological analytic which makes use of such assertions' should be cautious (*Ibid.*). Indeed '[t]he word "I" is to be understood only in the sense of a non-committal *formal indicator*, indicating' that ontically *Dasein* may be what 'I' am, but that this 'I' does not necessarily tell us everything of the ontological character of *Dasein* – specifically 'who' *Dasein* is (*Ibid.*, 151–152).

In order to demonstrate that, ontologically, the isolated (sovereign) 'I' is not the 'who' (or subject) of *Dasein*, Heidegger turns again to look at the structure of Being-in-the-world, the pre-theoretical condition of possibility of existence. In its average, everyday Being-in-the-world, *Dasein* is typically *absorbed* into the world. This means that *Dasein* is unreflectively engaged with the ready-to-hand things that are the condition of possibility of the worldliness necessary for existence. However, *Dasein* is not a lone individual given a context by the things that exist solely for him/her. This is precisely what Heidegger is getting at when he stresses the shared/public nature of the spatiality of existence constituted in and through (built) things. Thus *Dasein*'s everyday absorption into the world is always already a being-with-others. This Being-with has an ontological priority over modes of Being in which *Dasein* interprets him/herself to comprise an isolated 'I'. It is thus this Being-with that must be explicated in order to understand the 'who' or subjectivity of *Dasein*.

In order to explicate the ordinary, everyday way of being-with-others, Heidegger returns to the way in which things constitute our average, everyday existence/world as fundamentally public/shared. Heidegger notes that *Dasein*'s average, everyday relation to things, *Dasein*'s 'staying with things' as he will put it in his later work, always already implies alterity – other beings with the character of *Dasein*. For example, in 'the work world of the craftsman … along with the equipment to be found when one is at work … those others for whom the "work" … is destined are "encountered too"' (Heidegger 1962, 153). That is to say, in the work-world the thing always implies the person for whom it is destined. Moreover, the thing always implies the person from whom it has originated. As Heidegger (*Ibid.*) puts it, there is an 'essential assignment or reference' to others in the ready-to-hand things with which *Dasein* is absorbed. This 'assignment or reference' signals that an experience of ineluctable alterity is attendant to Being-in-the-world. Heidegger offers several examples of the ways in which that alterity may be felt. For example, for a tailor, a garment has a

> reference to possible wearers ... for whom it should be 'cut to the figure'. Similarly, when material is put to use, we encounter its producer or 'supplier' as one who 'serves' well or badly. When, for example, we walk along the edge of a field ... the field ... shows itself as belonging to such-and-such a person, and decently kept up by him; the book we have used was bought at So-and-so's shop and given by such-and-such a person, and so forth. The boat anchored at the shore is assigned in its Being-in-itself to an acquaintance who undertakes voyages with it; but even if it is a 'boat which is strange to us', it is still indicative of others.
>
> (*Ibid.*, 153–154)

The things that constitute the condition of possibility of *Dasein*'s worldliness thus imply a co-existence of entities with the character of *Dasein* ('others'). Even where an object does not have such a place in an economic chain (such as the 'boat which is strange to us'), there is always the intimation of alterity. Moreover, one could speak of building, and their locales, in a similar manner. Ultimately, '[t]he others who are thus "encountered" in a ready-to-hand, environmental context of equipment, are not somehow added-on in thought to some Thing which is proximally just present-at-hand; such "Things" are encountered from out of the world in which they are ready-to-hand for others – a world which is always mine, too, in advance' (*Ibid.*, 154). In this way, it is correct to say that '[t]he world of *Dasein* is a *with-world* [*Mitwelt*]' (*Ibid.*, 155). This is what Heidegger refers to as '*Dasein-with*' (*Mit-Dasein*). *Dasein*-with is a fundamental Being-with that characterises Being-in-the-world. Worldliness consists of the intimation of alterity in all that constitutes the world. And this alterity takes the form of others who are entities with the same character as *Dasein*.

Now it could be said that this accords with the Cartesian-Husserlian view that the world is always a with-world, but that the individual encounters the world first and then others. However, Heidegger argues that the primordiality of *Dasein*-with reverses the priority of such a formulation. Indeed, the fact that *Dasein*-with is a fundamental attribute of Being-in-the-world indicates that Being-with (*Mitsein*) is a pre-ontological characteristic of *Dasein*.[2] This Being-with is prior to the Being-alone on which the philosophical tradition has previously grounded ontology (the 'I' usually being first and foremost 'I alone'). Indeed, Heidegger goes on to note that Being-alone should be regarded as merely a deficient mode of Being-with:

> The phenomenological assertion that '*Dasein* is essentially Being-with' has an existential-ontological meaning. It does not seek to establish ontically that factically I am not present-at-hand alone, and that others of my kind occur. If this were what is meant by the proposition that *Dasein*'s Being-in-the-world

is essentially constituted by Being-with, then Being-with would not be an essential attribute which *Dasein*, of its own accord, has coming to it from its very own kind of Being. It would rather be something which turns up in every case by reason of the occurrence of others. Being-with is an existential characteristic of *Dasein* even when factically no other is present-at-hand or perceived. Even *Dasein*'s being-alone is Being-with in the world. The other can *be missing* only *in* and *for* a Being-with. Being-alone is a deficient mode of Being-with ... On the other hand, factical Being-alone is not obviated by the occurrence of a second example of a human being 'beside' me ... Even if these and more are present-at-hand, *Dasein* can still be alone. So Being-with and the facticity of Being-with one another are not based on the occurrence together of several 'subjects'.

(Heidegger 1962, 156–157)

It is important to understand the implications of Heidegger's demonstration of the primacy of Being-with over Being-alone. Were this primacy not to be shown (as Heidegger has done through his explication of the assignments and references to alterity inherent to equipmental wholes), others would only ever be said to be factically/ontically present on a case-by-case basis. This would mean that the assertion of heterogeneity would rest on being able to show that, *in a given factical case*, others were indeed present or implied. However, as Heidegger notes, when we find ourselves alone, recognition of that state rests upon our prior knowledge of Being-with. That is to say, alterity is a constitutive attribute of Being because *Dasein*'s world is always already a *with-world*. Whenever *Dasein* makes that world into an 'alone-world', this is only possible through a negation of the *with* that characterises the world.

It is for this reason that the concept of Being-with, or *Mitsein*, set out by Heidegger is so important. *Mitsein* establishes that being-with-others, or heterogeneity, is an existential condition, a horizon against which all other modes of Being are articulated. The articulation of non-heterogeneous modes of Being is only possible through a disavowal of the Being-with that is constitutive of existence. The importance of the concept of *Mitsein* lies in noting, therefore, that Being-in-the-world-with-others is the primary ontological condition. *Dasein*'s subjectivity – the 'who' of *Dasein* that Heidegger has been investigating – is thus not the sovereign, unencumbered 'I' that comes into existence alone and enters into a world where, as an antecedent, ontic fact it encounters others. As such, this sketch of the subjectivity entailed by Heidegger's ontological schema offers a radical re-interpretation of the nature of the heterogeneity at stake in urbicide. Significantly, the notion of *Mitsein* suggests that urbicide is a covering-over of an essential heterogeneity in order to give the impression that separateness and homogeneity are the norm. It is precisely, then, to the role of *Mitsein* in the understanding of urbicide that I want to turn.

Urbicide as the deprivation of Being-with

Urbicide demonstrates the manner in which forms of political violence such as that practised by ethnic nationalist movements represents a denudation of Being of its constitutive Being-with: a denial of the ontologically primary heterogeneity of existence. To destroy a locale constituted by elements of the built environment is not to destroy the co-existence that characterises Being-in-the-world, but to cover it over. After all, destruction is never complete – ruins, memories and histories always remain. This covering-over effects a denudation of existence of its essential Being-with. If the destruction is successful, sustained, or allowed to go unchallenged over a long period of time (that is, if the ruins are left to lie), then the denudation of Being-with is naturalised. In such circumstances, a mode of *Dasein* that is predicated on the covering over of Being-with results in a mode of existence that suggests that Being-with did not exist in the past and cannot exist in the future.

It is precisely this covering over of Being-with that can be seen in conflicts such as the 1992–95 Bosnian War and exemplified in the destruction of the *Stari Most*. In the case of the Old Bridge in Mostar, the destruction was aimed at reducing the locales that gathered the city to rubble. These locales constituted the city as a shared, and thus heterogeneous, built environment. The destruction aimed to cover over this sharing of municipal spatiality. In this case, it is possible to see the manner in which urbicide has two phases. In the first phase, this destruction is targeted at removing the things that constitute the locales which gather existential spatiality and constitute it as essentially heterogeneous. The ethnic cleansers operate with the hope that, in destroying these locales, Being-with, the heterogeneity constitutive of existence, will be similarly destroyed. The second phase of urbicide is aimed at covering over this heterogeneity with the suggestion that in the absence of the buildings there can be no Being-with, no co-existence. And yet, as I have shown, co-existence is constitutive of Being-in-the-world. In order to destroy this Being-with, it would be necessary, finally, to destroy the experience of the world.

Whilst destroying buildings destroys specific gatherings, it can never destroy Being-with itself. If, as I have argued, Being-in-the-world and the locales of the world mutually constitute each other, what is lost in urbicide is the reinforcement that a specific instance of Being-in-the-world gains from the locales in which it is constituted. The Being-with that is an ineluctable feature of Being-in-the-world is not lost, however, but merely covered over. This is disclosed most clearly in those cases in which the rubble is removed to create greenfield sites. Ethnic cleansers hope to deny the existence of a locale and thus to deny any Being-with that it may have embodied. And yet, Being-with persists. The destruction and the rubble that covers it over must continually work to deny this Being-with. Ethnic nationalist programs must continually reinforce, through necessarily violent means, this covering-over of Being-with. This is the purpose behind ethnic nationalists continuing to destroy houses intended for returnees, and protesting against the reconstruction of destroyed buildings.

If a covering-over is left uncontested for long enough, it is, of course, possible that this specific denudation of Being-with will be accepted as an ontic mode of

Being-in-the-world. After all, *Dasein* has accepted the notion of the 'I' as the subject of philosophy precisely because it has been affirmed repetitively throughout the history of Western civilisation until it appears natural. The rubble of Bosnia is a different story, however, since it is a visible reminder of an attempt to cover over Being-with. Such rubble discloses an assault on the community in which Being-in-the-world is always implicated. But more importantly, even after the rubble has gone, Being-with will still constitute the horizon of intelligibility of Being. And attempts to denude Being of its Being-with will still have to pursue, and cover over, Being-with with violence.

At stake then in urbicide is not any specific, ontic heterogeneity but the possibility of alterity itself. Urbicide, though it is manifest as an assault on particular differences, comprises a radical ungathering of the world in order to contest the very Being-with that characterises existence. Urbicide is thus a radical rejection of *Mitsein*, an attempt to institute the individualist schemas of traditional metaphysics in order to deny the shared and public nature of existence and the ineluctable opening towards alterity that characterises Being.

Such an explanation offers a powerful account of the political stakes of urbicide. Moreover, it indicates the resources that ethnic nationalism must mobilise to refashion the world in its own image. However, such an account treats heterogeneity as a single, general phenomenon, unamenable in its very pre-theoretical character to closer, more detailed delineation. As such, Being-with simply names the constitutive trace of alterity at the heart of Being-in-the-world. Noting this trace and the manner in which it is targeted is no idle feat and offers powerful resources for scholars of political violence. However, in order to say more about what urbicide attempts to achieve in such an assault on Being-with, we need a more nuanced picture of the nature of this existential heterogeneity. It is in order to sketch out such an account of the nature of heterogeneity that I will turn to Jean-Luc Nancy and his reformulation of the Heideggerian question of Being-with.

Nancy and the question of community[3]

Jean-Luc Nancy's work is explicitly concerned with the questions raised by the concept of *Mitsein*. For Nancy, the task bequeathed philosophy by Heidegger is to think through the implications of the constitutive heterogeneity that structures existence. However, according to Nancy, Heidegger fails to address this conceptual problematic due to the manner in which his philosophy privileges *Dasein* and, ultimately, encourages a retreat from the thought of difference. For Nancy, therefore, the conceptual contours of the being-with that characterises being remains largely unelaborated. It is thus this elaboration of being-with – or the task of outlining a co-existential analytic – that occupies Nancy in much of his work.

As Simon Critchley notes, 'Nancy is attempting an existential ontology of being-with which has the ambition of being a first philosophy' (Critchley 1999, 239). And yet if the theme of such thinking is to be heterogeneity, it would be at odds with this thought to see this first philosophy as the kind of monological ground that first philosophies (all of them ontotheologies) have aspired to be

(Nancy 2000, xv–xvi). In this sense then, this first philosophy is to be seen much more as an 'ethos', a 'social ontology' (an inquiry into the logic or being of the heterogeneous *socius*), or perhaps simply a response to the question that hangs in the air in the wake of *Being and Time*: the *Mitseinsfrage* (the question of the meaning of being-with).[4]

Nancy's responses to this *Mitseinsfrage* are multiple and dispersed across his work. Whilst *Being Singular Plural* represents the fullest attempt he has made to sketch out a co-existential analytic as first philosophy it is not, for my purposes, the most eloquent of his responses to the question of the meaning of being-with. In *Being Singular Plural*, Nancy addresses the question of the meaning of being-with out of the context of the social that is said to determine this ontology. That is to say, Nancy addresses being-with in a formal sense, outlining the principal philosophical contours that a thinking of the constitutive nature of being-with would follow. And yet, this formal thinking of being-with seemingly neglects the manner in which being-with is co-existent with community. That is to say, when we speak of being-with we are always already speaking of being-with-others. In this sense, Nancy's most eloquent outline of the constitutivity of being-with is to be found in his most explicit reflection upon community: *The Inoperative Community*.

For Nancy, thinking about community demands a confrontation with the dominant strand of thinking about community in the canon of Western philosophy: the metaphysics of presence/subjectivity. According to Nancy, this is explicitly framed as a confrontation with the problems bequeathed to any thinking concerning community by political theories that privilege the individual subject. The problem faced in such theories is the manner in which being-with is taken to be either ancillary to individuality or to be minimised/eradicated in order to grant sovereign autonomy to the individuals who compose the *socius* or the empirical phenomenon of community. Neither of these understandings of being-with can grasp the constitutivity of the 'with'. If the *with* is seen as either ancillary to, or a contingent (and undesirable) limitation of, transcendent autonomy, there can be no meaningful explanation of the manner in which being-with is constitutive of existence. That is to say, such understandings confront heterogeneity as an accidental rather than essential property of being. And in doing so, these understandings deny themselves a cogent account of the existential fact of community. Indeed, insofar as these understandings account for the sociality of political subjectivity, it is not in terms of a constitutive inclination towards alterity, but as a grudging acceptance (albeit as a contingent, ancillary, accidental aspect of being) that political subjects appear to co-exist empirically.

But, as Nancy notes, such understandings neglect the manner in which being-with/community constitutes a horizon from which any understanding of existence/being unfolds. To put it more clearly, such understandings are an attempted negation of the community that is constitutive of existence. And yet this negation is never complete, but only ever a covering-over, effacement or destruction (that leaves ruins and memories). In order to understand Nancy's argument concerning the way in which these conceptions of community cover over or disavow being-with, it is necessary to quickly sketch out his understanding of community.

'Community', according to Nancy, is the name given to that in which our 'being-in-common' is revealed. The Western philosophical tradition – the metaphysics of presence/subjectivity – understands the 'common' of this being-in-common as a 'substance uniformly laid out "under" supposed "individuals", [or as a substance] uniformly shared out among everyone like a particular ingredient' (Nancy 1991, xxxvii): an understanding of being-in-common as a common substance of being. Community thus understood is either a sharing in a common substance of Being (from the Christian sacramental figure of communion with the divine, to the Marxist notion of the privileged agent of history), or an aggregation of entities that are substantially/essentially the same (that is, *in essence*, identical – most commonly seen in the notion that humans are 'born free and equal').[5]

In the schemas of the metaphysics of presence/subjectivity, the realisation or bringing to presence of a common substance of being is taken to be the organising principle of community. That is, community is the realisation of the transcendent substantial essence of being. Hence from Rousseau through to Hegel and Marx, the structure of communal existence is organised around the realisation of a common substance of being (through, variously, the social contract, the dialectic of *Geist*, or the emancipation that will arise from the proletarian revolution). The important thing to note is that in such accounts, the common substance of being is *immanent* to the various communal arrangements of being. Community is the name for the conditions under which a pre-existent, immanent substance is to be realised. Community thus names the problematic of the conditions under which immanence is to be realised. As such community is, for the modern metaphysics of presence/subjectivity, not an experience in itself but the conduit through which an immanent substantial essence of being is realised. 'Community' thus refers to a problematic of overcoming the supposed constraints and limitations that empirical contingency places upon the realisation of such substance.

The problem raised by this conception of community as realisation of an immanent substantial essence of being is central to Nancy's understanding of the political. Simply stated, the problem is that, since the essence of being-in-common – the common substance of being – is taken to be simply *immanent* to community, what it is to be *in-common* is never questioned. That is, discussions of community focus on the problematic of realising (bringing to full presence) a supposedly pre-existent substantial essence of being. This means that in discussions of community, it is only the mechanism of the realisation of this common substance of being that is discussed. The nature, or even desirability, of the posited common substance is not questioned.

This understanding of community as the realisation of an immanent common substantial being is rooted in the metaphysical assertion that there is an essential identity which constitutes what it is to *be*-in-common. For example, it might be presupposed that the *being*-in-common of community lies in *being* 'human'. Hence 'humanity' becomes installed as the common substance of being that defines community. The problem that concerns Nancy is that politics becomes reduced to questions concerning how an immanent substance of being (such as 'humanity', or 'individuality') is to be realised. Questions concerning the meaning of this immanent substance (e.g., 'humanity'/'individuality') are suspended as it becomes consensus that this is simply the essence of being. Community is thus that mechanism which realises this immanent substantial essence of being. To challenge this idea is to contest what is taken to be 'common sense'. After all, once the immanent substance of being is defined, all contrary understandings of being must be taken to be contingent (and thus temporary) confusions or mis-recognitions of being. What sense, it will be argued, does it therefore make to elaborate alternative understandings of being, as the essence of being will, in the end, transcend all such empirical contingencies.

Understandings of community guided by the metaphysics of presence/subjectivity thus harbour two distinctly pernicious problematics. Firstly, as I noted, in taking a certain concept to be the essence of being, discussion of the meaning of that concept, its contours, and its consequences, is suspended. The installation of a certain concept as the embodiment of the essential identity of being takes the form of a naturalisation of a certain consensus. And in insofar as this concept is taken to be the substance of being, it becomes an entirely incontestable concept. This concept becomes a reiterable marker of the foundation on which an ideal system would be constructed. Thus, for example, in discourses about democracy or human rights, the concepts of freedom and humanity are reiterated as markers of the common substance of being without any close scrutiny of their meaning or specificity. To scrutinise them would be to realise that they are historically specific, born of certain historico-conceptual junctures, and thus far from the universal essences that such substances are purported to be.

Secondly, insofar as a concept is taken to be the immanent substance of being, all other competing concepts are either marginalised or reduced to the status of contingent impediment to the realisation of that essence. Moreover, questions of what it is to be-*in-common* are reduced to discussions not of the nature of being but the technical refinements of empirical contingency that must be accomplished in order to realise the essence of being. In this way, the modern metaphysics of presence/subjectivity embed a bureaucracy into modern society that delivers the most profound depoliticisation. Community becomes the mere refinement and perfection of the concept taken to embody the essence of being. This is precisely what is proper to bureaucracy: the refinement *ad infinitum* of a system for the realisation of a supposedly universal essence. Bureaucracy is blind to the consequences of such technical perfection without limits: capable of marginalisation, institutionalisation or even destruction in order to remove the empirical contingencies that prevent the realisation of the substance of being. The modern metaphysics of presence/subjectivity thus proceed in step with a profound depoliticisation of the question of community and a terror hidden behind the banal face of bureaucracy.[6]

This definition of community as the bureaucratic/technical realisation of an immanent common substance of being comprises what Nancy refers to as 'the *figuration of the political*'.[7] 'Figuration' denotes the manner in which the metaphysics of presence understands community. That is, the metaphysics of presence/subjectivity understands community as the realisation of a figure: a concept taken to be the embodiment of the universal/substantial essence of being, the realisation of which both grounds the technical bureaucratic organisation of society and suspends the question of community (what it is to be-in-common). Figuration is thus that through which the metaphysics of presence is able to represent itself to itself: as objective, as substance, as presence.[8] The *figure* of, for example, 'the human' becomes the image through which the metaphysics of presence represents its presence to itself. There are, of course, many such figures: legal person; state; *demos*; citizen; subject; object; rationality; and so on.

Figuration, immanentism, totalitarianism

Figuration accomplishes an important function throughout the history of the metaphysics of presence/subjectivity. Nancy (1991, 3) refers to this as the operation of 'immanentism'. Immanentism is the foreclosure of the question of community (what it is to be-in-common) that is performed in taking a particular figure as the substance immanent to being and thus the principle according to which society/community is to be organised. Moreover, the immanentist figuration of the political transforms community into *communion* (either sharing of common substance, or being of common substance) and makes this communion into a *work*, something *to be accomplished*.

How should we understand this immanentism, this community understood as a communion that is a work to be accomplished? At the level of fundamental ontology, the figure of the substance of being that institutes the communion-work must be conceived of as absolute. For the modern metaphysics of presence/subjectivity to come to presence, it must represent itself to itself as the universal (and thus only) substance/essence of being-in-common: the single measure of the common substance of being. The figure must have meaning beyond relation with other figures in order to be the (properly universal) foundation in which the communion-work originates. For if the figure is defined in relation (to anything), then the founding moment is complicated by exteriority. The figure constituted by exteriority is merely a value, dependent on relational definition for its meaning – a meaning, therefore, that cannot be the *single* (universal) measure of the common substance immanent to being.

The figure/figuration is, therefore, according to Nancy, a resolution of a contradiction central to the modern metaphysics of presence/subjectivity. Specifically it is the resolution of the contradiction raised by the desire for presence, particularly for a fullness of presence. This contradiction is elaborated by Nancy (1991, 4) as the paradox of being-alone. The metaphysics of presence offers, insofar as it proffers the possibility of a fullness of presence, a vision of the subject of being existing alone. Universal substance does not derive its meaning (or value) in terms of a differentiation from an other, but exists, fully present in and for itself. In these terms, figures of full presence offered by the metaphysics of presence must represent presence as the possibility of being-alone. And yet, Nancy notes, the possibility of being-alone is framed in terms of a relation. That is to say, being-alone is a mode of being-with defined as a standing apart from, or existing in the absence of, others.

It might be possible to assert that such a separation is possible: that the realisation of a figure might allow the subject of being to enclose itself and thus divide itself from its others. And yet even this enclosing, insofar as it is a closure *from* others, is a relation. To be properly alone (or as Nancy (1991, 4) puts it, to 'be alone being alone') requires that this relation established by the enclosure of the subject of being be enclosed itself. That is, the enclosure itself must be separate from the others it closes itself off from and thus the relation severed. It is precisely this impossible double enclosure that the immanentist metaphysics of presence attempts through figuration. That this double enclosure is impossible can be seen by noting the manner in which the enclosure must always be a closing off from alterity (a general otherness or specific others). Any enclosure is thus a relation, since if there were truly no alterity with which a relation existed, there would be no need for enclosure, no need for figuration and the simple existence of presence.[9]

And yet immanentism is precisely this operation of an impossible double enclosure continually asserting/performing representations of the fullness of the subject of being. Moreover, the paradox of the double enclosure that lies at the heart of the metaphysics of presence/subjectivity is both that which necessitates immanentism and that which fuels the desire for the accomplishment of the communion community in which fullness of presence is achieved through the figure. The immanentist metaphysics of presence/subjectivity posits the figure as that with which all subjects of being have a communion and then organises the society/community as a perpetual work to enclose this community in order to establish being as present in and for itself. That this is an increasingly violent work should be noted. The enclosure on which such immanentism is predicated is, precisely, an exclusion: an exclusion of the alterity in relation to which the enclosure that establishes presence is performed. Figuration, this enclosure, is thus a laying-out of boundaries, a drawing of a line that encloses a conception of the substance of being that all those in the society/community share. It is a bounding on which the fiction of the substance of being existing in and for itself is based.

It is in relation to this (en)closure that Nancy talks of immanentism as *totalitarianism*. By this Nancy does not mean that figuration is performed by some sort of party who take it upon themselves to exterminate all those who are not included in the figuration. Rather, all communities conceived of according to figuration are totalitarian *in form*; atrocities such as the Holocaust are historically specific instances of the extremes of which figured communion-communities are capable. The totalitarianism of the communion-community, conceived of as the work demanded by figuration, arises from the manner in which the figure is taken to permeate all being-in-common such that politics is reduced to the technical accomplishment of the realisation of immanence.

The consequence of this totalitarianism of the figure can only be the evaporation of the political into a technicism according to which it is no longer necessary to question being-in-common.[10] According to this technicism, a mere calculation of the ways in which to achieve the realisation of immanence is taken to be all that is required. Hence, in our present time the political evaporates into technical discussions concerning the manner in which society can best be engineered to suit to operation of a supposedly free market, or to correspond to the discursive regimes of science. Or the political evaporates into legalistic arguments concerning the minutiae of government. For some, of course, immanence has already been realised and all that remains is to broaden the geographic reach of that immanence (cf. Fukuyama 1992).

Shared community

It is precisely this immanentist communion-community that is the target of Nancy's critique in *The Inoperative Community*. In order to appreciate Nancy's critique it is necessary to underline the manner in which figuration is a *work*, a technical operation to secure the enclosure of the community. *Work* is, in Nancy's terms, an operation that proceeds according to the *telos* of the figure. That is to say, the figure establishes a ground for an operation of enclosure. This operation holds the realisation of the figure as its *telos*. This *telos* or horizon (in the sense of enclosure) is simultaneously the *logos* of the communion-community: that which expresses the horizon of enclosure towards which the technical operation of realisation is orientated, and the foundation on which the being of the communion-community is grounded. A figured communion-community thus *works* to secure the enclosure established in the figure. It is, properly, an *operative* (in the sense of *working*) community whose technical organisations function to secure the enclosure of the figured community.

It is in contradistinction to this operative (working), figured communion-community that Nancy outlines the notion of the 'inoperative' community. This inoperative community is not a dysfunctional or poorly implemented communion-community. Nor is it a principle of disruption of the communion-community. In fact, it is not posed strictly in opposition to the communion-communities established by the modern metaphysics of presence/subjectivity. For if it were to be posed in opposition to the communion-community, Nancy would be accepting at least the terrain on which the modern metaphysics of presence/subjectivity operates. In contradistinction, Nancy elaborates a first philosophy that challenges the principal assumptions of the modern metaphysics of presence/subjectivity concerning community. This first philosophy suggests that community itself can never be made operative, can never properly work (in the sense of realising a figure). It suggests, contrary to the modern metaphysics of presence/subjectivity, that community is not a sharing of substance. Indeed it suggests that the very notion of community as a gathering of those who share an essential substance of being is mistaken.

Instead Nancy suggests that community should be understood as the name of an existential condition of inoperability, a constitutive heterogeneity that leaves any enclosure continually unravelling in the 'loose ends' (Miami Theory Collective 1991) of an exposure to alterity. In this sense, Nancy is questioning the very idea of community as a bounded expression of substantial identity that has governed the history of Western thought and is instead suggesting another understanding of what it is to be always already implicated in community. And this 'other' understanding is derived in response to the question of what it is to be-in-common.[11] Thus

Nancy is responding to the constitutive heterogeneity of existence recognised by Heidegger in the concept of *Mitsein*. Moreover, this response directly challenges Heidegger's subsequent privileging of *Dasein* over *Mitsein* by asserting that the principal question is not that of being, but that of being-with, or being-in-common (a sharing of the public spatiality of existence that I have previously demonstrated to be constituted in and through buildings and at stake in urbicide).

Being-in-common – the existential condition that underlies community – can only be seen as being-with: being-separate only makes sense in relation to a being-in-common that is a being-with. That is to say, community is the experience of being-self *by virtue of* being-with: this is the being-in-common that is revealed in community (Nancy 2000, 94). Such a being is never absolute; it cannot perform the separation required to bring itself to presence without relation. Community is thus the name of a relation, an originary exposure to alterity, an identity that consists precisely in the impossibility of self-identification but which draws its sense from the being-*with* that is the condition of possibility of being-*in-common*. Community in this sense is not communion, but communication.

This conception of community radically re-orients our understanding of being-in-common from the enclosed figure (commonly realised in the nation-state or ethnic national group) to an understanding of being-in-common as a constitutive relation with alterity. This constitutive relation – a constitutive heterogeneity, since it constitutes existence as always already a relation with others – is a communication in so far as it is an opening to, and receiving of identity from, alterity. Which is to say that this relation is not a crossing-over of a pre-existent distance between the self and other. Rather it is a constitution of self and other in and through sharing. And since sharing is at once a distinction and a relation, it is proper to see this relation with alterity occurring precisely at those places where the distinction that makes possible the relation (and thus sharing) takes place.

The relation is, strictly speaking, a surface of contact between self and other that is at the same time both relation (a shared surface is in common) and yet a distinction (the surface separates self from other). It is in this sense, therefore, that the relation is best seen not as a conduit through, or crossing of, a distance separating self and other but a line shared between self and other. The line that separates self and other is thus in-common (it is part of both self and other) and yet is a line of distinction that separates (and thus constitutes) self and other. It is in this sense that community is a communication since the boundaries the self has in-common with the other are precisely those from which the self derives presence/meaning. The difference of self and other is thus *communicated* in and through this shared boundary. In this sense being is, for Nancy, an ecstatic event, a communication/constitution of self from beyond the self across the boundary of self–other that is both shared and yet separates.

In this sense, community is not the name of a distinct, separate territorial domain, space or association. 'Community' is the proper name of the constitutive communication of difference experienced in and through being-*in-common*. Community is the network of communications (in the sense of exposure to alterity) in which a differentiated articulation of contingent singularities (the social terrain) is constituted. Thus being is, in Nancy's phrase, 'singular plural'. Or rather, to give it proper articulation, 'community' is the event/experience of 'being singular plural' (Nancy 2000, 28–41).

Community is therefore 'a reticulated multiplicity, which produces no result': an inoperative network of singularities constituted by the loose ends of a communication of difference constitutive of self and other (Nancy 2000, 9).[12] And yet this communication of difference constitutes a limit that establishes a distinction of self and other that is co-existent with a sharing of a common distinctive boundary. And in this sense, the self is always already in-common with the other and thus any attempt to enclose the self and put distance between it and the other are perpetually unworked. The sharing constitutive of this being singular plural continually unworks the attempts of the metaphysics of presence/ subjectivity.

Nancy thus asserts that community is the proper name of the constitutive heterogeneity – the being singular plural that characterises existence – that structures/constitutes Being-in-the-world (to use Heidegger's terminology). In this sense, Nancy contests the notion inherent to the metaphysics of presence/ subjectivity that community is ancillary to the substantial essence of being, a contingent and wholly secondary aspect of Being-in-the-world. That is, he contests the idea that being is a transcendental substance existent prior to the world in which it always finds itself and thus sees community not only as an empirical fact, but also as a fundamental aspect of existence. Moreover, he answers the question of the nature of community by outlining the sense in which community is not the association (forced or voluntary) of individuals, but, rather the name of the being singular plural in which the self is constituted by virtue of being-with others: 'It can no longer be a matter of treating sociability as a regrettable and inevitable accident, as a constraint that has to be managed in some way or another. Community is bare, but it is imperative' (Nancy 2000, 35–36).

Excursus: heterogeneous heterogeneity and political plurality

In *Being Singular Plural*, Nancy claims that philosophical enquiry into being comprises a 'co-existential analytic' (Nancy 2000, 93–99). For Nancy, the question of what is 'between us' thus comprises a first philosophy. Insofar as this betweenness implies difference, it also implies that being is always already heterogeneous. Heterogeneity is thus the existential condition at the core of Nancy's philosophical schema. Named in this way, however, heterogeneity takes on the contradictory appearance of a singular existential condition. Moreover, the relation of such heterogeneity to the political plurality at stake in violence such as urbicide is simply assumed: the singular condition of heterogeneity is assumed to imply difference and, in turn, difference is thought to translate into, for example, the plural ethnicities that populate the imaginaries of those participating in (and observing) urbicidal events. To a certain extent I have this compounded problem due to my apparent willingness to substitute, on occasion, 'difference' or 'plurality' for 'heterogeneity'. At this stage, therefore, it is worth offering a brief clarification on both the heterogeneity of heterogeneity and the nature of political plurality implied in my argument.

One way to approach the question of the heterogeneity of heterogeneity and the nature of political plurality might be to draw upon Heidegger's distinction between the ontological and the ontic. We might argue that heterogeneity represents the kind of ontological difference Heidegger refers to when he discusses the difference between Being (*das Sein*) and Beings (*das Seiende*) (Inwood 1999, 46–49). As such, heterogeneity would be a singular irreducible difference constitutive of the question of Being. Such a reading might regard plurality as an ontic matter. However, this interpretation has the appearance of resurrecting a metaphysical distinction between essence and existence (appearance). Such a distinction runs counter to the existentialist theme in Heideggerian and post-Heideggerian thought. Indeed, it runs counter to Heidegger's own statement in *Being and Time* that '[t]he essence of *Dasein* lies in its existence' (Heidegger 1962, 67). It is with this in mind that I have turned to Nancy's post-Heideggerian existentialism in order to understand the heterogeneity implied in Being-with.

The heterogeneity that Nancy refers to in his co-existential analytic is derived from a notion of being unfolding from shared divisions. A shared division comprises the boundary that both being and otherness have in common. It is the line where being reaches its limit and across which lies the beginnings of alterity. This line is shared insofar as it is common, but a division insofar as it marks out the moment at which being ends and alterity begins. Such a line is, more correctly, a surface of contact. Difference is thus not that which is encountered, but rather that to which we are always already exposed by sharing a common boundary. It is because being unfolds from, and thus cannot disavow, these shared divisions that it is characterised as always already being-with. An irreducible and pervasive alterity (or difference) thus not only haunts existence but is constitutive of being-with, according to Nancy.

This alterity gives rise to singularities and hence to a heterogeneous existence. Each instance of being-with that emerges from this multiplicity is singular. That is to say, each and every instance of being-with comprises a distinctive unfolding from the particular division it shares with its other. The reticulated multiplicity that Nancy speaks of is thus not the division of an existential field into equal and similar units, but rather the emergence of a series of unique networks of identity and difference from multiple, intersecting shared divisions. In total, this field of singularities is multiple, or heterogeneous. Heterogeneity is thus the fundamental characteristic of this being-with. And since this heterogeneity is a collection of singularities, it is itself heterogeneous. It is not a plurality of identical units, but a multiplicity of singular beings-with.

Political plurality, as I refer to it in this argument, could be said to be the manner in which these singularities are expressed in aggregated political entities. Though heterogeneity is heterogeneous, political expressions emerge that aggregate various singularities into expressions of simple difference. Such expressions privilege one aspect of any given singularity and invite others to identify with this aspect. Ethnicity, nation, class, race have thus served as ways to aggregate and express the heterogeneity characteristic of being-with as simple difference. And yet plurality is not a simple reduction of heterogeneity: it is an expression of it. Plurality is expressed in and through unstable dialectics of inclusion and exclusion (Walker 1999, 173) that both simplify the complexity of the heterogeneity that characterises being-with and aggregate and organise singularities. On the one hand, these dialectics of inclusion and exclusion are necessary precisely because the multiplicity of singularities (or heterogeneous heterogeneity) that characterises (co)existence requires simplification and aggregation if it is to give rise to the agonistic interplay of forces that we call politics. On the other hand, such dialectics are unstable precisely because they are founded on an existential heterogeneity. They are partial and temporally limited simplifications of complex intersecting singularities and, as such, are always subject to the eruption of an existentially prior heterogeneity. Plurality is thus a response to, and yet always reveals, heterogeneity. Ultimately then, plurality, though a simplification of heterogeneity, is also a good indicator of its existential importance. In other words, plurality indicates the priority of the heterogeneous heterogeneity that characterises existence. It is with this in mind that in my argument I often use heterogeneity and plurality interchangeably, treating the latter as that which derives from, fails to contain, and often dissolves into the former. Or to put it another way: plurality is that which empirically poses the existential problem of the heterogeneity of heterogeneity.

Urbicide and community

Nancy can thus be said to provide an answer to the *Mitseinsfrage* left unanswered by Heidegger: specifically, that community is the name of the experience of fundamental heterogeneity that is an existential condition of all being. Nancy reorients the question of being away from notions of presence and subjectivity to construct a philosophy predicated on difference, communication and inoperability. Nancy's work thus radically recasts the classical figure of the metaphysics of presence/ subjectivity – community construed as a sharing of substantial commonality – as an experience of the constitutively heterogeneous nature of existence. Nancy extends the original insights found in Heidegger's elaboration of the notion of *Mitsein*, to argue for the constitutively heterogeneous nature of existence, providing a sketch of the nature of the heterogeneity at stake in urbicide.

Insofar as the built environment is constitutive of an always already shared/ public spatiality which is the condition of possibility of heterogeneity, it is constitutive of the conditions of possibility of a fundamentally inoperative community. The built environment is that which gives to being its fundamental openness to alterity. Nancy provides us with an outline of the nature of this openness – its fundamental inoperability and its contestation of the figures of the metaphysics of presence/subjectivity. Urbicide is thus the destruction of that which represents the conditions of possibility of such an inoperative community. Indeed, urbicide is the deliberate targeting of that which contests and challenges the work of various immanentist figures – *ethnos* and nation in particular. An account of the nature of the heterogeneity at stake in the shared/public spaces of the built environment, which takes this difference to be an inoperative community – an originary exposure to, and relation with, alterity – thus provides a further insight into the stakes of urbicide. Not only is urbicide an assault on shared/public space, or a covering-over of being-with, but it is part of the project or work of an immanentism. The politics of urbicide are not only a denial of heterogeneity, but a destruction of constitutive relations with alterity in order to constitute immanentist, figured notions of political community.

Such a sketch is, however, nothing more than the bare outline of the meaning of urbicide. Having sketched out the manner in which the built environment is constitutive of shared/public space, I have demonstrated the manner in which urbicide is an assault on the conditions of possibility of heterogeneity. Moreover, in showing that the heterogeneity at stake is a fundamental openness to alterity that constitutes existence as an inoperative community, I have outlined the manner in which urbicide is not merely a destruction, but a project for contesting such essential being-with. However, it is necessary at this stage to elaborate further the political and conceptual stakes of the argument that I have advanced. It is to such an elaboration that I will turn in the next two chapters. In examining the political and conceptual stakes of urbicide, I will be concerned to address both the insight into the politics of urbicidal destruction and the conceptual implications for scholars of political violence of conceptualising destruction of the built environment as a distinct form of political violence.

5   The political stakes of urbicide

> Mostar joined the ominous club of divided cities ... in which the bridges are replaced by walls ... [Mostar was thus] reduced to a battleground of opposing political interests, with its architecture and urban fabric turned into ... military targets. The two sides in Mostar ... allied along ethnic lines ... breach the basic covenant of the city: to be open for all. Thus they engage in the futile game of claiming what they can never get.
>
> (Modrcin 1998, p. 79)

Previous chapters have traced a two-fold movement in understanding the phenomenon and concept of urbicide. In Chapters 1 and 2, I outlined the distinctive nature of such violence, beginning with an account of the manner in which it falls outside of conventional understandings of the destruction of the built environment according to notions such as military necessity, collateral damage, the destruction of cultural heritage, or the particular cultural characteristics of certain communities. I argued that the concept of urbicide enables us to perceive the distinctive logic of such violence and trace out its characteristics. Specifically, I argued that urbicide, understood as a distinct form of political violence, represented the destruction of the built environment *qua* that which comprises the conditions of possibility of a particular existential quality: heterogeneity.

In Chapters 3 and 4, I then turned to the question of the manner in which the built environment constitutes the condition of possibility for existential heterogeneity. Drawing on Martin Heidegger's account of spatiality and dwelling, I argued that buildings are constitutive of the spatiality that characterises existence. Since buildings are fundamentally public, this spatiality is always already shared with others and thus contains the possibility of heterogeneity. According to Heidegger and Nancy, heterogeneity comprises a Being-with, or sharing of the world with others. This Being-with, or sharing, is understood as a fundamental relationality in which identity (the presence of an entity) is constituted only in relation to difference. Self and other are not pre-existing entities that exist side-by-side (and thus are contingently forced to enter into a relation), but rather identities that are established in and through the constitution of a relation. These identities unfold from a shared boundary that marks where self finishes and other starts and vice versa.

This heterogeneity comprises an existential condition in which relationality and alterity perpetually unwork the presence of an identity. As public artefacts, buildings constitute the condition of possibility for such sharing precisely by holding open the possibility of others existing in the same spaces and places that they constitute. Buildings thus constitute all identity as a relation with the possibility (actualised or potential) of alterity. In other words, by being in principle available for all, buildings make those identities constituted through the spatiality they establish relate to the possible others that might also be constituted in and through that spatiality. The identity constituted in the locales established by buildings is thus perpetually unworked by the alterity that comprises a possibility of the latter's public availability.

Urbicide is thus an assault on buildings *qua* that which, as the fundamentally public artefact that constitutes existential spatiality as shared, is the condition of possibility of heterogeneity. The mutually constitutive relation between buildings and heterogeneity is the defining characteristic of 'the urban' and, as such, 'urbicide' is an appropriate term for such violence. The term 'urbicide', like that of 'genocide', is deployed with the aim of indicating a coordinated pattern of violence that attacks a particular class of entities for their collective characteristics rather than their individual specificity. In the case of genocide, the aim is to outline a coordinated attack on individuals and/or cultural artefacts as elements constitutive of collective identity, such as ethnicity or nation; in the case of urbicide, it is to reveal a coordinated pattern of attacks on buildings *qua* elements that are constitutive of the heterogeneity that defines urbanity.

I have suggested that such violence comprises a disavowal of heterogeneity, a covering-over of a fundamental existential plurality, by political subjectivities predicated on concepts of homogeneity and purity. Moreover, I have suggested that ethnic nationalism is precisely such a political subjectivity and, as such, its intimate involvement with urbicidal violence can be traced to the concepts of homogeneous, pure territory around which it is constituted. Such a proposition is, however, a broad brush outline of the meaning of urbicide. It ceases with the rubble of urbicide, presuming that it is enough to indicate that destruction of the built environment is a disavowal of heterogeneity.

This leaves the consequences and legacies of urbicidal violence largely unexamined. I will refer to these consequences and legacies as the 'stakes' of urbicide, since they are what is in the balance in any event of urbicide. These stakes represent what can be lost and/or transformed in urbicidal violence. Understanding the stakes of urbicide is thus essential if we are to grasp and, in and through such understanding, contest the aims, consequences and legacies of such violence. I will argue that there are two primary stakes of urbicide, loosely classifiable as the political and the conceptual. On the one hand, the political stakes of urbicide refer to the way in which the political is put at stake in urbicide, in particular the ways in which political subjectivity is transformed in and through such violence. The conceptual stakes of urbicide, on the other hand, refer to the general conceptual imaginary that underlies both the perpetration and (mis)understanding of the destruction of the built environment. These conceptual stakes thus comprise the manner in which a distinctive imaginary is reinforced by such acts of violence. I will treat these stakes in turn: examining the political stakes in this chapter, and the conceptual stakes in the following chapter. The present chapter will thus comprise an examination of the manner in which the political is put at stake in urbicide, the transformation of political subjectivity effected by such violence, and discussion of empirical examples that illustrate this argument.

The political stakes of urbicide: the territorialisation of antagonism

Agonism and the political

In referring to the 'political' stakes of urbicide (that which is put in danger in the event of urbicide and which can be lost in and through destruction), a particular assumption is being made about the nature of politics and the political that requires further explication. It is necessary, therefore, to enquire into what Philippe Lacoue-Labarthe (1990, 17) refers to as 'the *essence* of things political'. In speaking of 'the *essence* of things political', I am referring to the characteristics that are taken to define the various phenomena that are designated as being 'political'. In this sense, 'the political' is much broader than the narrow notion of 'politics' found in modern societies/states. In such societies/states, 'politics' refers simply to the mechanisms of representation and organisation by which polities are governed. It is, however, a mistake to confuse the mechanisms of governance extant at a specific historical juncture as being co-extensive with, and exhaustive of, all of the characteristics that define what can be said to be properly *political*.

We must ask, therefore, what it is that allows us to say of events that they '*are* political': what defines events that have the characteristic of 'being-political'; or, more simply, what is the *being-political* that is to be found in 'things political'? That such an enquiry is relevant to an analysis of urbicide could be said to be 'common-sense' insofar as urban destruction would in everyday parlance be referred to as either 'politically motivated', part of the 'politics' of ethnic nationalism, or 'political' violence. And yet, what is it about this destruction that designates it as *being* a properly political event? After all, the violence itself is exterior to what we would ordinarily, in liberal-democracies, refer to as 'politics'. Indeed, the idea of a 'political settlement' is often counterposed to such violence. The idea operative in attempts to reconcile warring parties is thus precisely an opposition between politics and violence/conflict/war. What is it, then, that necessitates speaking of 'the political' being at stake in urbicide?

Things political, I would contend, are characterised by an *agonism*: a struggle, conflict or combat (though not always in the literal sense). Here, I am drawing on Foucault's (1982, 222) notion of 'agonism' derived from the Greek αγωνισμα, meaning combat, contest, struggle or sport. Agonism refers to 'a relationship which is at the same time reciprocal incitation and struggle; less of a face-to-face confrontation which paralyses both sides than a permanent provocation' (*Ibid.*). For Foucault, agonism is a characteristic of power: only insofar as there is incitement (i.e., a provocation) of government to modify the actions of others is there a field of possibility for practices of power.

The concept of agonism is further developed by William Connolly in his discussion of 'agonistic democracy'. 'Agonistic democracy', according to Connolly (1991, x), 'affirms the indispensability of identity to life, disturbs the dogmatization of identity, and folds care for ... diversity ... into the strife and interdependence of identity\difference'.[1] Connolly thus emphasises the way in which provocation and incitement characterise the interdependent networks of identity and difference that arise out of the relational heterogeneity of existence. In Nancy's terms, the constitutive heterogeneity of existence comprises an agonistic relationality in which the relation of self and other is formed in and through a perpetual provocation to delineate where the former ends and the latter begins. The relation between self and other is thus a mobile boundary, and the action of either self or other can put that boundary into question, provoking the need for redefinition of the relationship (and of the identities that result from the distinct form of that relationship). The sharing of divisions that I outlined in the previous chapter is thus the constitution of an agonistic, relational network of identity\difference.

Combining Nancy, Connolly and Foucault, we could sketch out the political character of this heterogeneous, relational agonism as follows. The constitutive heterogeneity of existence that comprises a sharing of divisions is a communication (Nancy 1991, 25) in which the meaning of self is given by, and at, the distinction from the other (a differentiation/division that can be neither recuperated into, nor alienated from, the self). In this sense the 'reticulation' (Nancy 2000, 9) of existence, its constitution as a network of singularities structured by the plurality/heterogeneity of existence, is a labile mosaic of inclusions and exclusions. The singularities of self, other, state, nation, *ethnos* and so on constituted at any given juncture are established precisely though the constitution of temporary and contingent limits of differentiation at which self and other are distinguished and thus constituted. These limits include what it is to be part of the identity of the self and other and exclude what is to be taken to be foreign to it. In this sense, the division shared by self and other is a mark of both inclusion and exclusion.

This differentiation, inclusion and exclusion, is precisely the operation on which the practice of power (and specifically government) is founded. Government is a classification and disciplining that is productive of particular/singular selves and others. Government constitutes the limits between itself and alterity – thus establishing a communal, or societal, identity – and then exercises power over those 'other' singularities (the mad, the criminal, the sexually deviant) in order to draw them into, or expel them from, the boundaries of the communal/social. And yet government is constantly provoked by the alterity with which it shares a constitutive division.[2] It can never escape this provocation, because it can only ever delimit itself with a shared division.

'The political' is thus defined as agonistic: that event in which a particular identity is put into question, leaving the location of its boundaries open to contestation (and eventually resolution). This is precisely the characteristic of things political, according to Nancy, Connolly and Foucault: the (necessarily impossible) struggle to constitute singular presence. Political events are, therefore, those instances in which an identity is contested by the alterity in relation to which it is always already constituted. Identities may become ossified over time, even naturalised, but they never exist in isolation from a constitutive alterity whose very existence contests their identity, threatens to undo their efforts at self-identity or presence, and thus to open up the social field to an alterity that will ruin the presence any identity has achieved.[3]

In this sense, the agonism of relational heterogeneity is the essence of the political. Without heterogeneity, and the alterity on which it is predicated, there can be no properly political events. Urbicide is an empirical attack upon, and attempt to efface, the constitutive alterity that structures existence. As such, urbicide attempts to re-constitute existence as being comprised of separate homogeneous, sovereign individuals/groups. This effacement of heterogeneity in the rubble of war is necessary precisely because exclusionary political programs, such as ethnic nationalism, are founded upon the myth of homogeneity. Projects such as ethnic nationalism are, therefore, constituted by myths of separateness, self-determination and ancient hatred. For such political projects to succeed, they must deny that they are constituted by alterity despite the historical and empirical evidence that they are always in a relation of some kind with others. To do so they attack the built environment, which, by its fundamentally public nature, constitutes existence as heterogeneous. In so doing, urbicidal ethnic nationalists seek to efface the permanent provocation of otherness that the built environment entails.

Insofar as urbicide represents an assault on heterogeneity, it targets agonism: seeking to efface the provocations of otherness in order to disavow the constitutive alterity that characterises all identities. It is agonism, therefore, that is put at stake in urbicide. If urbicide is successful, the provocation of otherness will be effaced. Moreover, insofar as it is characterised by agonism, urbicide comprises an assault upon, and attempt to disavow, the political. In other words, the 'essence of things political' is also at stake in urbicide. As such then, agonism comprises the political stakes of urbicide.

From agonism to antagonism

The agonistic relation of identity and difference is thus the political stake in urbicide. Or, rather, in attacking this agonistic relation, urbicide puts the political itself at stake. If the heterogeneity constituted by the built environment is lost through destruction, so is the condition of possibility of the political that this heterogeneity – insofar as it is an agonistic relation of identity and difference – represents. In putting agonism at stake, then, urbicide constitutes a direct assault on the political. Such an observation raises two questions, however. On the one hand, it raises the question as to how exactly agonism and the political are effaced. On the other hand, it raises the question of what such destruction achieves. It is to these two questions that I will now turn, beginning with an account of the manner in which Foucault's conception of power might help us to understand what the destruction of agonism and the political achieves.

Foucault distinguishes between the exercise of power and conditions of domination or confrontation (1982, 221; 2000, 283–284). Confrontation seeks to eliminate the freedom necessary to the exercise of power (i.e., the freedom necessary to engage in the provocation from which power – understood as an attempt to modify the provocative actions – originates). In confrontation, force is not exerted as a response that seeks to engage with, and modify the action of, a provocation. Rather, confrontation represents an attempt to eliminate the freedom to act and, as such, is characterised by violence. In confrontation, rather than engaging in an interdependent relationship characterised by provocation and response, parties separate from each other and refuse to yield to one another.

Confrontation eliminates agonism and thus the political. It is in this sense that Foucault distinguishes the political relation of power from the depoliticised relation of confrontation. Confrontation is thus an elimination of the political insofar as it is the face-to-face opposition of one figure to another rather than a relation in which mutually interdependent, singular identities acknowledge their shared divisions and engage in a struggle to define identity characterised by provocation and response. The freedom to act is negated by the figuration of either party insofar as the party presents itself not as a provocation to the other but as an essential substance un-amenable to governance. In this situation, each figure presents itself as a thing with a substantial essence and the opposing party is reduced to exerting force upon that thing. As well, the division shared by both parties is taken to be an unbridgeable gap that thwarts the exercise of governmental power over actions. This is the reduction of provocation or contestation to confrontation. It is, I would argue, the translation of agonism into antagonism.

This translation of agonism into antagonism is a strategy to secure figuration. It is an attempt to efface the political insofar as it attempts to translate both division into separation and provocation into confrontation. This is a dual event insofar as the translation of division into separation is a necessary precursor to confrontation and to the extent that the constitution of a confrontation is necessary for the establishment of a separation. Antagonism brings a figure to presence insofar as it disavows the shared division between itself and its others by constituting that division as a separation. In constituting the figure and its others as separate figures confronting each other, antagonism is also a depoliticisation. Insofar as agonistic provocation is reduced to antagonistic confrontation, the political is reduced to technical management of such oppositions (albeit a technics that is, properly, a violence). The being-in-common of being singular plural is thus effaced.[4]

It is precisely this effacement of the political through its translation into the politics of confrontation that is at work in the logics of urbicide. Urbicide targets buildings because they are conditions of possibility of the provocation of alterity that constitutes agonism. Insofar as buildings are that which constitute existential spatiality as fundamentally heterogeneous, they are also that which constitute existence as agonistic. It is in the network of relations constituted by buildings that the shared divisions which give rise to self and other are constituted. The destruction of buildings is thus an attempt to efface the shared division they constitute and the provocation of alterity that any identity is thus constitutively open to.

Such an assault on alterity, or the agonistic provocation that otherness comprises, is particularly necessary for those forms of identity that are predicated on homogeneity. Forms of identity such as ethnic nationalism are predicated on the notion that their identity is pure or homogeneous. Such purity or homogeneity can only be realised if the relation with alterity that provocation represents is disavowed. Instead such identity rests on the notion that it can have presence in and for itself, in other words without deriving any of its identity from a relation with alterity (as such a relation would contest its homogeneity). As such, this identity seeks to disavow not only alterity, but also the provocation of such otherness. It is thus a disavowal of the political. Instead such identity seeks a world in which provocation is minimised either through the elimination of otherness or its subjugation to technical rules that offer no provocation. Only if ethnic nationalism can achieve this disavowal of the political can it avoid the provocation that would otherwise question the purity and homogeneity of its presence.

The territorialisation of antagonism

The disavowal of the agonism of the political through the constitution of antagonism represents the achievement of urbicide. However, this leaves an important question unexamined, namely how this antagonism is actually constituted. In one sense, we have proceeded in reverse order in this examination of the political stakes of urbicide, from a general discussion of the political nature of the agonism at stake in attacks on the built environment to the more specific question of how the attack on urban fabric actually effects the loss of these stakes. It is my contention that this later question returns us to the central theme of Chapter 3: namely, the manner in which spatiality is at stake in urbicide. In Chapter 3, I demonstrated the manner in which Being-in-the-world, or existence, is ineluctably spatial. I also showed that insofar as this spatiality is constituted by buildings, it is fundamentally shared/public. It was on this basis that I argued that existence is constitutively heterogeneous. If it is the conditions of possibility of a shared existential spatiality that are attacked by urbicide, what is the fate of this spatiality? It is my contention that the constitution of antagonism through urban destruction discloses precisely the manner in which spatiality is at stake in urbicide.

At this point it is necessary to point to a distinction between *spatiality* on the one hand, and *space* on the other hand. Space has traditionally been conceived of as a homogeneous medium bounded within certain limits. From the earliest Greek origins of the metaphysics of presence to Newton and Kant, space has been conceived of as analogous to the interior of a vessel – a given space, within particular bounds, contained, and finally a medium in which things may be located and through which they may move (Casey 1998, 54). Spatiality, on the other hand, refers to the relationality, dimensionality and orientation that comprises Being-in-the-world. This spatiality is quite unlike the space in which objects are located. Spatiality does not provide an *a priori* set of co-ordinates in relation to which any object can be located. Rather, spatiality comprises a relational engagement with things that is constitutive of the worldliness of Being-in-the-world. That is, spatiality contains no co-ordinates and is not prior to Being-in-the-world. Rather, it comprises, as I discussed in Chapter 3, the complex networks of relations that constitute Being-in-the-world as an everyday engagement with, and an orientation towards, the things with which it is concerned. In this sense, spatiality is not an abstract medium, or universal substance, but a set of relations established by the everyday concerns of Being-in-the-world. Heidegger refers to the distinction between space and spatiality when he notes that although the spectacles on someone's nose may be closer in terms of space than the picture that they are looking at on the opposite wall, the picture is closer in terms of spatiality because it is that with which *Dasein* is concerned (Heidegger 1962, 141). In other words, although the distance moved through a purported medium may be greater from subject to wall than from subject to the end of their nose, the relationship is stronger between subject and glasses than it is between subject and picture.

Heidegger notes a specific existential priority between space and spatiality: namely that space is derived from spatiality. Space is generated by the establishment of a common measure against which the relations of engagement that constitute existential spatiality can be measured (inches, feet, miles, centimetres, metres, kilometres and so on). This is what Heidegger means when he says that spatiality affords

> the possibility of measuring things ... according to distances, spans, and directions, and of computing these magnitudes. But the fact that they are *universally* applicable to everything that has extension can in no case make numerical magnitudes the *ground* of the essence of spaces and the locales that are measurable with the aid of mathematics.
>
> (Heidegger 1993a, 357–358)

Spatiality is thus the ground of spaces. Space comprises the reduction of the existential spatiality of Being-in-the-world to arbitrary magnitudes.

Moreover, spatiality is, as I have demonstrated in Chapter 3, fundamentally shared/public. That is to say the things in engagement with which spatiality is constituted are available to each and every singular instance of Being-in-the-world. Space, however, is a different proposition. Space is a substantial medium providing the co-ordinates of locations within given limits (i.e., a thing may be said to be located in the space of the room). It is, therefore, a metaphysical concept, a homogeneous substance. In one sense, space admits of heterogeneity insofar as any object can be located within it. However, space is not shared in the way that spatiality is. Indeed, the fundamental rule of this medium is that no two objects can occupy the same space (whereas a specific object can be articulated into spatial relations by more than one *Dasein*). The closest to sharing possible in space is for two things to be adjacent to, or touching, one another. And yet these things are differentiated as having no common border, but rather as touching one exterior surface against the other.

This is precisely the sense in which antagonism presents the confrontation of opposing parties – as the being-adjacent, or touching of two bounded entities in which the surface where touching occurs is not a common surface, but the meeting of two exterior surfaces and, hence, despite touching, an indication of the separation of both entities. It is not hard, therefore, to see that the antagonism constituted in and through urbicide is co-extensive with the constitution of homogeneous, ethnic national entities that are represented as existing side-by-side in the medium of territorial space (but never as occupying the same space). That is to say, antagonism is the translation of shared existential spatiality into adjoining, but bounded, spaces (or territories). Understood in this way, antagonism is a territorialisation of figuration. Put simply, figuration demarcates a territorial space, bounds it, and admits of no heterogeneity other than that of a confrontation with opposed/ antagonistic territorial spaces.

It is precisely this territorialisation of antagonism that can be seen in urbicide. For example, the destruction of the Old Bridge in Mostar created a zone of separation (the Neretva Canyon) between west and East Mostar that is the territorialisation of an antagonism between Bosnian Croats and Bosniacs that is vital to the performance of the presence of the Bosnian Croat ethnic statelet of Herceg-Bosna. Thus in and through the destruction of the Old Bridge, the Bosnian Croats translated the agonistic provocation of heterogeneity that the urban environment of Mostar comprised into the antagonistic separation of 'Croat' West Mostar and 'Muslim/Bosniac' East Mostar. This separation and antagonism was achieved by reconfiguring the urban terrain as separate entities, thus lending credence to the claim that these were substantially separate parties opposing one another in a confrontation. The destruction of mosques, front line streets, public places and finally bridges followed this logic, destroying the shared spatiality of Mostar in an attempt to establish two distinct, opposing entities who shared nothing, had no being-in-common.

The destruction of the urban environment is thus a laying waste of the locales whose spatiality cannot be recuperated to ethnic nationalist spaces. The spaces that ethnic nationalism seeks to construct are territorialisations of the figures of ethnic presence on which they are predicated. It is in this sense that mosques (and to a lesser extent churches) are destroyed as reminders within the territories carved out by ethnic nationalists of the heterogeneity on whose disavowal these spaces rest. Moreover, and perhaps more importantly, it is the residential districts of Bosnian towns – the public squares, parks, shops and so on – that are locales whose fundamentally public and, hence, heterogeneous, spatiality cannot be recuperated to these projects of the territorialisation of figures. And, hence, an assault on these shared locales is an integral part of the campaign by ethnic nationalist forces to bring to presence the figures of ethnic identity. In this way, ethnic nationalist forces hope to create the depoliticised confrontation in which figured ethnic groups live in adjacent, but not common, spaces (touching at, but not sharing, their borders). Hence, it is necessary, argue the forces of ethnic nationalism, to legitimate ethnic cleansing, partition Bosnia, and deny the heterogeneity constitutive of existence.

And yet, as I suggested in Chapter 4, the territorialisation of figuration in and through antagonism unravels in a variety of places. Antagonisms have to be continually re-territorialised in order to maintain the spaces of ethnic-nationalist figuration. This re-territorialisation takes the form not just of a continuing post-war urbicide, but also of continued expulsions predicated on the antagonistic state of affairs (International Crisis Group 1997). This continuation of what constitutes an 'unstable dialectic of inclusion and exclusion' (Walker 1999, 173) is a perpetual unravelling of territorialised antagonisms necessitating their re-territorialisation.

The political, agonism and shared spatiality thus return perpetually as an ineluctable trace of alterity/heterogeneity necessitating this continual play of re-territorialisation. In the laying (or not) of a foundation stone for a mosque, the rebuilding of the Old Bridge in Mostar, or the refurbishment of the homes of returnees, the traces of the heterogeneity constitutive of existence return to haunt ethnic nationalism. Of course, as long as the antagonistic play of confrontation is allowed (particularly by the so-called 'international community') to remain the *status quo*, this return of the political will be fleeting. And yet, the point to note is that it is precisely this constitutive heterogeneity glimpsed in brief moments prior to the re-territorialisation of figures of ethnic identity that is at stake in urbicide. It is this heterogeneity that is disavowed in urbicide. And that is the same as saying that the logic of urbicide is the reduction of the agonism of the political to the antagonism of territorial politics.

Revealing the political stakes of urbicide

One can see the political stakes of urbicide in a number of instances of conflict and post-war reconstruction. In the latter context, the stakes of urbicide are equally stark as the destruction secured under cover of war is either contested or consolidated. To demonstrate this I want to outline three cases where the territorialisation of antagonism at stake in urbicide is revealed. These examples are indicative of the general logics of urbicide and cast revealing light on the issues at stake. Of course, such a sample of cases does not provide a general template for consideration of all such cases. However, these cases will demonstrate the ways in which each case of the widespread and deliberate destruction of the built environment can be addressed in order to outline what is at stake in the logics of urbicide.

I have chosen cases from the post-Cold War era. Whilst urbicide is not confined to the post-Cold War period, it is in this era that the question of the destruction of urbanity has become a focus of concern for scholars. It seems appropriate, therefore, to concentrate upon the period when highlighting the issues that are being addressed in the use of the concept of urbicide. Furthermore, whilst each of these cases is part of wider, evolving dynamics of conflict (which are still developing in the contemporary period), I have abstracted each case from contemporary dynamics to examine how a particular historical instance highlights what is at stake in the logics of urbicide. None of the cases pretends to represent a complete picture of the general conflict within which they occur (or possibly even of the limited events they discuss). However, each reveals the ways in which the territorialisation of antagonism and its unworking are at stake in urbicide.

House-burning in post-war Bosnia

The stakes of urbicide were revealed in the aftermath of the 1992–95 Bosnian War by 'minority returns' and the violence deployed to prevent such a process. The 1992–95 Bosnian War was characterised by both the killing and the forced displacement of ethnic groups. Comprising a logic of violence euphemistically referred to as 'ethnic cleansing' (Shaw 2007, 48–62), this killing and displacement followed a typical pattern of depopulation and re-population.[5] A town or village would be 'cleansed' of a particular ethnic population and then resettled by members of the 'cleansing' group. The Bosnian Federation town of Drvar provides an exemplary instance of this dynamic. As the International Crisis Group notes,

> Before the war ... some 9,000 people lived in the town and some 17,000 in the municipality, of whom 97.3 per cent were Serbs and 2.7 per cent 'others'. In 1995 ... Drvar fell to Croat forces and its Serb population fled. The new Croat authorities ... repopulated the municipality with displaced Croats ... The current civilian population in Drvar municipality numbers between 5,000 and 6,000. Of these, only 79 are Serbs, all elderly people who chose to remain after the Croats took control of the area – 68 in the outlying villages and 11 in town.
>
> (International Crisis Group 1997, 2)

Such 'ethnic cleansing' comprises the disavowal of agonistic heterogeneity through the creation and consolidation of territorialised, antagonistic ethnic enclaves. It is thus the disavowal of the political. After the conflict ended, the problematic posed by refugees and internally displaced persons (IDPs) was central to the project of post-war reconstruction.[6] According to the Dayton Agreement, both the Bosnian Federation and Republika Srpska were to facilitate the return of refugees to the place from which they had been displaced. A right of return was thus established that placed a duty upon both entities to ensure that displaced persons were assisted in returning to their former towns and villages. These measures were intended to reverse the consequences of war-time destruction and displacement. The intent was, thus, to reverse the effects of ethnic cleansing and to restore Bosnia's pre-war ethnic heterogeneity. As such, these returns would constitute the revivification of the agonism characteristic of the political.

However, despite the undertakings made in the Dayton Agreement, returns were hindered in the post-war period by both violence against returnees and the destruction of buildings to which displaced persons could be returned. It is in the latter violence against the buildings that would provide the basis of return that the stakes of urbicide are revealed. The town of Drvar provides stark evidence of this violence. In October 1996, thirty-five houses were destroyed after Bosnian Serbs displaced during the war returned to see their properties. Then, in May 1997, another twenty-five houses were destroyed 'after an international delegation ... met with local authorities ... to discuss the return of displaced Serbs to the area' (International Crisis Group 1997, 1). This violence was not confined to Drvar, however. The International Crisis Group notes that '[t]he vandalism in Drvar is sadly not an isolated event but part of a sustained campaign [across Bosnia-Herzegovina] to prevent the return of minorities' (*Ibid.*).[7] Indeed, the destruction of houses and places of worship across Bosnia *after* the signing of the Dayton Agreement demonstrates that urbicide is not confined to situations of conflict.

In the case of Drvar, and in the other cases where ethnic nationalist objections to minority returns spilled over into violence, the destruction of houses intended for returnees disclosed more than the simple destruction of the place where that returnee was to live. Indeed, those who saw this destruction as simply an obstruction through the elimination of places of residence forgot that it is always possible to rebuild a house, or to refurbish another, and that the destruction of a house itself need in no way prevent the return of displaced persons.[8] Rather, the destruction of the buildings to which displaced persons were to return discloses the manner in which those buildings are constitutive of a shared space that fosters heterogeneity. Indeed, the destruction of such houses is best understood as an instance of urbicide since the house is destroyed not simply to intimidate the returnee, but as the condition of possibility of the heterogeneity constitutive of urbanity.

Returns are the return of heterogeneity to territories that were homogenised through ethnic cleansing. In this sense, they contest the fiction of antagonistic separation that is at stake in urbicide and consolidated through so-called ethnic cleansing. The return of heterogeneity is possible precisely because the urban fabric of these towns and villages comprises always already shared spaces, and thus harbours an ineluctable possibility of alterity. It is only possible to remove this possibility of alterity by removing the shared spaces of that urbanity. And it is precisely because they are constitutive of the shared space that it is buildings that are destroyed. House-burning thus exposes what is at stake in urbicide precisely at the moment where the urbicidal regime stands to lose that which it thought it had secured. At stake then is the consolidation or reversal of a fiction of separation achieved through the conversion of agonism into territorial antagonism. This territorialisation of antagonism is secured through the destruction of the buildings that constitute existence as an agonistic heterogeneity.

In and through urbicide, a separation is effected between ethnic groups. This separation is a territorialisation of boundaries. These are not the shared boundaries constitutive of being-in-common, but dead zones between groups that naturalise the idea that there is no sharing or commonality between different ethnicities. This separation is then consolidated by an urbicidal program of destruction within the territory carved out by the zones of separation. This program achieves a homogeneity that disavows the existence of heterogeneity within the territory controlled by the ethnic nationalist figuration, thus giving the fictive appearance of presence to the ethnic nationalist figure.

This is precisely what is at stake in instances of post-conflict house-burnings where buildings were destroyed in order to prevent minority returns. Such cases are significant insofar as they demonstrate the lengths to which it is necessary to go to efface agonistic heterogeneity. The space constituted by the buildings that comprise the elements of towns and cities is always already a shared space. As such, this means that towns and cities such as Drvar are the sites of an ineluctable agonistic heterogeneity – even in the wake of sustained 'ethnic cleansing'. The territorialisation of antagonism thus, eventually, leads to the destruction of any building construed to offer the possibility of return, or the possibility that the identity constituted through the antagonistic separation of one ethnic nationalist community from its others could be revealed as a violent fiction.

As such, then, return is an intensely political process – a revivification of the agonism characteristic of the political. Attempts to prevent return demonstrate the political stakes of urbicide insofar as they comprise attempts to efface the political and the agonism that characterises it. Returnees are a provocation that demonstrates the relational, communicated nature of identity. Their houses are precisely that which provides the condition of possibility of the communication of such difference and the establishment of relational networks of identity\difference. As a form of violence that seeks to efface the political, relational character of identity, ethnic nationalism thus seeks to continue its assault upon the urban environment in order to consolidate its territorialised antagonisms.

The demolition of Palestinian homes

The political stakes of urbicide can also be seen in the demolition of Palestinian houses by Israel. The Israeli Committee Against House Demolitions (ICAHD) has argued (with reference to reliable sources) that since 1967 Israel has demolished in excess of 18,000 Palestinian houses (Halper 2007). As B'Tselem notes, Israel destroys Palestinian homes for three reasons: 'operational, administrative and punitive' (B'Tselem 2004, 7). Operationally, Israeli military forces demolish Palestinian homes that are built in zones regarded as particularly sensitive or important. In practice, such demolitions occur in the areas surrounding settlements, roads servicing settlements, international and internal borders, the separation barrier, crossing points on the separation barrier (or borders), or other military installations. These military demolitions comprise the clearing of houses from territory in order to remove the presence of Palestinians. B'Tselem attributes 60 per cent of the demolitions of Palestinian homes carried out between 2000 and 2004 to such 'clearing operations' (B'Tselem 2004, 7). In the period from the beginning of 2004 to August 2007, B'Tselem attributes the demolition of 1,753 houses to this form of destruction (B'Tselem 2007a). Such destruction is accomplished through the use of technology such as the D-9 bulldozer, whose capabilities for destroying the urban environment were demonstrated in the 2002 assault on Jenin (Graham 2004, 195–209).

Administratively, Israel operates a system of planning permission that makes it extremely difficult for Palestinians to build homes. Restrictions on planning permission are exacerbated by difficulties in registering land and thus proving ownership. In such circumstances, many Palestinian houses are built illegally. Israel has demolished homes deemed to be built illegally (i.e., without permission) in large numbers. For example, between 1987 and 1998 over 2,200 homes built without permission were demolished (B'Tselem 2007b). More recently, in East Jerusalem 305 houses built without permits were demolished between 2004 and

2007 (B'Tselem 2007c). Finally, the Israeli Defence Force (IDF) has a policy of demolition as a punishment for suspected involvement in militant or terrorist activity. These demolitions target the homes of those involved in planning or implementing such attacks, and their families. This policy has been acknowledged to have failed in deterring attacks (Shalev 1991; Myre 2005) and is arguably illegal (principally by virtue of comprising a collective punishment). Overall this punitive destruction is disproportionate to the military objectives sought and, as such, seems to fall under the logic of urbicide.

The destruction of Palestinian homes exhibits the two central dynamics that comprise the political stakes of the logic of urbicide. On the one hand, demolition for military purposes comprises a clearing of zones of separation (cf. Hass and Harel 2001). These zones, around access roads, the separation barrier, borders and settlements, constitute a disavowal of the agonistic relationality that characterises existence. This separation is central to the constitution of an Israeli identity that is understood as existing in and for itself, without relation to its Palestinian other. The agonistic, provocative relation that constitutes the existential condition under which Israeli and Palestinian identities are constituted (or communicated through shared divisions such as the Green Line and separation barrier) is effaced by such separation. As such, then, this separation gives rise to the fiction, or figuration, of an Israeli identity free from any constitutive alterity.

On the other hand, however, the consolidation of such a fictive figured identity necessitates the constitution of antagonism and subsequent homogenisation of the territorial spaces to which these antagonisms refer. Separation cannot merely be an inert fact, but is rather constructed as the representation in spatial terms of the intractable antagonism that exists between two distinct, unmixable, and thus unrelated, entities. This antagonism rests, however, on the homogenisation of the territorial entities claimed by each party. Thus Israel has administratively worked to ensure that the territorial space claimed by their figure of identity is homogenised. Israel is not simply separated from Palestine, but traces of alterity within Israeli territory (e.g., Palestinian homes built without permits) are removed through demolition. This second dynamic comprises the consolidation of the disavowal of the political: the lasting effacement of the agonistic relationality the latter comprises.

Seen as such, Israeli destruction of homes should be understood to comprise a logic of urbicide. Seen as urbicide, the demolition of Palestinian houses is exposed as a covering-over of being-in-common and a territorialisation of an exclusionary politics that shares a basic presumption with ethnic nationalism: namely an ontopolitics that posits territorial self-determination as the only possible option for security of identity. Moreover, if this destruction is seen as urbicide, it becomes clear that it is precisely this territorialisation of separation that must be contested if the disavowal of the political is to be resisted.

Grozny

The final case that I want to discuss – the second Russian assault on the Chechen capital Grozny in 1999–2000 – demonstrates that a far more devastating outcome is at stake in urbicide: urban annihilation. The dynamics of separation and homogenisation effected by urbicide reach their apogee in Russia's Chechen campaign. At stake in this urbicidal conflagration is the complete effacement of agonistic, relational heterogeneity.

In the 1990s and early twenty-first century, Russian nationalist identity was both constituted in relation to, and contested by, Chechen ambitions for independence (Lieven 1998, 369–384). Chechen claims for independence – an alternative form of political being than that offered by Moscow – represented an agonistic provocation of Russian nationalist identity. Nationalist ideas of the extent of Russian control over Chechnya existed in relation to such claims. The nationalist imaginary was thus shaped by a relation of denial of Chechen aspirations for self-determination. One example in particular highlights the relational, agonistic character of this relationship: the destruction of residential blocks in Moscow in September 1999. These blasts were blamed upon Chechen terrorists (Gentleman 1999). However, this attribution of responsibility has been disputed, especially by Chechens who argue that these incidents constituted a mechanism for reviving Russian military designs to subdue the breakaway republic. Regardless of whether this attribution of blame is correct, however, the exclusionary force of the discourse is unmistakable.

Relationality can be overcome through a disavowal and effacement effected through a conversion of agonism to antagonism: a separation of self from other and their figuration of independent and opposed entities. The discursive construction of the Chechens as terrorists was thus an attempt to construct a moral and political gap between Chechen and Russian identity. It was an attempt to circumscribe the extent of Russian identity by making clear the moral and political separateness of Chechens. However, this discursive othering cannot fully break the relation that mutually constitutes Chechen and Russian nationalism. Constructing the terrorist threat externalises Chechen identity and gives an impression of separateness but does not fully break the relation no matter how much it makes it look like a gulf rather than a surface of communication. One reason for the failure of such discursive separation lies in the fact that the moral and political criteria for construing the Chechens as other are constituted by the Russians. Thus the Chechens only exist as separate for, and in relation to, the Russians.

It is in such a context that the Russian urbicidal assault in Grozny in 1999–2000 is to be understood: as a strategy for the disavowal and effacement of the relational, agonistic provocation of Chechen identity. Insofar as the destruction of Grozny comprises an effacement of its agonistic heterogeneity in the course of a strategy of homogenisation (i.e., the removal of alterity from Russian soil through the extension of the latter's rule across Chechnya), it exemplifies the logic of urbicide. Russian forces failed to fully enact such a strategy in the 1994–96 war (Farby and Magnusson 1999; Oliker 2001, 5–32). However, during this early conflict the stakes of urbicide were already evident (Human Rights Watch 1995). The capital Grozny was damaged out of all proportion to military necessity. During this campaign it became clear that Russian tactics were to destroy the urban fabric. However, this destruction was out of all proportion to the number of Chechen fighters actually sheltering in Grozny. Rather, it seemed that Russian forces were destroying Grozny because it harboured heterogeneity itself. The buildings of the capital city established a fundamentally public/shared space that harboured an alterity intolerable to the Russian project to exclude difference and homogenise the identity of the Federation.

Ultimately, this fear was proved well founded insofar as the city remained open to Chechen resistance and ungovernable by Russian forces (Hills 2004, 151–153). The fundamentally public/shared character of this urbanity proved both too elusive and too agonistic for the Russian homogenising claim. Despite this, Russian forces returned to Chechnya in 1999 to finish what had been started earlier. In October 1999 the stakes of urbicide were starkly set out when Russian forces announced their intention to raze Grozny (Hoffman 1999, A1; Human Rights Watch 1999). Russian forces clearly identified Grozny with an ineluctable (and, hence, un-pacifiable) alterity. In this context, the urbicidal destruction of Grozny constituted a program of homogenisation that was the necessary adjunct to the territorialisation of Russian identity. This territorialisation is predicated on the ontopolitical claim that Russian identity exists in and for itself within its territorial boundaries. Such an ontopolitics requires the effacement of the relational nature of such identity. The logic of urbicide is precisely such a homogenisation in which buildings are destroyed *qua* the conditions of possibility of agonistic being-in-common. In this way, the heterogeneity that characterises the Russian Federation is disavowed/effaced.

This is the end point of urbicide: a relentless and total destruction of urban fabric that lays waste to all that can possibly offer testament to the heterogeneity proper to existence. Urbicide will naturally, if left unchecked, tend towards this infinite ruination of the urban fabric.[9] Since the urban fabric always already constitutes existence as relational and heterogeneous, it always offends figures of territorialised identity. As we saw in previous examples, it is possible, through a territorialisation of antagonism, to disavow the provocation of the city. However, insofar as this provocation is intractable and insistent, such conditions of confrontation are perpetually unworked. The territorialisation of antagonism must, therefore, be effected through a sustained work of urbicide, destroying and controlling those built things that threaten to uncover the relational agonism characteristic of existence. In Grozny, this provocation proved too insistent and ineluctable for the Russian Army. The logical consequence is a total destruction of the city, a laying waste to the very possibility of heterogeneity. Insofar as there is no city, there can be no provocative, agonistic relationality.

This instance of total devastation of the urban environment is a fitting point at which to bring to a close the discussion of the political stakes of urbicide. In the devastation of Grozny, it is possible to see those stakes thrown into stark relief. The rubble of Grozny exposes the manner in which the territorialisation of being-separate is accomplished through the ruination of the built things that constitute existence as fundamentally public/shared. The stakes of such urbicide are thus the agonism of the political itself. In this context, it is worth noting Jean-Luc

Nancy's caution concerning the danger of failing to contest this disavowal of the political:

> if we do not face up to such questions, the political will soon desert us completely, if it has not already done so. It will abandon us to political and technological economies, if it has not already done so. And this will be the end of our communities, if this has not yet come about. Being-in-common will nonetheless never cease to resist, but its resistance will belong decidedly to another world entirely. Our world, as far as politics is concerned, will be a desert, and we will wither away without a tomb.
>
> (Nancy 1991, xli)

6   The conceptual stakes of urbicide

From the political to the conceptual

The political stakes of urbicide reveal the manner in which identity is constitutively structured by an agonistic relation to alterity. This relational agonism is constituted through the sharing of public buildings as nodes in networks of relational spatiality. The destruction of such buildings comprises an attempt to destroy these relational networks, to disavow the constitutive role of alterity and to efface the agonistic interdependence of identity\difference by inscribing in its place a territorial antagonism predicated upon an image of separation.

Recognising the political stakes of urbicide requires us to understand the constitutive impossibility of an identity existing in and for itself. It thus requires a particular reorientation of our understanding of the nature of politics and, hence, political violence. This recognition has two interlinked consequences. Firstly, it requires us to understand the consequences of the mutual interdependence of materiality (in the form of buildings) and identity. The impossibility of bringing identity to presence in and for itself is attributable to the role played by buildings in constituting the relational spatiality of Being-in-the-world. Such identity is structured both by its relation to others as well as by the role material things play in constituting Being-in-the-world. In other words, not only is an openness to alterity constitutive of existence, but so is a relation with material objects. Separation from these objects, and their treatment as contingent features of a world encountered by a preconstituted individual, is a primary feature of many understandings of politics and political violence. These figures of thought disavow the constitutive role played by materiality (in this case buildings) in order to maintain their fictions of individuals existing in a world where things have merely instrumental value. Understanding the political stakes of urbicide thus entails questioning such a disavowal of the constitutive interdependence of materiality and identity.

Secondly, recognising the political stakes of urbicide requires us to adopt a critical stance towards those understandings of politics and political violence that proceed from figures of separateness. Figures of separateness – whether the figure of territorial separateness found at the heart of international relations, or the autonomous individual at the heart of liberal political theory – have guided many understandings of politics and political violence. However, the previous chapter's argument shows that such figures are inscribed over, and constitute a disavowal of, the agonistic heterogeneity of existence. Recognising the existential priority of such heterogeneity will necessarily entail adopting a critical stance in relation to such figures.

Understanding the political stakes of urbicide thus has wider, conceptual entailments. Both consequences of recognising the political stakes of urbicide entail questioning a wider conceptual imaginary that structures much thinking about politics and political violence. The disavowals of the constitutive relation between materiality and identity and between identity and otherness share a common intellectual horizon: they are *anthropocentric* in their figuration of politics as that which is engaged in by autonomous individuals for whom both the material environment and otherness are contingent and secondary features of existence. I will treat each of the two anthropocentric figures in turn, arguing that such anthropocentrism comprises the conceptual stakes of urbicide. If successful, urbicide comprises the inscription of anthropocentric figures over the constitutive heterogeneity of existence.

The conceptual stakes of urbicide: anthropocentrism

Anthropocentrism and the material environment

Anthropocentrism can be defined, broadly, as an implicit or explicit assumption 'that human reason and sentience places the human being on a higher ground' (Seckinelgin 2006, 31). This assumption is the ground for a conceptual division between human beings and nature, or, more broadly, between human beings and all the other non-human elements that comprise the world and which, whether living or non-living, are seen merely as the context within which human lives are lived. Such a conceptual division has led to an understanding of the world in which the activities of human beings are understood to be of paramount interest and engagements with the remainder of the world are construed solely in terms of the uses to which humans put their material context.

The identification and critique of 'anthropocentric bias' has been developed primarily within discussions of environmental politics (Seckinelgin 2006, 31; Taylor 1986; Routley and Routley 1979, 36–59). This is hardly surprising insofar as one of the central concerns of environmental politics has been to overcome the division between mankind and the environment that has resulted in the latter being conceived of as an instrumental resource for the gratification of the former. Overcoming such an anthropocentric conceptual division is necessary in order to see the material world as a complex ecology in which human beings are part of, not distinct from, nature (Seckinelgin 2006, 9–10).

The 'anthropocentric bias' (Seckinelgin 2006, 31) is not, however, confined to environmental politics. Indeed, 'human-centered' understandings of the environment are representative of the anthropocentrism at the heart of enlightenment thinking.[1] According to such a proposition, the distinction between humanity and its environment reflects a wider set of cultural discourses in which anthropocentric principles are deeply embedded. Though the roots of this anthropocentrism can, according to Giorgio Agamben (2004), be traced to Aristotle's *De Anima*, its Enlightenment formalisation (and, hence, the source of its grip upon contemporary cultural discourse) is attributed to Descartes and Kant (Seckinelgin 2006, 86–108). This 'anthropocentric bias' in modern reason holds that, by virtue of being the sole entity endowed with reason, the human takes priority over all other entities (living or non-living).

This anthropocentrism has exercised a strong grip on modern thought, defining not only our understanding of nature, but also our philosophical, political and ethical discourses. From the anthropocentric 'Copernican turn' of Kant's *Critique of Pure Reason* to the centring of discussions of the nature of the *polis* on the reasoning and discursive capacities unique to humans, accounts of what it is to be human have consistently taken to be of secondary concern the material amongst, in, around and through which our lives are lived: resources at the disposal of human subjects to be deployed instrumentally to satisfy their requirements.[2]

Such an account of anthropocentrism resonates with Heidegger's discussion of 'enframing' in 'The Question Concerning Technology' (Heidegger 1993b). Heidegger notes the manner in which modern technology has led to the conception of nature as a 'standing reserve'. That is, nature is understood as a realm of objects, fundamentally different to, and put at the disposal of, human beings. The relationship of humanity to nature is thus one of instrumental use. For Heidegger, the instrumental enframing of nature in the modern era poses grave dangers, not least that the proper sense of *techne* is obscured, thus effacing the manner in which an authentic technological relation can disclose the truth of Being. Such a technological relation with nature obscures the manner in which Being-in-the-world is, as I have shown in Chapter 3, constituted in and through objects. Indeed, it is in relation to the objects that are constitutive of locales that dwelling (as Heidegger refers to Being-in-the world in his later work) is constituted (Heidegger 1993a). Thus to understand objects as separate from, and at the instrumental disposal of, humanity, effaces the existentially constitutive role such things play.

Indeed, recognising the logic of urbicide exposes the unsustainability of understanding buildings merely as objects with instrumental value for humanity. Rather, human existence is constitutively structured by the things that form the locales from which the spatial networks that constitute experience unfold. The creation of an identity that separates the human from those relational networks is the work of a substantial cultural discourse that culminates in the modern understanding of technology. This is a cultural discourse that effects a two-dimensional separation: humanity from nature and the individual from his/her environment. To put it more precisely, the separation of humanity and nature is embodied in the figure of the individual whose relationship with the things around him/her is understood not as constitutive but, rather, as contingent and instrumental. This anthropocentric discourse obscures the constitutivity of material objects in Being-in-the-world and, therefore, individual identity.

Contesting this anthropocentrism requires contesting the model of ecology that posits humanity and nature as separate domains of existence. Insofar as this separation is embodied in the figure of the individual, it requires contesting the figure of the individual as a sovereign entity in an instrumental relationship with the environment in which s/he exists. Indeed, it requires contesting the notion that the individual is separate from the things that are constitutive of his/her existence.[3] As such then, this leads us to the second of the anthropocentric figures at stake in urbicide: the individual. Just as the separation of the human and the material is at stake in urbicide, so is the separation of the individual as a political subject; a separation the gives rise to another anthropocentrism in which the body of the individual becomes the referent object for political understanding. It is to this second anthropocentrism at stake in urbicide that I will now turn.

Anthropocentrism and the autonomous individual

The constitution of the individual as the political subject comprises the inscription of an anthropocentric figure that is understood as being existentially prior to both the environment and the society in which s/he exists. The individual is conceived as a sovereign, autonomous entity unencumbered by existentially prior relations with things or others. Such an assumption is anthropocentric insofar as it reduces the environment and society to secondary concerns, mere contingent, empirical facts rather than ontological characteristics. This anthropocentric notion of individuality can be most clearly seen in liberal political theory.

Liberal political theory conceives of being-with-others as an empirically unavoidable, yet essentially subsidiary, aspect of Being. That is to say, despite acknowledging the facticity of being-with-others (which is the motivating force behind liberal attempts to reconcile the various competing claims to political entitlement), liberal political theory argues that this empirical situation is not an essential aspect of Being. Indeed, liberal political theory begins with the proposition that individual, sovereign, and free political subjects are the components from which any being-with-others is contrived (Nancy 1991, 3–7). This understanding of Being leads liberal political theory to conceive of political subjects as 'unencumbered and antecedently individuated ... [and thus] prior to society' (Mulhall and Swift 1996, 167). Society, community, or being-with-others is thus, whilst factually the case, a contrivance that is supplementary to the basic state of human existence.

Liberal political theorists are right, of course, to protest against the misconception that they are ignorant of the empirical facticity of society (Caney 1992). However, it must be noted that this is not my point. My point here is that the ontology underlying liberal political thought conceives of Being in terms of a sovereign, free individual existing prior to Being-in-the-world – at which point the individual becomes encumbered and constrained by the empirical contingencies of human existence. It is precisely on the basis of this ontological assumption that liberal political theory conceives of being-with-others as a secondary characteristic of Being. Being-with-others arises through either the contingencies of empirical circumstance or a voluntaristic association. That is, either it is the case that we *must* be with others because contingent empirical circumstance is such that we co-exist in the same space as others, or we *choose* to be with others (often in a contractual way).

It is this ontological assumption about the nature of the political subject that leads to the liberal conception of sharing. Since individuals exist prior to Being-in-the-world with others, sharing can only be conceived of as an antecedent allocation of goods to these subjects. This allocation is deemed necessary for two reasons: 1) because, although their existential qualities are prior to the contingencies of the world, it is an empirical fact that subjects exist in the world with others; and 2) as things are part of the empirical contingency of the world, they are not intrinsically related to the subjects that inhabit the world – the subject is, since it is sovereign, existentially unfettered by any relations with things despite its empirical entanglements with questions of allocation of goods. The free, sovereign individual can own goods either solely or jointly, but cannot share in a more fundamental sense. To share in a more fundamental sense would be to violate the principle that the individual is essentially sovereign and free. Indeed, it would entail a constraint of freedom through the establishment of an ontological relation to others.

The problem with such a conception of sharing, and the being-with-others it entails, is that there can be no essential heterogeneity attendant to it. Heterogeneity may be an empirical fact of existence and yet it is not an ontological aspect of political subjectivity. Thus the heterogeneity that characterises urban environments can only be seen as an empirical contingency. Correspondingly, the destruction of buildings cannot be conceived of as the destruction of the conditions of possibility of heterogeneity. That is, since heterogeneity is only empirically contingent to the urban experience, there is no essential link between the buildings that comprise urbanity and the heterogeneity that is characteristic of this urbanity. Indeed, though it is the case that empirically urbanity is characterised by heterogeneity, there is, according to the ontological assumptions of liberal political theory, nothing about the structure of existence that would support the assertion that the destruction of urban environments *necessarily* comprises a destruction of heterogeneity. Although it might be conceded that, in the majority of empirical cases, heterogeneity might be so destroyed, it is not the case that *each and every time* a systematic assault on urban fabric occurs it is heterogeneity that is at stake. This is because heterogeneity, or being-with-others, is a contingent and entirely subsidiary aspect of human existence and, hence, has no essential conditions of possibility the destruction of which would, in each and every case, lead to the invocation of the concept of urbicide.

The contingent nature of heterogeneity can be attributed to the essential *anthropocentrism* of the ontological assumptions that underpin liberal political theory. More broadly, it is these ontological assumptions that are at stake in urbicide. Insofar as urbicide is successful, it disavows the constitutive heterogeneity of existence. Moreover, insofar as it is successful, it inscribes an antagonism that naturalises notions of homogeneity and separateness that consolidate the figure of the individual (as the figure that embodies separateness and homogeneity) as the primary subject of politics and political violence. Unless we recognise and understand the logics of urbicide, we will fail to note the problems implicit in the inscription of such a figure over the essential heterogeneity of existence: the principal problem being that the individual is conceived of as a human person unencumbered by any relationships and thus entirely free, or sovereign, with regard to their lives.

The consequences of the anthropocentric priority of the person

Whilst the individual human person may appear to be a common-sense starting point for a political theory, such anthropocentrism has two distinct consequences: that violence is only significant insofar as it affects the person; and that violence is primarily determined by the choices of individuals. I will treat each consequence in turn.

Firstly, the seemingly innocuous assumption that the human person comprises the subject of politics leads to a central concern with the business of human individuals. The principal consequence of this concern is that ethics and politics concern themselves almost wholly with the conduct of humans towards other humans. This means that political problems are identified as being those in which persons are affected. The consequence of this concern is that liberal-anthropocentric political theories devalue the theoretical importance of phenomena such as the destruction of the urban environment. Indeed, such destruction is only of consequence insofar as it affects human individuals, makes them homeless, and deprives them of their sense of cultural identity through the loss of what is considered to be heritage. Where there is thought to be no direct consequence for human individuals, then no political problem arises.

It is for this reason that the destruction of the homes of prospective returnees in Bosnia (discussed in the previous chapter) is conceived of as an act of intimidation rather than as an attack on the conditions of possibility of heterogeneity. Moreover, it is why the destruction of Dubrovnik (a site listed on UNESCO's World Heritage List as part of the cultural heritage of humanity) – conceived of as an assault on the sense of cultural identity and civility possessed by persons in both Croatia and the larger world – is more important than the destruction of villages across Bosnia and Kosovo which have no buildings purporting to be of cultural significance. Indeed, in the case of the destruction of cultural heritage, the irony is that anthropocentrism reads such destruction not as an assault on buildings but as an attack on individuals (and their collective groupings), as it is an attack on an identity possessed by those individuals through the existence of the buildings. Anthropocentrism thus displaces the meaning of the destruction of urban environments from the loss of those environments to the purported loss of identity suffered as a result by human persons. The destruction of buildings is not seen as something to be examined in its own right for the meanings it discloses, but rather as something that only matters insofar as it is instrumental in causing an injury to the identity of human persons. This means that anthropocentrism cannot admit that, in each and every case of destruction of buildings, the conditions of heterogeneity are under attack. Rather it is limited to assessing each case of destruction in order to determine whether some person or group has suffered an assault on their identity through the destruction of cherished buildings. It is precisely in this way that no one mourns the loss of ugly buildings, since their loss is not thought of as important for any person's or group's identity.[4]

However, this perception that a political problem is defined by its being a problem for human persons is not the only consequence of anthropocentrism. There is, as I noted, a second consequence of anthropocentric understandings of politics and political violence: since the basic unit of analysis for such theories is the sovereign individual, the basic motivating force behind political action is taken to be choice. Moreover, such choice is conceived of as the execution of the *intent* to exercise one's freedom to choose in a particular manner. This means that every political problem must be traced back to the *intent to choose* a particular course of action.

The effect of the centrality of anthropocentric assumptions for such accounts of politics can be seen in the hegemony of the concept of 'intent' in international jurisprudence. The effects of the widespread anthropocentric assumption that political problems can be explained via the intent of sovereign individuals are at their starkest in the problematic juridical definition of genocide. The 1948 UN Convention on the Prevention and Punishment of the Crime of Genocide clearly states that genocide consists of the 'intent to destroy, in whole or in part, a national, ethnical, racial or religious group' (Roberts and Guelff 2000, 181). The consequence of such a definition is that, for any individual or group to be found guilty of genocide, this intent must be demonstrated. Moreover, and more importantly, it means that where intent cannot be demonstrated, genocide cannot be deemed to have occurred.

That this problem of intention derives from *anthropocentric* assumptions should be made clear. It is because an idealised image of the human person is taken to constitute the political subject that the concept of intent is given such prominence. Intent is the logical corollary of the notion of sovereignty. Anthropocentric understandings of sovereignty hold that the ideal human person is unencumbered by the constraints of being-with-others and thus is free to choose. Choice, of course, postulates the existence of an intent to exercise one's freedom in a particular way. For the model of unencumbered sovereign agency on which anthropocentrism relies to work, it must be the case that it is the subject who causes their actions to occur in the way that they do. The ideal is that every action of the self is derived from, and ordered by, the self. Such an assumption has distinct consequences for understandings of political violence such as urbicide. For example, the International Criminal Tribunal for the Former Yugoslavia issued indictments for crimes committed against the urban fabric of Bosnia only where it could be shown that the intent to 'wantonly destroy cities or towns' existed (Roberts and Guelff 2000, 569). This means that it has not been possible to assert that, in each and every case in which an assault on the urban environment occurred, urbicide (or an assault on the conditions of possibility of heterogeneity) occurred. One can only argue for the consequence of destruction on a case-by-case basis where intent to destroy can be shown.

Excursus: anthropocentrism and reconstruction

The anthropocentrism at stake in urbicide manifests itself as the inscription of the two-fold separation of individuals from their material environment and from the alterity always already implicit in community. As such, it comprises the conceptual hegemony of the figure of the sovereign individual understood as autonomous, unfettered by relationality. Anthropocentrism is, of course, not limited to the context of urbicide. Indeed, anthropocentric conceptual regimes have dominated modern thought. That said, the inscription of a hegemonic anthropocentric political imaginary comprises the specific conceptual stake of urbicide. Thus, although one can find anthropocentrism in contexts other than the destruction of the built environment, in the latter circumstances it will be a pronounced element of the violence. Indeed, the inscription of an anthropocentric conceptual schema will be at the heart of urbicidal violence.

It is worth, at this stage, illustrating the manner in which such inscription occurs. I will focus on a 'response' to urbicide: the reconstruction of built environments scarred by urbicidal destruction. I will argue that an anthropocentric conceptual horizon is inscribed that effectively disavows the relational heterogeneity constituted by the built environment. This latter heterogeneity is precisely what is under attack in urbicide. This case thus demonstrates neatly what is put at stake in urbicide and what its loss represents.

Urban reconstruction is at the heart of a return of agonistic heterogeneity in the wake of ethnic nationalist conflicts such as the 1992–95 Bosnian War. It is reconstruction, and an associated program of returns, that contests the disavowal of heterogeneity characteristic of urbicidal ethnic nationalist violence. Insofar as reconstruction contests the logics of urbicide, it also demonstrates the manner in which the built environment is constitutive of heterogeneity. Put simply, insofar as reconstructing buildings contests the urbicidal disavowal of heterogeneity it is an explicit recognition that buildings are constitutive of heterogeneity. Indeed, it is only because it comprises a reminder of the manner in which buildings constitute existence as fundamentally shared that reconstruction can comprise a challenge to ethnic nationalist urbicide. The provocation of reconstruction thus exposes both the manner in which urbicide disavows agonism and the manner in which buildings constitute existential spatiality as fundamentally heterogeneous.

However, post-war reconstruction is not necessarily recognised in such terms. Indeed, in many cases reconstruction is taken to be the simple repair of equipment for living. This might not sound so objectionable insofar as it is important to house populations and meet their basic needs through infrastructure. However, amongst those engaged in reconstruction there is a common perception that reconstruction is a technical problem exterior to political problems such as ethnic nationalist violence. This framing of the problem of reconstruction as a technical problem exterior to political problems fails to properly comprehend the stakes of urbicide.

This failure can be attributed to the anthropocentric imaginary that dominates agencies tasked with reconstruction. It is perhaps not surprising that anthropocentrism dominates the process of post-conflict reconstruction; after all, reconstruction is undertaken by agencies that construe their mission to be 'humanitarian'. That is, these organisations take their role to be one of intervening in a (post-)conflict context to ameliorate the life circumstances of fellow human beings (on the basis that, as human beings, they deserve a better standard of life replete with the individual rights the international community sees as indicating such a 'better' standard of life). As David Campbell (1998b) notes, such humanitarianism is predicated on a humanist model that conceives of sovereign individuality as the basis of human life. This humanism is thus always an intervention to uphold (or implement) rights or entitlements considered to define the conditions of possibility of such sovereign individuality. Such humanitarianism thus inscribes, by prioritising their needs, an anthropocentric separation of the individual from their material environment and society. As such, it covers over, or disavows, the heterogeneity that is at stake in urbicide. Humanitarianism thus fails to recognise what is at stake in urbicide.

Since human life is claimed to comprise sovereign individuality, the things with which humans engage are taken to be mere materiel (or equipment) put at the disposal of humans and forming the background against which they live out their lives. Buildings, infrastructure and monuments may be seen as enabling conditions for human life, but are ultimately secondary to that life. Humanitarian projects reduce reconstruction to mere engineering projects. These projects are removed from all discussion of the political and given over to technicians as a problem to be solved, rather than a condition of possibility of being-in-common to be restored.[5] Indeed, Bosnia has given rise to a number of programs for the reconstruction of urban fabric that propose technical formulas by which to replace the urban spaces destroyed in war time.[6] In this way, urban reconstruction has been taken out of its properly political position and reduced to technical programs. This is an exclusion of urbanity from the figure of humanitarian reconstruction by removing it from political consideration and placing it in the hands of technicians who proceed according to a plan that simply seeks to replace the equipment lost in conflict.

The problems encountered by the European Administration of Mostar (EUAM), in the initial post-war period, in attempting to contest the antagonistic division of the city, provide a good illustration of the anthropocentrism of humanitarianism. The urbicide perpetrated in Mostar (largely by Bosnian Croat forces) left the built environment of the city devastated. The damage was not restricted to specific buildings but covered housing stock, public buildings, commercial buildings, public spaces and monuments. During the war, the *Bulevar Nardone Revolucije* on the west bank of the Neretva had become the front line of fighting. This street was reduced to rubble and formed a 'natural' zone of separation that delineated the two antagonistic halves of the city. With the city antagonistically divided, there was little point in crossing from one half of the city to the other. The destruction of the *Bulevar*, and the establishment of a dead zone between east and West Mostar, effectively naturalised an antagonistic separation of identities. Indeed, it appeared that Mostar had split into two separate cities with few spaces of commonality between them. This would have represented the complete naturalisation of a territorial antagonism disavowing any being-in-common between Bosnian Croats and Bosniacs.

With damage to the urban environment of Mostar widespread (although disproportionately divided between east and west with more extensive and serious damage done to the east), the question of reconstruction was a pressing one for the EUAM. The EUAM set about reconstructing the city, concentrating on the restoration of housing stock and the repair of basic infrastructure. This project was tasked to engineers who treated it as a technical problem ancillary to the political work being carried out by the European Union Administrator, Hans Koschnick. In the context of the insistent demands of post-war reconstruction (such as the provision of shelter in time for the onset of winter), larger questions of the relationship between these buildings and the political process of contesting ethnic nationalism remained largely unexplored. For example, the *ad hoc* reconstruction of houses meant that no specific plans were considered to build new housing stock that might foster heterogeneity. The rebuilding of houses in both east and West Mostar resolved the demand for shelter and yet in no way problematised the *de facto* partition of the city.

It is in this light that plans drawn up by students from Columbia University in the post-war period are particularly interesting (Plunz, Baratloo and Conrad 1998). These plans were guided by the aim of restoring, through urban development, the heterogeneity proper to Mostar. All of the projects considered the way in which urban planning should, in a way not effected by the EUAM, contest the present partition of the city. One point raised by these projects is particularly worthy of mention. It was noted that there were two options when planning urban development in post-war Mostar. On the one hand, development could continue in a north–south direction (*Ibid.*, 43). The problem with such development is that the line of antagonism established during the conflict ran north–south through Mostar. Hence development in a north–south direction would not problematise this line of antagonism. Indeed, it would encourage the parallel development of two distinct halves of the city without ever transgressing the line of separation.

On the other hand, east–west development might offer the promise of contesting the line of fracture and, hence, fostering the uncovering of the heterogeneity of Mostar. That is to say, if West Mostar develops to the east, and East Mostar to the west, the line separating the two will at some point be transgressed and its naturalised status as a line of separation and antagonism will be called into question. In this sense, plans to develop the *Bulevar* and, in particular, to disrupt its function as a line of separation were deemed worthy of particular consideration (*Ibid.*, 62–69). The student plans aimed to disrupt the straight line of separation that the *Bulevar* presented. By disrupting this line and developing the commercial and residential potential of the area to the east and west, movement across this line would be encouraged, thus contesting the antagonistic disavowal of heterogeneity it represents. Such a project acknowledges the need for contesting the antagonisms constituted in and through urbicidal violence, and, as such, challenges the anthropocentric assumptions that guide much reconstruction. Instead of thinking of reconstruction as an ancillary activity that supports the individual, these projects construe intervention in the urban environment as key to revivifying the heterogeneity of existence. For these projects, existence is a complex ecology in which the individual always already exists in a complex relation with the built environment and the others who share it.

The stakes of urbicide are thus the inscription of a hegemonic anthropocentric conceptual horizon that, by conflating political subjectivity with the figure of the individual, naturalises the separations which, in turn, naturalise the territorialisation of antagonism. This anthropocentrism consolidates the disavowal of the hetero-geneity effected in urbicide by naturalising these dual dimensions of separateness. Refusing to lose what is put at stake in urbicide demands contesting such anthropocentrism by prioritising the question of the contestation of antagonism. By prioritising the contestation of antagonism, it is possible to refuse to see such a question as ancillary, as well as noting that existence is relational and thus heterogeneous and not comprised of sovereign individuals instrumentally utilising resources for their gratification.

In the context of such a contestation of antagonism, the reconstruction of the *Stari Most* became, for obvious reasons, something of a touchstone (Boyes 2003, 18). For those involved in rebuilding the bridge, the project was a vital element in rejecting the ethnic nationalist division of the city of Mostar (Pasic 1994, 66). Indeed, the opening of the new bridge in July 2004 'meant the "radical Croatian project" of the past decade was finished' (Traynor 2004, 19). That is to say, the rebuilding of the Old Bridge was taken to constitute an important symbol of the recovery of the agonism proper to Mostar. And yet, in the absence of other plans to foster the recovery of the agonism proper to the city's locales, such a project, whilst symbolic, may prove to be simply a gesture (though no doubt an important gesture).

This feeling was summed up by a European Union (EU) official in 1994, some ten years before the bridge was rebuilt, who stated that '[t]he bridge should be rebuilt at the end of the reconstruction' (Traynor 1994, 8). The bridge would thus be the last act of the contestation of ethnic partition, a crowning of this achieve-ment. It would symbolise the successful restoration of pre-war heterogeneity. Moreover, the EU official cautioned that rebuilding the bridge might encourage the idea that heterogeneity had returned to Mostar. It might, therefore, cause a false sense of accomplishment that could misrecognise a certain symbolism for the actual recovery of the being-in-common proper to Mostar.[7] In the wake of the completion of the rebuilding of the Old Bridge in 2004, such a warning seems apposite. Despite rebuilding the bridge, progress in contesting the division of the city along ethnic nationalist lines remains slow in Mostar (International Crisis Group 2003; Connolly 2007, 30). Part of the blame for such slow progress can be attributed to the manner in which the anthropocentric assumptions of reconstruc-tion agencies fail to contest the basic disavowal of heterogeneity on which ethnic nationalist politics are predicated, instead consolidating the figure of the sovereign individual upon whom the antagonisms that characterise the post-conflict partition of Bosnia are founded.

Such anthropocentric reconstruction treats urbanity (that which is characterised by heterogeneity) as a secondary aspect of political reconstruction. The tight grip of this anthropocentrism means that the stakes of urbicide have remained largely invisible in post-Dayton Bosnia. Since the urban environment is not considered to be constitutive of existence, but merely that against which sovereign individuals exist, the manner in which its destruction announces the disavowal of agonism has not been comprehended. And so long as this is the case, the return of agonism is overlooked: projects do not seek to reconstitute fundamentally shared/public locales, but merely to provide the equipment with which the separate ethnic nationalist enclaves can continue to live as they are.

Reconstruction projects thus expose the manner in which an anthropocentric imaginary is inscribed by urbicidal violence. This anthropocentric imaginary understands the sovereign individual as the primary figure of political discourse, treating the individual's relationship with the built environment and community as secondary, contingent phenomena. The predication of reconstruction agencies' efforts upon this figure of the individual consolidates the work of urbicide. That is to say, the failure to treat reconstruction as more than a technical, non- or extra-political problem, ensures that the disavowal of heterogeneity at the heart of both urbicidal violence and the anthropocentric imaginary it inscribes remains uncontested. That is to say, the manner in which the built environment constitutes a fundamentally shared spatiality in which subjectivity is always already relational (and thus structured by alterity) remains unacknowledged.

Recovering the stakes of urbicide – contesting the loss of that put at risk by such violence – demands the recognition of the manner in which buildings constitute locales that are public and, hence, the condition of possibility of relational networks of identity\difference. As such, it requires contesting the double separation of the individual from the built environment and their community inscribed in anthropocentricism as much as it requires the contestation of the territorial antagonisms carved out via the ruination of the built environment. The contestation of anthropocentrism requires the acknowledgement of the complex ecology of existence in which identity and difference are constituted in and through the locales established by built things. Existence is thus decisively shaped by the subject's relation to built things. Moreover, insofar as these locales are public, and thus shared by potential others, existence is definitively shaped by community (being-with-others). As such, anthropocentrism represents an idealised and ultimately deficient picture of subjectivity. Recognising this and responding accordingly represents the challenge put forward by urbicide. Put differently, at stake in urbicide is a disavowal of the heterogeneity of existence. Ensuring that what is put at stake in urbicide is not lost demands contesting the anthropocentrism that goes hand-in-hand with such a disavowal.

Conclusion: drawing the political and conceptual stakes together

The political and conceptual stakes of urbicide share the motif of *separation* in common. For the political stakes of urbicide, it is separation that is achieved in and through the territorialisation of antagonism. For the conceptual stakes, it is the separation of human and material, individual and community that underlies anthropocentrism. In both cases this separation constitutes a disavowal and efface-ment of heterogeneity. Urbicide effects such a disavowal through the destruction of precisely that which is the condition of possibility of heterogeneity: buildings. If separation – in the guise of disavowal of heterogeneity or anthropocentrism – is at stake in urbicide (i.e., what might be lost if such destruction is successful), con-testation is the only response through which we stand to be able to safeguard the heterogeneity that would otherwise be disavowed. Recognising and understanding the logics of urbicide thus necessitates contesting the inscription of these figures of separation. The task is precisely to prevent the naturalisation of such figures and, hence, to prevent the naturalisation of separation.

This separation (embodied in the disavowal of heterogeneity and/or anthropocentric understandings of politics and political violence) is contested by the ontology revealed by the concept of urbicide. The naturalisation of ethnic nationalist enclaves, the separation of humanity from the environment, and the positing of individuality before society are contested by the existential heterogeneity at the heart of the concept of urbicide. The concept of urbicide thus reveals both a radical ecology, in which the spatiality of Being-in-the-world is constituted in and through relations with things, and a relational understanding of political subjectivity, in which identity is constitutively structured by difference. That is, the concept of urbicide de-centres our understandings of political subjectivity and political violence. It demonstrates that identity is a spatial Being-in-the-world that is constituted through relations to the buildings that structure our everyday environment. Such an understanding inverts the normal, anthropocentric ecology that assumes such buildings comprise a mere environment, contingent to the essence of individual being. Moreover, it demonstrates that, through the public nature of such buildings, Being-in-the-world is always already a being-with-others. And, as such, identity is constituted, in an ineluctably political agonistic relation to difference. Urbicide thus requires us to put aside the figure of the sovereign individual and develop an understanding of the subject as decentred and constitutively structured by alterity.

It is worth briefly noting two entailments of this position that would otherwise remain largely implicit. Firstly, critiques of anthropocentrism have, like critiques of Enlightenment humanism, been criticised as anti-human (Seckinelgin 2006, 32). However, a critical stance towards, or contestation of, the 'anthropocentric bias' (*Ibid.*, 31) that has affected the majority of scholarship on political violence, does not represent a turning away from concerns with the well-being and security of those affected by urbicide. In this regard it is worth revisiting Martin Heidegger's comments regarding his critique of humanism. Heidegger noted that his

> opposition [to humanism] does not mean that [his] thinking aligns itself against the humane and advocates the inhuman, [nor] that it promotes the inhumane and depreciates the dignity of man. Humanism is opposed because it does not set the *humanitas* of man high enough.
>
> (Heidegger 1993c, 233–234)

For Heidegger then, there is more to humanity than humanism can comprehend. Similarly, a non-anthropocentric approach to political violence would argue that there is more to the constitution of a *polis* than the gathering of *anthropos*. That is, the various non-living entities that anthropocentric accounts see as simply the backdrop against which political community is enacted are, in fact, to be seen as constitutive features. And, hence, the destruction of such 'material' must be an attack on that political community. In that sense, in order to understand the insecurities of political communities, it will not be enough to focus solely on the threat of harm or displacement experienced by human bodies.

Secondly, it should be noted that the recasting of scholarship concerning political violence in order to overcome the 'anthropocentric bias' that has historically shaped its conceptual horizon, is consonant with a wider rethinking of the intellectual terrain of security and conflict studies. In particular, in the post-Cold War era scholars have both redefined the agenda of security studies and identified new, historically specific, forms of war.[8] On the one hand, the emergence of concepts such as environmental and human security onto the agenda of security studies have demonstrated that security is a more complex phenomenon than the traditional focus on the military protection of sovereignty implied. Moreover, these 'new' concepts of security imply that the referent object of security cannot be understood in a wholly anthropocentric manner.[9]

On the other hand, the identification of 'new' forms of war (i.e., forms of conflict specific to the contemporary era) has suggested that the traditional conception of war shaped by Clausewitzian ideas should be rethought. Whilst much of this literature has focused on the impact of transnational interconnections upon the conflicts of the post-Cold War era, there has been growing interest in the emergent nexus of urbanisation and war. The conjoint fact of the increasing urbanisation of the global population and the perception that wars of the future will increasingly be fought in a built-up terrain, previously thought to be proscribed as a target or arena of war, has led to a concern with the manner in which violence in and against the built environment will be central to understanding wars of the future (Graham 2004; Hills 2004).

This literature seeks to move beyond the 'anthropocentric bias' and note the manner in which an understanding of post-Cold War conflict must take into account the assault on buildings, logistics networks and communications infrastructure. That is, these accounts argue that in order for scholars of political violence to understand the impact of contemporary conflict upon individual victims, the range of referents of political violence must be expanded beyond the anthropocentric horizon to include the fabric that comprises the city and defines the nature of the lives lived in its environs.

Deployments of the concept of urbicide thus combine concern for the heterogeneous community lost in the naturalisation of ethnic nationalist enclaves through urban destruction with a desire to broaden the agenda of studies of political violence. Ultimately, this is what is at stake in the study of urbicide. Whilst heterogeneity and anthropocentrism represent the stakes of urbicide itself, this nexus of non-anthropocentric humanism and a decentring of the traditional agenda of scholarship concerning political violence represents what is at stake in the concept of urbicide. Failing to recognise this concept as a distinct form of violence represents a failure to grasp both possibilities.

Conclusion

By way of conclusion I want both to restate and to extend my argument. I will start by recapitulating the broad features of the logic of urbicide as I have outlined them in the preceding chapters. Following this recapitulation of the logic of urbicide, I will reflect on several conceptual questions that this account of urbicide raises. This will give me the opportunity to clarify four issues relating to the definition and utilisation of the concept of urbicide: 1) the relationship between the built environment and heterogeneity; 2) the relationship between the built environment and urbanity; 3) the relationship between assaults on the 'experience of the city' and urbicide; and 4) the utility of the term 'urbicide'. I will then restate the stakes of urbicide via Nancy's characterisation – in *Being Singular Plural* – of the city and philosophy as opposing principles (Nancy 2000, 23). Finally, I will conclude by reflecting on the manner in which, at the point in human history where urbanity has become the predominant mode of existence, urbicide offers a particularly potent challenge for scholars of global politics.

Recapitulation

I began this book by examining the manner in which the built environment has been targeted for destruction in post-Cold War conflicts. Whilst such destruction has been witnessed in events such as the assault on the *Stari Most*, it cannot be restricted to a (relatively) small group of iconic buildings. Indeed, such iconic instances of violence are merely a subset of a wider, deliberate assault on the built environment that has targeted the full spectrum of buildings. Whilst the loss of iconic elements of the built environment has received significant amounts of attention (to the point where their destruction becomes iconic), this violence has not been seen in the context of widespread and deliberate destruction of buildings. I argued therefore that we should recognise the need for an analysis of the nature and meaning of this widespread and deliberate assault on the built environment. That is, we should see this destruction as a distinct form of political violence. I argued that urbicide (the 'killing of urbanity') would provide the necessary concept for both identifying a distinct form of violence and understanding its conceptual contours.

In my subsequent argument, I outlined both the need for such a concept and the meaning and stakes of such violence if understood through the lens of urbicide. Broadly speaking, the argument makes six distinct points (each roughly corresponding to a chapter in the book):

1   I began my examination of the need for a concept of urbicide by addressing extant accounts of the nature of violence directed at buildings. I argued that at present urban destruction is primarily understood in terms of military necessity (or the lack thereof), as an attack upon cultural heritage, or as a metaphor symbolising or embodying Balkanist stereotypes. I demonstrated, however, that these understandings of urban destruction are insufficient. The notion of military necessity leaves us with a crude recognition that the destruction of villages, towns and cities in Bosnia was not necessary. However, it gets us no closer to understanding the nature of this destruction. Whilst the concept of the destruction of cultural heritage is of some utility in the case of particular buildings, it privileges certain forms of destruction and ultimately fails to note the widespread and deliberate destruction of the built environment in general. Understanding urban destruction as a product of particularly 'Balkan' traits problematically attributes this form of violence to an aberrant hatred of culture. As such, it fails to get to grips with precisely what is destroyed in attacks on the built environment.

2   I argued, therefore, that in order to understand widespread and deliberate destruction of the built environment, it is necessary to uncover the distinct *logic* of such violence. I argued that the nascent concept of 'urbicide' provided a resource that would enable delineation of the nature and stakes of this logic. Urbicide is the killing or slaying of 'the urban'. In this sense, it has lexical and discursive similarities with the concept of genocide (particularly their shared discursive reference to a notion of annihilation). However, insofar as their referents diverge, urbicide signals an attempt to name a form of violence distinct to that of genocide. More specifically, urbicide is the destruction of buildings *qua* that which constitutes the conditions of possibility of a distinctively 'urban' existential quality. Following Wirth (1996), I argued that the urban is characterised by heterogeneity. Urbicide is thus an assault on buildings as the conditions of possibility of heterogeneity.

I suggested that heterogeneity is at stake in urbicide precisely because buildings constitute urban space as always already shared space. That is to say, it is the always already shared nature of urban space that bequeaths it the heterogeneity at stake in urbicide. An understanding of how this is the case, and the relationship between buildings (as the target of urbicide) and heterogeneity (as the stakes of urbicide) thus constitutes the principal task of the argument in this book. In particular, we must ask what it is about buildings – what spatiality they are constitutive of – that makes them the conditions of possibility of heterogeneity (and thus the target of urbicide). It is only in addressing this specific issue that we will find the meaning of urban destruction (specifically, what is lost in urban destruction, and what this loss means).

3   I suggested that it was in the work of Martin Heidegger that we might find a way to approach such questions. According to Heidegger (1962; 1993a),

existence is constituted in and through the (built) things with which Being (understood as *Dasein*, or Being-in-the-world) engages in everyday activity. These things are constitutive of a spatial existence: a relational network that contains both distance, direction and orientation. These relational networks are referred to in Heidegger's later work as the 'locales' in which we dwell (Heidegger 1993a, 354–356). Buildings are fundamentally public things: available to anyone as nodes in spatial networks. Because this spatiality is constituted in and through things that are fundamentally public, it is an always already shared existence. That is, every relational network is predicated on nodes/buildings that, in being available to all, always offer the possibility that there will be an other that also constitutes their Being-in-the-world around the same object. Existence is, therefore, according to Heidegger's understanding, fundamentally heterogeneous. It is this heterogeneous existential spatiality that is at stake in urbicide. The destruction of buildings is the destruction of things that constitute the spatiality in which we exist. This destruction is a deliberate targeting of these things precisely because they constitute existence as fundamentally heterogeneous. In destroying these things, heterogeneous existence is destroyed.

4   Although Heidegger's argument provides a productive account of the manner in which the destruction of buildings comprises the destruction of the conditions of possibility of heterogeneity, it leaves the question of the nature of that heterogeneity largely unexamined. I argued that we must examine Heidegger's understanding of heterogeneity through an exposition of his concept of Being-with. According to Heidegger (1962, 153–157), Being-with is an existential feature of all Being-in-the-world. This Being-with is a consequence of the sharing of the world that is constitutive of all existence. It is in the things through which we conduct our lives that we find the ineluctable trace of the other. According to this account, heterogeneity is a characteristic of existence, rather than a contingent feature of the world (as some political theories understand it to be).

However, Heidegger failed to develop this understanding of Being-with. I turned, therefore, to Jean-Luc Nancy's understanding of being-with as the fundamental characteristic of existence. Nancy (1991) understands being-with as an existential characteristic co-extensive with community (which, for Nancy represents the experience of being-in-common that marks being-with others). For Nancy, community (or being-in-common) is a reticulated network of exposure to alterity. That is, being-with others comprises the constitution of networks of identity and difference in which self is defined in relation to others and vice versa. These networks of identity comprise a series of boundaries that mark out where self begins and other ends (and vice versa). Each boundary is shared, a place in which self and other are mutually constituted rather than separate surfaces that adjoin. This is a sharing that is always already a division – a sharing of a boundary that also marks the division of self from other, identity from difference. Being-with is thus the communication of identity at shared boundaries.

Two consequences follow from Nancy's understanding of heterogeneity. Firstly, Nancy notes that giving any identity presence (i.e., creating a sense of its objectivity and self-sufficiency) requires the creation of an immanent figure that disavows its relation to alterity. Figuration grounds politics on the assumption of a given identity and, without questioning the presence of this identity, seeks to perfect that identity. Secondly, since heterogeneity is constitutive, it is not possible (despite the work of figurative, immanentist political programs) to disavow the relation with alterity. Thus identity is perpetually unworked by being-with others. Indeed, this is why community is, according to Nancy (1991), *inoperative*: unable to complete the work of figuration.

It is this heterogeneity that is attacked in urbicide through the destruction of the buildings that, through being fundamentally public elements of the constitution of existential spatiality, are constitutive of the conditions of possibility of being-with others. That is to say, urbicide is an assault upon the constitutive relationality of existence and the manner in which it unworks immanentist figurative politics. It is a disavowal through violence of the constitutive relation of identity to alterity. As such, it is the tool of exclusionary regimes such as ethnic nationalism for whom the disavowal of constitutive heterogeneity is central to enacting their identity politics.

Points 3 and 4 thus constitute an outline of the *logic* of urbicide. Specifically an outline of: a) the manner in which buildings, through their fundamentally public character, constitute the condition of possibility of heterogeneity; b) the nature of this heterogeneity (a being-with that comprises a sharing of divisions which gives rise to networks of identity and difference); and c) the effects sought by urbicidal assaults on the built environment – specifically a disavowal of the constitutive relationality that underlies all identities.

5   The question thus remains what the stakes are of such a logic of violence. That is, in any event of urbicide, what stands to be lost if the destruction is successful? I argued that there are two 'stakes' of urbicide: one political, the other conceptual. Indeed, the political itself is put at stake in urbicide. The political can be characterised, following Foucault (1982), Connolly (1991) and Nancy (1991; 2000), by *agonism*. This agonism – a constant provocation – is precisely that which the relation of identity and difference sketched out in my account of heterogeneity comprises. This relation of identity\difference is agonistic insofar as the shared division through which each term derives meaning is both a provocation to establish a boundary as well as the product of a struggle to define precisely where that line lies. Insofar as urbicide comprises a disavowal of the relation with alterity that is constitutive of this heterogeneity, it is an assault upon agonism and, thus, the political itself. Urbicide seeks to reduce the agonism of the political to a sterile confrontation through the territorialisation of *antagonism*.

In confrontation, the impression of the separation of two parties is con-veyed through the manner in which no agonistic interplay exists (Foucault 1982, 222). Naturalisation of such an impression of separation allows identities founded on the disavowal of their relation to alterity (e.g., ethnic nationalism) to be consolidated. Moreover, this is a reduction of the political interplay of agonism to the politics of technocratic administration: from the political question of the constitution of identity to the technical question of how to administrate separate domains. In urbicide, then, the political itself is at stake. I illustrated these stakes of urbicide in relation to several empirical examples.

6   The separation effected by the territorialisation of antagonism resonates with a wider conceptual horizon at stake in urbicide. I referred to this wider conceptual horizon as 'anthropocentric' and argued that there are two distinct ways in which such anthropocentrism is at stake in urbicide. Firstly, in disavowing the relationality constituted in 'staying with things' (Heidegger 1993a, 353), this violence seeks to disavow the constitutive role that the material environment has in the political constitution of identity. Such a disavowal can be seen in the naturalisation of the notion that it is people, not the things in and through which they live, that are the central concern in contexts of violence. Such a concern, whilst understandable, effaces the constitutive role of buildings, and thus fails to recognise the essential heterogeneity of existence that the built environment constitutes. Such 'humanitarianism' is not humanitarian enough in its failure to see the essential heterogeneity of human existence (Heidegger 1993c, 233–234; Campbell 1998b).

Secondly, anthropocentrism can be seen in the installation of the individual as the principal figure of political analysis. This figure is understood to be essentially pre-existent of the world. That is to say, the individual's essential characteristics are independent of the historically contingent circumstances s/he finds him/herself in. As such, this not only compounds the impression of the separation of the human and the environmental, but also gives rise to the notion that heterogeneity is, whilst empirically the case, ontologically contingent. This gives rise to a notion of community as a voluntary association in which identity is constituted free of relations to alterity. This is the anthropocentric assumption at the heart of ethnic nationalist arguments that territorial disaggregation of existing plural communities comprises the recognition of the fundamental right to territorial self-determination.

These then are the conceptual stakes of urbicide. It is this conceptual horizon that is put in the balance in any urbicidal event. If successful, urbicide will inscribe anthropocentric assumptions as the hegemonic figure for politics. It is important, then, to contest not just the political separation that urbicide seeks to effect but also the conceptual separation that is at the core of anthropocentrism: of the human from the environment and the individual from community. Contesting such anthropocentrism requires decentring our understandings of political subjectivity and reorienting our studies of security and conflict to examine the ways in which complex structures of existence, rather than the simple integrity of sovereign territory, are at stake in political violence.

Excursus: some clarifications

This argument outlines the logic and stakes of the urbicide witnessed in post-Cold War conflict. It notes a specific relationship between war, the built environment and heterogeneity and argues that the destruction that characterises this relation deserves to be recognised as a distinct form of violence, which requires a particular response. Recognising the relationship that urbicide entails, however, raises certain important questions. Specifically it raises questions about: a) the relationship between the built environment and sharing; b) the relationship between the built environment and urbanity; c) the relationship between war and urbicide. It seems appropriate, therefore, to suspend the narrative for a moment and allow an excursus to clarify the issues raised in these questions.

These questions do not comprise a problematisation of the core relationship that underlies my account of the logics of urbicide. Rather, they constitute questions that pertain to possible extensions of the argument. Thus the question concerning the relationship of the built environment and heterogeneity asks whether it is only in the destruction of buildings that we see an assault on heterogeneity. The question concerning the relationship of the built environment and urbanity asks whether the concept of urbicide, here linked to an assault on the physical architecture of the built environment, could be extended to assaults on the wider socio-political experience that characterises urbanity. Finally, the question of the relationship between war and urbicide asks whether the concept of urbicide could be extended to address instances of the destruction of the built environment in contexts other than war or its aftermath (such as the context of the modern, capitalist development of cities).

These questions pose critical counterpoints that address both the limits and possible extensions of this argument. In each case, addressing the question entails outlining the ways in which the concept of urbicide may be extended and thus noting the limits of the present argument. Ultimately, insofar as they indicate the limitations of the concept of urbicide as it is presently elaborated, these questions problematise the utility of the concept of urbicide. To put it bluntly, if the current formulation of the concept is limited in the way these questions reveal, does it still hold utility for analysts of political violence? Whilst this question was partly addressed in Chapter 2, it is posed again here. Thus this is the fourth and final question that should, therefore, be addressed in clarifying the argument made above.

The built environment–heterogeneity relationship

The first question to arise in relation to the outline of the logic of urbicide given in my argument is that of the relation of the built environment to heterogeneity. Specifically, it could be argued that my argument posits a strong relationship between buildings and heterogeneity, posing this relation as constitutive, necessary and exclusive. That is, it could be argued that my argument sees buildings as the sole ground of heterogeneity. As such, this would mean that heterogeneity is only associated with buildings. At least two problems can be derived from this observation.

Firstly, it could be argued that such an understanding of the constitution of heterogeneity represents a historically or culturally specific understanding coloured by the role played by cities in modernity. In other words, the notion that the built environment constitutes existence as heterogeneous could be said to be derived from a very particular historical and cultural understanding of the role that the city plays in human society. This idea is supported by studies that show the manner in which the idea of the city is historically and culturally constructed (Williams 1973).

In itself, however, such an observation does not problematise my argument in a significant sense. Indeed, as I have noted at various points in the argument, I regard the question of the relation between the built environment and heterogeneity to be of particular concern in the present, post-Cold War era. That is, I have acknowledged that this relation is to be seen as historically and culturally specific. In this sense, such an observation offers a caution, rather than a significant problematisation of the argument. It cautions us to recognise that the relationship of the built environment to heterogeneity that is constitutive of a certain being-with-others is a historically contingent mode of Being-in-the world. This does not, ultimately, seem out of keeping with the philosophical sources I have drawn upon to sketch out this relation, each of which remarks on the modern inflection of Being-in-the-world (specifically, the technological ways in which its truth is covered over).

Of course, this means that the question of extending urbicide to historically ancient examples is far more contentious. Indeed, I would be careful about seeing references that treat the biblical destruction of Sodom and Gomorrah or the Roman annihilation of Carthage (Musabegovic 1994, 48–49) as urbicide as more than metaphorical or heuristic uses of such terminology. The logic of urbicide, set out here, is thus not intended to comprise a universal, trans-historical ontological prescription. That said, I would argue that the relation between buildings and heterogeneity posited here applies globally to instances of widespread and deliberate destruction of cities in the twentieth and twenty-first centuries.

The second problem raised concerns the exclusivity of the relation posited between buildings and heterogeneity – specifically, that it appears heterogeneity pertains only to the built environment. In cases where there were no buildings, therefore, heterogeneity would not be said to exist. However, although I have – for obvious reasons – focused on the constitutive role played by buildings (after all, concern with what is lost when buildings are destroyed animates the entirety of this argument), I have noted that it is a 'staying with things' that is constitutive of the dwelling which is always already a Being-with others (Heidegger 1993a, 353). It would be possible, therefore, to examine the ways in which other 'things', apart from buildings, structure existence as always already open to the possibility of alterity.

Indeed, such an examination would show that, regardless of the presence of the built environment, Being-in-the-world is always already constituted in relation to things (after all, if there are no things there is no world). And these things always entail a constitutive relation to alterity (for example, cloth entails a relation of tailor to wearer whether or not both are present at hand (Heidegger 1962, 153–154)). I would argue, therefore, that it is necessary to note that existence is constitutively heterogeneous as a consequence of the manner in which Being-in-the-world is constituted in relation to things. However, I would not regard this extension of the class of things that are constitutive of heterogeneity to comprise a substantial problematisation of my argument. On the contrary, it seems to me to comprise an argument for the extension of the logic of my argument to a wider consideration of the constitutive role played by things in the heterogeneity of existence.

Acknowledging that other 'things' apart from buildings could constitute the heterogeneity of existence does not, however, diminish my argument that there is something specific that inheres in the destruction of buildings. Moreover, it does not, to my mind, problematise the notion that there is a particular relationship between buildings and heterogeneity that is put at stake in a distinctive manner by such destruction. In other words, whilst things other than buildings may entail relations with alterity (which could be lost in their destruction), acknowledging this does not problematise the notion that built things entail a specific relation with alterity and thus that their destruction is distinctive. Two observations might be made in this regard.

Firstly, it is hard to find widespread and deliberate destruction of things other than buildings. The most obvious case would be books, works of art and religious objects. Widespread destruction of such things, however, seems to conform to existing understandings of the ways in which genocide targets the objects that form the material substrate of a particular social or political group. Destruction of things other than buildings could also be said to occur in military actions such as carpet bombing and scorched earth policies. Insofar as such destruction occurs in terrains where buildings are largely absent, it can largely be assimilated to notions of military necessity and/or collateral damage. Whilst such actions may be degenerate (and thus a violation of the laws of war (Shaw 2003, 23–26)), they stem from an attempt to target the resources of the enemy and force him/her to capitulate. Objects are thus destroyed not for their role in the constitution of heterogeneity but for their logistical value. Thus whilst these cases of the destruction of things other than buildings can – despite their role in constituting existence as heterogeneous – be understood according to extant explanations of political violence, the destruction of buildings offers a case that cannot be understood according to extant categories, suggesting that it is a distinctive mode of violence and should be treated as such.

Secondly, I would argue that the rationale for treating the destruction of buildings as a distinct form of violence stems from the distinctive role that buildings play in constituting existence as heterogeneous. Buildings differ from other classes of 'thing' in the way that they orient macro understandings of space. Whilst all things comprise nodes that gather relations of identity and difference, it is buildings that allow us to make sense of the relations that exist between different nodes. Buildings and the built environment provide the macro environment in which nodes are embedded. An assault on the built environment thus offers distinct possibilities for the loss, disavowal or effacement of heterogeneity. As such then, whilst buildings are not the only things that constitute existence as heterogeneous, they do so in a distinctive way and thus assaults on the built environment should be treated as a distinct form of political violence.

The built environment–urbanity relationship

The second question that requires clarification is that of the relation of the built environment to urbanity. Three questions arise concerning this relation: (a) Can we reduce the built environment to buildings?; (b) Is the built environment always urban?; and (c) To what extent does my argument conflate the built environment and the city? These questions, albeit in different forms, address the same issue, namely the extent to which the built environment, urbanity and the city coincide. I have treated these questions at reasonable length in Chapter 2 and so will not repeat arguments that I have made there. However, it is worth supplementing the comments made elsewhere in the hope of clarifying my argument.

These questions address the complex relation between the built environment conceived of as an ensemble of material things and the experience of urbanity that is largely assumed to pertain to the city. Most urban social theories acknowledge this complex relation by arguing that the built environment comprises more than just an ensemble of buildings. The 'built environment' in this sense circumscribes both material structures and the forces, dynamics, exchanges and so on that are distinctive to such an environment (e.g., see Saunders 1986; Harvey 1985; Harvey 1989). In my argument, however, I have used 'built environment' to refer solely to ensembles of buildings. On the one hand, this could be construed as a neglect of important dimensions of urbanity. However, my argument is not an urban social theory, sketching out the complexity of the experiences relating to 'urbanised' societies. Rather, this argument comprises an exploration of a logic of political violence and, as such, is concerned with the destruction of specific things and what is at stake in their loss. I have, for purposes of my own investigation, reduced the built environment to built things.

This reduction is not made in ignorance of the various ways in which urbanity and the city are discussed in urban social theory. Common to all of these discussions is the notion that the phenomena under examination are characterised by difference, plurality and, hence, heterogeneity. I have spoken about this heterogeneity in general terms, concentrating instead on the manner in which buildings constitute the condition of possibility for such a constitutive alterity. This has privileged the constitutive role of buildings and, thus, might be (rightly) construed as an assertion that the experience that forms the principal subject matter of urban social theory is a consequence of 'staying with built things'. In this sense, I have argued that the domain of urban social theory is defined by a constitutive 'staying with (built) things'. This does not, however, comprise a reduction of the complexity of the urban to an ensemble of buildings. Indeed, the various contingent ways in which difference manifests itself in urban places and spaces requires careful investigation. However, the destruction of buildings comprises a distinct logic that strikes at such heterogeneity whatever its forms.

Of course, this means that I have expanded the definition of urbanity by arguing that where built things are constitutive of existence, the heterogeneity that pertains to such Being-in-the-world is precisely what we refer to as 'urbanity'. As such, urban social theory cannot be confined to the 'city' and the built environment must be understood to be always constitutive of a heterogeneity that we can refer to as urbanity. Of course, buildings are most numerous in cities and thus the constitution of relations of identity\difference most dense there. It is thus to be expected that urban social theory might treat such locales as its central case. However, less dense ensembles of buildings are similarly constitutive of heterogeneous existence and thus cannot be excluded from 'urbanity'. In a way, the extension of the urban beyond the concentration of the city is a historical development. Indeed, the articulation of buildings into sprawl has given rise to the notion that urbanity has become globalised. In other words, there are no spaces in which Being-in-the-world is not constituted as heterogeneous in and through a constitutive relation with buildings. This would mean that the threat to buildings posed by urbicide had become a problem of global magnitude and importance.

Peace-time urbicides

The acknowledgement that 'urbanity' comprises a complex phenomenon predicated upon, but contingent to, the material buildings that are its condition of possibility is the source of another question concerning urbicide: Can the logic of urbicide be expanded to apply to those peace-time episodes of urban planning and development that damage the perceived character of the city? Such a question is raised by writers such as Huxtable (1972, 12–14), for whom urbicide represents the destruction of the integrity of the urban experience through planning.

Whilst I would argue that urbicide need not occur in the context of war, it is characterised by the widespread deliberate destruction of buildings in order to disavow of agonism in and through the constitution of antagonism. Of course we can find examples of such violence in peace-time – Marshall Berman's description of the destruction of New York neighbourhoods would constitute such an example (Berman 1996). However, this logic cannot, to my mind, be extended to cover the demolition of buildings that occurs as part of the everyday renewal of the city. For renewal to become urbicide, destruction must be widespread and deliberate and accomplish the territorialisation of an antagonism. Urban development projects such as the original construction of the World Trade Center might decisively alter the aesthetic, social or economic patterns of the city (Huxtable 1972, 27–31), but they do not comprise the disavowal of agonistic heterogeneity. As such, although my argument expands the field of instances that could be considered 'urban', it retains the concept of urbicide for a specific type of violence.

On the utility of the term 'urbicide'

The need for these clarifications might be taken to problematise the utility of the concept of urbicide. It might be argued that, insofar as it is necessary to add such caveats, the concept's utility is outweighed by the need for extensive clarification. Such an observation is primarily directed at the lexical reference to urbanity that the '*urbi-*' of urbicide entails. Indeed, it could be argued that so much clarification is needed to define the concept of urbanity referred to in my use of 'urbicide' that the latter loses its utility. Is there, however, a lexically more elegant term to refer to urbicide? The phenomenon under consideration comprises the widespread destruction of built environments. Moreover it comprises the destruction of heterogeneity through this widespread violence. Both built environments and heterogeneity are principal characteristics of urbanity. Whilst it might be possible to search for alternate terms, it seems unlikely that a single term would be able to describe this complex process.[1] Urbicide, whilst needing clarification, seems therefore to have utility. It has the added benefit of already circulating in discourses about the widespread destruction of built environments in post-Cold War conflicts.

This discussion of the utility of the concept of urbicide contains echoes of the various debates concerning the concept of genocide. The *genos* of genocide similarly requires substantial clarification for the concept to have utility. However, there is a minimal consensus that the phenomenon of the destruction of social groups represents a sufficiently distinct (and grave) form of political violence for the concept of genocide to have utility in scholarly and political discourse. I would argue, similarly, that although the urbanity of urbicide requires clarification, the concept has utility for identifying the logic and stakes of a distinct form of political violence. Here I would agree with Shaw (2007, 12) that it is both necessary to classify political violence and that 'concepts must be used coherently': hence, the necessity to clarify urbicide at such length. I also agree that '[w]e need to remember classification is the beginning, not the end of analysis' (*Ibid.*, 13). Indeed, the question of the utility of the term 'urbicide' obscures the more important issue, the analysis that follows from identifying a widespread and deliberate destruction of built environments that constitutes a nameable and, therefore, distinct form of political violence. It is to the logic and stakes of such violence that I hope the concept points, albeit with 'approximation' (Shaw 2007, 12; Eltringham 2004, 7).

It is to the stakes of urbicide that I now want to turn. Having restated and clarified my general argument I want briefly to outline, by way of conclusion, two extensions of the preceding analysis. Firstly, I want to sketch out a philosophical conclusion that might be drawn from the argument. Following that, I will bring the argument to a close with some brief reflections on the perilous position of the city in an era of globalisation and the urgency of considering urbicide as a grave threat to global urban life.

The city and philosophy

The ontopolitical claim

In *Being Singular Plural*, Jean-Luc Nancy notes that, 'as long as philosophy is an appeal to the origin, the city, far from being philosophy's subject or space, is its problem' (Nancy 2000, 23).[2] Nancy's comment elegantly captures the stakes of urbicide. The 'philosophy' that Nancy is referring to – that philosophy that seeks to ground ontology on an essential foundation – is shorthand for the conceptual imaginary that underlies exclusionary political forces such as ethnic nationalism. According to such conceptual imaginaries, being is founded on a particular principle and thus predicated on a notion of homogeneity and purity. All that cannot be attributed to such a foundational principle cannot be seen as proper being and, hence, must be excluded.

Such an 'appeal to an origin' comprises an ontopolitical claim. According to William Connolly, an 'ontopolitical' claim 'invokes a set of fundaments about [the] necessities and possibilities of human being, about, for instance, the forms into which human beings may be composed and the possible relations humans can establish' (Connolly 1995, 1). These are claims concerning the *onta*, 'the really existing things', or rather, claims concerning the basis on which such 'really existing things' are possible (Connolly 1995, 1). These claims articulate the 'conditions of possibility' of all that really exists, the limit beyond which what is taken to really exist has no proper grounding. It is precisely the fact that these claims set out the conditions of possibility of really existing things that makes them inherently political. In assuming that reality is grounded in a particular manner, a limitation of the possibilities of existing things is imposed. This limitation rules that really existing things have a specific ontological character and thus certain existential possibilities are ruled out.

This is the logic of ethnic nationalism: a politics that seeks to ground being on the proposition that identity is derived from the exclusive possession of territory. Ethnic nationalism's 'appeal to an origin' takes the form of a claim to territorial sovereignty for supposedly pre-existent and naturally homogeneous ethnic groups (cf. Campbell 1998a, 80–81). In this sense, ethnic nationalism attempts to delimit the agonism of heterogeneous existence by appealing to a metaphysical ideal that posits ethnicity as a pre-existent human attribute. Moreover, ethnic nationalism asserts that since ethnicity is a pre-existent attribute of each and every individual, the natural state of affairs is for individuals to aggregate in homogeneous groups. Preventing such aggregation is taken to be an artificial and contingent constraint of the real basis of human existence.

It is this ontopolitical claim that legitimates ethnic nationalist claims to self-determination for the aggregation of the various enclaves they have carved out through violent means into statelets. Ethnic nationalism thus both seeks to eradicate traces of difference in the territory claimed as its possession and fails to recognise as full being those forms of identity not grounded on a possessive relation to territory.[3] Ethnic nationalism thus represents an exemplary instance of an ontopolitical claim. Moreover, ethnic nationalism demonstrates the manner in which the ontopolitical comprises an appeal to an origin that runs contrary to the existential heterogeneity of the built environments it confronts.

Urbicide and ontopolitics

Insofar as urbanity, and in particular the buildings that are its conditions of possibility, reveals the ineluctably shared and heterogeneous nature of existence (our being-in-common), it comprises a constant, agonistic provocation to the ontopolitics of ethnic nationalism. In order to assert its appeal to an origin, ethnic nationalism thus strikes at the conditions of possibility of the agonism that constantly provokes it: the (built) things that constitute existence as fundamentally shared (a being-in-common). As I argued in Chapter 5, this assault attempts to naturalise the claim that ethnic groups are naturally distinct and separate by constituting the relationship between groups as an antagonism. This is an attempt to deny the network of identity\difference in and through which these groups are constituted. This naturalisation of separation covers over the agonism of existence, transforming it into the antagonism of territorially distinct entities locked in confrontation.

As I noted in Chapter 4, this is precisely what Nancy refers to as *figuration*: an appeal to a figure that is taken to be the origin, or universal/transcendent substance of being. The figure establishes an 'unstable dialectic of inclusion and exclusion' in and through which the fiction of being-separate rather than being-in-common is instituted (Walker 1999, 173). In this way the figure is the institution of a community understood as a communion – a sharing (in or out) of a universal substance that is the origin of all those who belong in the community. The communion-community only exists insofar as it is able to clearly delineate those who are included in, and those who are excluded from, the communion: those who either partake, or are the embodiment, of the posited substance of being. When the figure is established, the community can claim to have achieved presence, to be able to exist alone, rather than in relation to others. And this can only be accomplished through the expulsion and then exclusion of that which is other than the figure. Every figure is, after all, defined in and through the agonistic networks of identity\difference, the being-in-common, that characterises existence and must thus suppress/cover over this agonism in order to achieve presence.

Figuration thus denies agonism, closing itself off from the other(s) in relation to which it is defined, and claiming a separateness predicated on an appeal to an ontological foundation. Moreover, when this separation is effected, the presence of the communion-community can be taken for granted by its members. The universal substance on which the figure is predicated is taken to be the natural origin of the community members, and, hence, never questioned. The communion-community thus becomes a technical-bureaucratic entity that works to refine the figure and never questions the appeal to origins made in this figuration. In this way the ethnic statelet, once established, never questions its substantial presence but works, with ever increasing ferocity, to refine its homogeneity – its separateness from its others. This work is the consolidation of the antagonisms through which the figure covered over the agonism of existence. Thus destroyed buildings are not rebuilt for lack of permits, minority returns fail to happen because of 'security fears', and non-ethnic institutions fail to operate because they are said to lack legitimacy. These are bureaucratic responses that effect a consolidation of the ethnic nationalist figure whilst never questioning the origin on which this figure is predicated.

Ontopolitical conceptual imaginaries can never, therefore, simply inhabit or regulate the city. The built environment, as condition of possibility of a fundamentally shared spatiality, is precisely that which continually unworks such articulations of an essential foundation for identity. Insofar as the built environment constitutes the city as public/shared and, hence, heterogeneous, foundational philosophies will always fall idle in its streets, squares and buildings, unable to perform the work of figuration. Despite this, foundational philosophies return again and again to work on the city. It is as if the city offends those who attempt to ground community on an essential foundation. The built environment has thus been subjected repeatedly to the ravages of projects inherently opposed to the intimations of alterity that it harbours. The ravages of this 'appeal to the origin' have been seen in diverse locations including, though not limited to, Mostar, Sarajevo, Vukovar, Beirut, Belfast, Hiroshima, the Occupied Territories (West Bank and Gaza), Dresden and New York.

It is in this sense that Nancy notes that 'philosophy is the problem of the city' (2000, 23). Philosophy, understood as an 'appeal to the origin', is a problem for urbanity insofar as it 'covers over … "community"' (*Ibid.*), reducing being-in-common to rubble that disavows the heterogeneous co-existence characteristic of the city. For Nancy, the issue is not so much whether a philosopher speaks explicitly of a/the city, but rather that a certain (problematic) relationship inheres between the appeal to an origin and a principle of fundamental heterogeneity proper to the built environment. 'The city' and 'philosophy' thus name two opposing, and yet inextricably related, principles.

Conclusion: the threat to urbanity in a global era

'The Year 2007 will mark a tuning point in human history: the world's urban population will for the first time equal the world's rural population' (UN-HABITAT 2006, 4). We have thus witnessed 'the advent of a new urban millennium: a time when one out of every two people on the planet will be a "city-zen"' (*Ibid.*). Although the urban–rural distinction is difficult to define, UN-HABITAT's *State of the World's Cities 2006/7* demonstrates the manner in which urbanity will define the lives of the majority of humankind in the globalised twenty-first century. This globalisation of urbanity is characterised by a ubiquity of the built environment witnessed in the expansion of slums (Davis 2006) and 'metacities' (UN-HABITAT 2006, 7). Under such conditions, the challenges of urbicide will be intensified. Agonistic heterogeneity, the constitutive feature of a Being-in-the-world constituted in relation to buildings, will face multiplying threats. It is, or course, impossible to foresee the precise forms in which such challenges will materialise. However, by way of conclusion, I want to indicate the central lesson my outline of the logics and stakes of urbicide holds for scholars of political violence in an era of global urbanity.

At the heart of urbicide – its central stake – lies anthropocentrism. Urbicide's success both depends upon and in turn installs, anthropocentric assumptions about the nature of existence. The failure to recognise that urbicide constitutes a distinct form of political violence rests upon an anthropocentric assumption that the material environment constitutes a mere resource for humanity (and thus is less important than that humanity). This assumption facilitates urbicide insofar as it effaces the role buildings play in constituting heterogeneity and thus deprives those contesting such political violence of a potent resource. Similarly, urbicidal forces seek to consolidate this anthropocentric separation of humanity from its environment insofar as they seek to disavow the relation to alterity that material buildings install at the heart of Being-in-the-world. If the way that buildings are constitutive of a relation to alterity is forgotten/effaced, urbicide is on the way to disavowing all relations to alterity. The naturalisation of an anthropocentric ecology that effaces the true constitutivity of material buildings is thus central to the success of urbicide.

Similarly, the anthropocentric assumption that the sovereign individual comprises the proper political subject is central to both the logic of urbicide and a failure to adequately address and contest that logic. Urbicide itself is predicated on a notion that agonistic heterogeneity is a contingent empirical phenomenon rather than a constitutive existential feature. This anthropocentric presumption that the essential nature of the political subject is fixed prior to engagement with the world is at the heart of notions of ancient hatreds and the need for self-determination (and thus partition). Insofar as anthropocentric political theories endorse the individual as the proper political subject, they share a political imaginary with urbicidal forces. They are thus powerless to contest the logic of urbicide in a meaningful sense. And it is for this reason that the cessation of conflict often safeguards gains made through urbicide, protecting the disavowal of agonistic heterogeneity that this violence has secured.

A contestation of anthropocentrism thus comprises the central lesson of an understanding of the logic and stakes of urbicide. This contestation of anthropocentrism must occur on two axes. Firstly, attention must be paid to the role the built environment plays in constituting Being-in-the-world. This requires the delineation of an ecology in which the constitutive role played by things in political subjectivity is acknowledged. In an era defined by the ubiquity of the built environment, the delineation of such an ecology represents an urgent task. Secondly, the figure of the individual and their correlate sovereign autonomy must be replaced with a co-existential analytic that delineates the constitutive heterogeneity of existence. This requires contestation not only of the centrality of the individual in political discourse, but also of figures such as territorial sovereignty. Underlying the figures of the individual and territorial sovereignty is the notion of separation, a notion in which the agonism of the political is reduced to the confrontation of territorial antagonism. Contesting anthropocentrism thus requires contesting such figures. In an era defined by the sprawl of meta-cities and the global interconnection of various urban centres and ways of living, the sense of our being-in-common is ever more pressing. Indeed, global urbanity is remarkable largely because it indicates that the majority of the global population faces a similar fate (though with differing outcomes). The community implied by global urbanity should thus initiate a thoroughgoing contestation of the anthropocentric figures of individual and territorial sovereignty.

This need for a two-fold contestation of anthropocentrism echoes with the transformation of scholarship concerning security and political violence currently underway in the academy. Recognition that the traditional determinants of the agenda of scholarship concerning security and political violence, such as the state and the national interest, are transformed in the context of the contemporary global order provides a context within which a non-anthropocentric understanding of the threat posed to global urbanity by urbicide can be elaborated. Such an understanding should account for the constitutive role played by materiality in political subjectivity and thus in political violence. Moreover, it should also delineate the complex patterns of interdependence that shape any subjectivity and defy the neat lines of territorial separateness upon which notions of security have been predicated. I hope that the argument I have outlined, and its understanding of the logics and stakes of urbicide, comprises a step in this important direction.

Notes

Introduction

1 Quote attributed to spokeswoman for the United Nations Relief Agency (Traynor 1993, 10).

2 'Bosniac' is more adequate in describing those who were the victims of such violence than 'Bosnian Muslim'. Just as the Jews were not the only victims of Nazi violence, so those who could be identified as 'Bosnian Muslim' were not the only victims of the Bosnian Croats (or indeed the Bosnian Serbs). Indeed, in many discourses 'Muslim' is deployed less as a descriptor of a specific, well-defined identity than as a 'catch-all' category for all those who found themselves to be opposed to, victims of, or excluded from, the Bosnian Croat or Bosnian Serb nationalist programs. See also in this regard Tone Bringa's comments on the evolution of *Bošnjac* identity (Bringa 1995, 34–36).

3 It is worth noting, following Grodach (2002, 68), that the frontline that divided Mostar was actually a short distance from the bridge on the western bank of the river and followed the *Bulevar Narodne Revolucije*. Whilst it is somewhat erroneous, therefore, to see the unbridged river as the dividing line between east and West Mostar, I would contest Grodach's diminishment of the importance of the destruction of bridge in the division of the town of Mostar. The destruction of the bridge was an important symbol of the division of the town. Moreover, whilst Bosnian Muslim/Bosniac militia may have held a frontline in West Mostar, the majority of the Bosnian Muslim/Bosniac population was forced onto the eastern bank and the destruction of the bridges over the Neretva prevented their return.

4 The Herceg Stephen Vukcic resisted the Turkish Army after their 1463 conquest of the majority of Bosnian territory. By 1482, however, Herzegovina was conquered by the Turkish Army (Malcolm 1994, 43–44).

5 Pasic (1995, 14) notes that 'its height in summer when the water is low was about 20 m'.

6 Jezernik (1995, 483) notes that '[t]here are some other theories of the origin of the name Mostar'. Among these other theories are the idea that 'Mostar derived its name from the towers of the bridge, popularly known as *mostare*', and that the 'name [is derived] from *most-tara* (tower on the left bank)'.

7 It should be noted that whilst Gunzburger Makas notes the ubiquity of the bridge as an iconic representation of Mostar and/or Bosnia, she argues that it was only the international community that understood this image to be iconic of a plural way of life. Moreover, she argues that this iconic meaning was ascribed only after the bridge's destruction: the bridge's loss being interpreted as the loss of that which embodied, literally and metaphorically, a multicultural way of life. This raises the question of what the icon represented prior to the bridge's destruction. Given that the icon was largely deployed as a symbol of so-called 'heritage' and that the heterogeneity attendant both to its history and environs was central to justifying the ascribing of cultural importance to this structure, it seems reasonable to argue that it was in some sense iconic of

a plural way of living (if not of the multiculturalism the international community wished to ascribe to it). It is also worth noting that Gunzburger Makas argues that the multiculturalism that comprises the referent object of the international community's interpretation of the bridge as iconic image is, in fact, a fiction. Whilst Gunzburger Makas is right to indicate that the notion of multiculturalism ascribed to the icon of the bridge by the international community is indeed a (historical) fiction, this does not mean that life in Mostar, or Bosnia, prior to 1993 was either ethnically segregated (as some apologists for ethnic cleansing might argue) or homogeneous (as those eager to stress the existence of a Bosnian or Yugoslavian identity might assert). In other words, to say that Bosnian life prior to 1993 was not multicultural in the sense intended by the international community is not to say that it was not plural.

8 On the 'unmaking' of Yugoslavia, see Denich (1993).
9 We should be wary of simplistic representations of the differences bound together by the bridge. For example, in the wake of the conflict it would be easy to say that the bridge united 'Muslim' East Mostar and 'Croat' West Mostar. However, as I have already noted, West Mostar only became substantially 'Croat' after a prolonged program of killing and displacement. Similarly, another simplistic representation might contend that the bridge bound together the eastern 'old' town (characterised by Ottoman-style buildings), and the western 'new' town (characterised by modern buildings). This is, however, an exceptionally broad and generalising division. Modern buildings exist on both sides of the river, and the old town (*Stari Grad*) spreads out from the *Stari Most* onto the western bank. Whilst the bridge could not be said, therefore, to unite two easily distinguishable parts, it could be said to comprise the structure at the heart of a complex plurality.
10 Although the *Stari Most* was never listed as a World Heritage Site by the United Nations Educational, Scientific and Cultural Organisation (UNESCO), the response to its destruction by a variety of bodies (including UNESCO) illustrates the manner in which it was regarded as an example of the heritage of humanity. See for example: the declaration by Federico Mayor, Director-General of UNESCO, in the Council of Europe's *War Damage: Fourth Information Report* (Council of Europe 1994); and the website documenting UNESCO's program to assist in the rebuilding of the bridge: http://www.unesco.org/opi2/mostar/ (Accessed February 2008).
11 The *New York Times* provided graphic evidence of the razing of Grozny in a series of satellite images commissioned in 1999 (*New York Times* 2000).
12 Drakulic is quoted in Pasic's *The Old Bridge* (Pasic 1995, 40). The same quotation is also used (though not clearly acknowledged) in Pasic's 'Why *Stari Most?*'(Pasic 1994, 66) and the UNESCO DRG website (http://www.unesco.org/opi2/mostar/).

1 Interpreting destruction of the built environment

1 Arendt's comment is made in *Eichmann in Jerusalem*, where she observes that the Israeli prosecutor's 'case rested on the assumption that [Eichmann], like all "normal persons," must have been aware of the criminal nature of his acts, and Eichmann was indeed normal insofar as he was "no exception within the Nazi regime." However, under conditions of the Third Reich only "exceptions" could be expected to react "normally" [that is, according to the norms of conscience to which the Israeli prosecutors were appealing]'. That is, to judge a regime of meaning according to what is 'normal' for others is not necessarily to grasp the logics according to which that regime operates. Eichmann was thus normal under the conditions of the Third Reich, and to account for his actions one has to understand the regime within which he was so 'normal', and within which a sense that his actions involved no moral wrongdoing could be established (Arendt 1994, 26–27).
2 During the drafting of this Convention, there was some disagreement concerning the protection of religious buildings. There was concern that the Convention would afford

protection to all religious buildings that were not used for military purposes. Some parties were keen to exclude this possibility, since it may include buildings that were of little cultural value, whilst other parties were keen to afford protection to all such buildings since they viewed religion as a principal aspect of culture itself. The prevailing interpretation of the Convention seems to indicate that all religious buildings can be afforded protection – although, in practice, it is those that have a notable position in the heritage of a culture (i.e., those of specific architectural or artistic merit, those of specific significance for a given religion, and those that are especially ancient) that are thought most deserving of protection (see Mose 1996, 202–204).

3 For a copy of the full text of the 1948 Genocide Convention, see Appendix 1 of Andreopoulos (1994, 229–233).

4 UNESCO's World Heritage List can be viewed at http://whc.unesco.org/en/list (Accessed January 2008). In drawing up the World Heritage List, UNESCO is advised by the International Council on Monuments and Sites (ICOMOS). Information regarding ICOMOS and its member national committees can be found at http://www.international. icomos.org/e_sumary.htm (Accessed January 2008).

5 The reverse logic is applied to those who destroy cultural heritage: since these buildings are designated as such, and thus in some way extraordinary, it is assumed that they must have been deliberately targeted. It is precisely this reversal of logic that gives rise to fierce contests over the definition of buildings and monuments as cultural heritage. That is to say, if one can define a building as cultural heritage, its destruction cannot be explained away as the consequence of expediency or excess. This can clearly be seen in the case of Serbian attempts to characterise NATO's 1999 offensive in Kosovo as an aggression akin to 'genocide'. These attempts paid particular attention to destruction or endangerment of cultural heritage, since it was argued that if it could be shown that NATO was destroying the physical basis of Serbian cultural identity, it would, *de facto*, hold that NATO was conducting a campaign aimed at destroying the Serbs themselves.

Two strategies were deployed by Yugoslav authorities and Serb organisations. Firstly, buildings that might otherwise not have been so designated, but had been damaged by NATO munitions, were defined as 'cultural heritage' in order to magnify the damage caused. Thus the television tower on Mt Avala in Belgrade, which was destroyed as part of NATO's (controversial) strategy of disabling communications and propaganda networks, was defined as cultural heritage by The Institute for the Protection of Cultural Monuments of Serbia (see http://www.yuheritage.com/nato_list.htm for a full list – with hyperlinks – of the 'cultural heritage' damaged or destroyed by NATO). The tower was built in 1965 and cannot really claim heritage status (though it might be accurate as the Institute claims to see it as an achievement of Serbian engineering). The designation of this destroyed building as 'cultural heritage' was intended to imply a deliberate attempt to destroy Serbian culture on the part of NATO.

Secondly, where a building had been reasonably defined as 'cultural heritage' (such as the ancient Orthodox monasteries in Kosovo), any damage by NATO munitions was deemed to be a deliberately targeted act of aggression. This is conspicuous in the case of monasteries damaged by the force of nearby detonation of bombs/missiles. Such damage is hard to define as an assault on cultural heritage. In many cases, the detonations were from munitions directed at legitimate targets and so the damage appears to comprise an unintended (and possibly unforeseen) consequence of military targeting. For claims concerning the amount of cultural heritage destroyed in Serbia and Kosovo, see the Federal Ministry of Foreign Affairs' *Whitebook* (now removed from the official ministry website, but available at http://www.balkan-archive.org.yu/kosovo_crisis/destruction/ white_book/ and http://www.balkan-archive.org.yu/kosovo_crisis/destruction/white_ book2/); and the *SerbiaInfo* article 'A Large Number of Cultural Monuments in Serbia Damaged' (http://www.serbia-info.com/news/1999-06/12/12509.html).

6 Article 2(b) of the statute of the ICTY provides for the charge of 'wanton destruction of

cities, towns or villages or devastation not justified by military necessity' (Roberts and Guelff 2000, 569). Indeed, this charge forms part of the indictment of Radoslav Brdjanin and Momir Talic (see International Criminal Tribunal for the Former Yugoslavia (ICTY) case number IT-99-36-PT; for an information sheet on the Brdjanin and Talic, or 'Krajina', case, see http://www.un.org/icty/glance/brdjanin.htm). Though this charge recognises that widespread destruction of the urban environment may be of significance beyond the destruction of cultural property, it still sees the rubble of war as being militarily unnecessary. That is to say, the destruction is not of significance in its own right, but points to the excessive force used by the 'ethnic cleansers'. The devastation of the urban environment is thus implicitly reduced to a signifier of brutality without being highlighted as a phenomenon in its own right. Thus, as I noted earlier, the question of what is disclosed in such 'wanton destruction' is not raised.

7 The Unis Co. buildings, next to the Holiday Inn in Sarajevo, provide the front cover picture for Silber and Little's *The Death of Yugoslavia* (Silber and Little 1995). For further examples of the modernist buildings destroyed in the siege of Sarajevo, see Association of Architects of Bosnia-Herzegovina (1993) and Association of Architects DAS – SABIH (1993).

8 For an account of semiology, the scholarly study that defines *the semiotic*, see Culler (1986, 90–106).

9 The similarity between the formulation of this section of my argument and Roland Barthes' *Mythologies* should not be interpreted as an endorsement of the latter's argument. Rather, this similarity arises because I think that the interpretation of urban destruction that I am outlining at this point conceives of the ruins of urban Bosnia in a manner comparable to that in which Barthes conceives of images: as forms/signs appropriated as the signifiers of certain concepts (Barthes 1973, 117–142).

10 I take the idea that 'Balkanisation' is 'transvalued' from a term in the lexicon of classical geopolitics to the status of motif for violent fragmentation from Der Derian (1992, 148).

11 This definition owes its wording to Bakic-Hayden and Hayden (1992). Bakic-Hayden and Hayden draw upon Edward Said's original definition of 'Orientalism' (Said 1991).

12 This view can be seen in the words of a spokesperson for the American Republican leadership, who stated: 'I see no reason to send young men over there to lose their lives over something we can do nothing about. These people have been fighting for centuries' (quoted in Campbell 1998a, 52).

13 For example, Sells claims that the *Stari Most* was 'a symbol of Bosnia's role in bridging cultures … its destruction is a symbolic separation of Croatia/Herceg-Bosna from "the Orient" of Serbs, Muslims, and Jews' (Sells 1996, 113).

14 For an exegesis of the manner in which 'peacemaker and paramilitary' can share common assumptions, see Campbell (1998a, Chapter 5). Campbell argues that a common 'political anthropology' underscored both diplomatic efforts to resolve the conflict and nationalist paramilitary efforts to ethnically cleanse and partition Bosnia.

2 The logic of urbicide

1 Extracts of this publication were published in 1993 as 'Mostar '92 – Urbicide', in *Spazio e Società/Space and Society* 16: 62, pp. 8–25.

2 In this essay, Berman explores at greater length themes that he touched upon in his comments on Robert Moses in *All That Is Solid Melts into Air* (Berman 1983, 290–312).

3 It should be noted that 'heterogeneity', like 'multiculturalism', is a contested category. In later chapters I will examine the nature of the heterogeneity through an elaboration of the Heideggerian notion of 'Being-with'. I will argue that heterogeneity in this sense comprises a fundamental openness to alterity. This contrasts with an (anthropocentric)

understanding of heterogeneity that takes it to comprise the existence, side-by-side, of different but essentially homogeneous groups.

4 Note that the notion of 'concept' used here is similar to Martin Jay's notion of the '*post facto* conceptual entity' (Jay 1992 quoted in Campbell 1998a, 40).

5 '[A]lthough Lemkin's conception [of genocide] included the physical extermination of targeted groups [indeed, the destruction of the European Jews was a central aspect of Lemkin's evidence of the genocidal policies of the Nazis], this was, in his view, *only the most extreme technique of genocide*' (Orentlicher 1999, my emphasis).

6 Here I draw on both Claude Lefort's definition of totalitarianism and Jean-Luc Nancy's idea of the totalitarianism of the immanentist figure (see respectively: Lefort 1986, 273–291; and Nancy 1991, 1–42).

7 Shaw's argument is a response to my essay within the same volume outlining the logic of urbicide in Bosnia (see Coward 2004, pp. 154–171). This argument is reiterated (albeit more briefly) in his *What Is Genocide?* (Shaw 2007, 75–76).

8 To this could be added the dynamic noted by Pratt (2000, 773), in which 'the slide in living standards in the 1980s drove urban populations to reactivate their rural kin ties … and, in some cases … forced young unemployed people back into the rural areas for survival' – thus further blurring any potential urban–rural distinction.

3 The built environment and shared spatiality

1 In his comments on William Connolly's *Ethos of Pluralization*, Stephen White (1998, 81 footnote 4) similarly, albeit briefly, indicates that the destruction of the urban environment in World War II forms the proper context in which 'Building Dwelling Thinking' should be understood.

2 For example, in *Being and Time*, Heidegger (1962, 137) speaks of the sun as a region: the sun 'has its own places – sunrise, midday, sunset, midnight'. These 'places' orient *Dasein*'s world: for example, 'the house has its sunny side and its shady side; the way it is divided up into rooms is oriented towards these …'.

3 This is the implication of Heidegger's comments in *Being and Time* that although the spatiality of *Dasein* can be reduced to measurements, these distances cannot fully capture the spatial relations on which they are based (Heidegger 1962, 140).

4 One could read Kenneth Hewitt's notion of 'place annihilation' – also elaborated in relation to Allied bombing – in a similar light (see Hewitt 1987; Hewitt 1983).

5 Ó Tuathail (1996, 39–43) provides an account of Cartesian perspectivalism, which documents the evolution within cartographic practice of a God's-eye view exterior to the map and constitutive of a point from which the mapped territory can be surveyed.

6 On the concatenation of 'ethnic' and 'nationalist' (to indicate the manner in which nationalism in Bosnia was predicated on an understanding of the national body as an ethnic body), see Campbell (1998a, 70–71) and Connor (1994).

7 Campbell (1998a) demonstrates the ontopological nexus of territory and identity on which ethnic nationalist politics rest.

4 The nature of heterogeneity: from *Mitsein* to *the inoperative community*

1 'Ready-to-hand' refers to the way in which *Dasein* encounters objects as usable in order to accomplish something. Such an understanding is pre-theoretical and not the result of reflection. 'Presence-at-hand', in contrast, refers to 'mere things' (Inwood 1999, 172) as they form the 'object of theoretical contemplation' (Mulhall 1996, 41). Objects perceived as present-at-hand are thus perceived not as having an immediately obvious use, but rather as things in themselves for contemplation.

2 Pre-ontological knowledge represents an 'implicit understanding of being as a matter of course' that *Dasein* has in its everyday absorption with the world. The pre-ontological comprises the structures of Being-in-the-world of which *Dasein* has a pre-theoretical

grasp, prior to any reflection upon them. Since *Dasein*'s absorption in equipmental wholes is pre-ontological, so must its relation to others be (King 2001, 20).

3 It is important to note in what follows that Nancy (and his translators) follow a different convention to that of Heidegger (and his translators) with regard to the word 'being'. To this point in the argument, I have followed a convention of capitalising 'Being'. In what follows, it will be necessary to mix this convention with that of Nancy's (where 'being' is not capitalised). This has the potential for confusion. However, despite the orthographic mixture, one should still read the same conceptual questions in both 'Being' and 'being'. It is also worth bearing in mind Pattison's (2000, ix) observation that '[t]he advantage of giving the lower-case "being" is that it brings out the verbal aspect of the term and avoids misreading it as a hypo-statised metaphysical concept. On the other hand, this could … lead to it being read simply as a present participle and not as a distinctive philosophical term.' It is important, therefore, to note in what follows that the lack of capitalisation does not indicate a conceptual difference between the two understandings of 'being/Being'. Rather, we should 'remember to hear the German "Sein"' in both 'being' and 'Being'.

4 Nancy (2000, 99) refers to the co-existential analytic as '*ethos* and *praxis*'. On Nancy's claim that *Being and Time* must be rewritten as a 'social' ontology, see Critchley (1999, 240). On the manner in which Nancy contests the privileging of the *Seinsfrage* over the *Mitseinsfrage* in *Being and Time*, see Devisch (2000).

5 In relation to the former notion that community is a partaking in a universal substance, see Ernesto Laclau's comment that 'the *privileged agent of History* [was] the agent whose particular body was the expression of a universality transcending it' (Laclau 1996, 23, italics in original). In relation to the latter idea that community is an aggregation of entities that are substantially the same, Article 1 of the Universal Declaration of Human Rights states: 'All human beings are born free and equal in dignity and rights. They are endowed with reason and conscience and should act towards one another in a spirit of brotherhood.'

6 The use of the term 'banal' here resonates, of course, with Hannah Arendt's reports from, and reflections upon, the trial of Adolf Eichmann. Arendt (1994) notes that the problem posed by the bureaucrat Eichmann is precisely how he could suspend all judgement regarding the question of community and serve as the technical instrument of the perfection of the supposed essence of being on which the Nazi 'community' was predicated. Eichmann's Nazism is exemplary of the bureaucracy of which I am speaking – it is an unquestioning technical management of the empirical contingencies (particularly the so-called 'Jewish question') that were taken to constrain the realisation of the homogeneous (racially pure) Nazi state founded upon the purported Aryan/ German essence of being.

7 I have taken the term 'figuration' from various points in the work of both Jean-Luc Nancy and Philippe Lacoue-Labarthe. It is given partial exegesis by Simon Sparks in his 'Introduction' to *Retreating the Political* (Lacoue-Labarthe and Nancy 1997), and is elaborated in Nancy's essay 'Myth Interrupted' (Chapter 2 of Nancy 1991).

8 Presence here is intended to invoke all the various strands of thought concerning being that could be said to be implicated in what Derrida has called the 'metaphysics of presence'. 'Presence' could be said to be a regime of representation of being as if it were immune to the effects of difference and contingency (cf. Derrida 1997).

9 It is precisely this point that Todd May fails to recognise when he argues that whilst it seems that enclosure is impossible, might it not be the case that 'individuals, while communicating, do so only for strategic reasons, and thus retain a strong form of "personal self-enclosure" while doing so?' (May 1997, 26). The retention of an individualist mode of thought in this statement is indicative of May's apparent misreading of Nancy's *Inoperative Community*.

10 Here I am explicitly echoing certain aspects of Heidegger's thesis concerning technology. For a thought-provoking set of essays discussing the general sense of exhaustion that

accompanies the end of politics implied in the technicisation of Being, see Campbell and Dillon (1993).

11 I take the notion of an 'other' understanding of community from Jean-Luc Nancy and Philippe Lacoue-Labarthe's invocation of a 'wholly other politics' (Lacoue-Labarthe and Nancy 1997, xix).

12 Reticulation refers to 'a division into a network or into small [spaces] with intersecting lines' (Oxford Paperback Dictionary 1983, 564).

5 The political stakes of urbicide

1 It is important to recognise that it is not by mistake that I have reversed the 'slash' that usually divides identity and difference. In writing identity\difference, rather than identity/difference, I am following William Connolly's formulation of the agonism of identity and difference (Connolly 1991). Connolly notes that his 'reason for the reverse slash was to indicate that identity does not just lean over difference, as people tend to assume. Difference both helps to constitute and recoils back upon identity'. (Email correspondence with the author, 12 July 2001). I would note that the reversed 'slash' is distinct in meaning from the forward slash used in either/or binary pairing. Either/or binary dualisms (such as inside/outside, domestic/international, self/other, identity/difference) have a semblance of closure. That is, the forward slash gives the impression that the terms of the dualism are independent of one another and, hence, separately constituted. These dualisms both restrict the possible forms that heterogeneous existence might assume (e.g., one must either be inside or outside, but not both, or neither) and give the impression that the two terms in the pairing have a pre-formed and closed identity. In reversing the slash I wanted to note (as Connolly does) that identity and difference are in a mutually constitutive relationship, not a forced opposition. Moreover, this relation is defined by a shared border of distinction at which identity unravels into difference, not by a separation that establishes an antagonism between a pre-constituted identity and an exterior alterity. It is important to note, therefore, that this reversal of the 'slash' is not a typographic error, and is motivated by specific intellectual concerns.

2 For Foucault, genealogy is a history of the provocations of government and the manner in which the alterity found in these provocations was either drawn into, or expelled from, the *socius*. This is what Foucault means when he argues that genealogy traces the '*insurrection of subjugated knowledges*' (1980, 81).

3 I am also drawing here on Ernesto Laclau's notion of 'dislocation'. Laclau (1990, 21) notes that 'identity … is merely relational and would therefore not be what it is outside the relationship with the force antagonising it, the latter is also part of the conditions of existence of that identity'. Laclau, in turn, is drawing on Ferdinand de Saussure's structural linguistics. If, following Saussure, identity is defined only in relation to what it is not, the other that an identity *is not* is both constitutive of, and antagonistic towards, that identity. That is, the other that an identity *is not* is both a condition of possibility of that identity and, precisely because it must remain what that identity *is not*, simultaneously the other that must be excluded if that identity is to achieve presence. The concept of 'dislocation' points to this contradictory logic at the heart of identity; 'every identity is dislocated insofar as it depends on an outside which both denies that identity and provides its condition of possibility [relational definition] at the same time' (Laclau 1990, 39).

4 It should be noted that my conception of antagonism draws on, and yet differs from, Ernesto Laclau's. I would read Ernesto Laclau's notion of antagonism as the realisation of a confrontation in the Foucauldian sense. For Laclau, antagonism is the realisation of hegemony by the aggregation of a series of competing claims into a single confrontation. Insofar as hegemony is achieved, the provocation of identity and difference is ossified in apparently fixed social relations that have the appearance of presence. However, given the constitutive dislocation of the elements from which hegemony is composed, it is

never entirely realised. This constitutive incompleteness echoes with my claim that the metaphysics of presence/subjectivity are perpetually unworked by the heterogeneity/ agonism that is constitutive of existence (see Laclau 1990, 33–36).

5 On the logic of ethnic cleansing, see Campbell (1998a; 2002b).

6 Refugees are defined as '[p]ersons originating from Bosnia and Herzegovina, currently hosted in third countries, with refugee status as defined by international law'. Displaced persons are defined as '[p]ersons having left their place of origin as a result of war or persecutions and currently accommodated in Bosnia and Herzegovina' (Office of the High Representative Reconstruction and Return Task Force 1998, Annexe 1).

7 For further documentation of the manner in which minority returns were prevented in the immediate post-war era, see International Crisis Group (1998a; 1998b).

8 I should note that here I am arguing in fairly general terms. It is clear that intimidation and physical violence against the persons of returnees remains the principle obstacle to minority returns. I would not want, therefore, to suggest that if a house intended for a returnee is destroyed it is simply a matter of finding another one. Indeed, the very fact that that house is destroyed may be enough to intimidate returnees and thus halt the minority return process. However, I do want to note that this destruction comprises more than the elimination of the residence of a given returnee. Those who understand house-burning to comprise the destruction of the house of such-and-such a returnee (and, hence, to prevent the return of that specific returnee) miss the point, since it is *in principle* possible for the returnee to be returned to any available property. Instead of seeing the destruction in the very narrow terms of a given house being destroyed because it could potentially house a specific family, we should ask in generic terms: 'Why destroy the buildings?' What is it that these buildings comprise that means they must be destroyed? Indeed, why is it that intimidation is not enough and destruction of the very urban fabric is necessary?

9 Evidence of the almost total ruination of Grozny can be found in the various graphics assembled online by the New York Times (New York Times 2000).

6 The conceptual stakes of urbicide

1 Taylor uses the term 'human centered' interchangeably with 'anthropocentric' (Taylor 1986, 11). The link between anthropocentrism and the Enlightenment is made explicit by Seckinelgin (2006, 86–108).

2 One of the best examples of the manner in which the human capacity for reasoned discourse is cast as the defining characteristic of the *polis* is Jurgen Habermas' notion of 'discourse ethics' (see, for example, Habermas 1990, 43–115). For a critical recasting of the question of what it is to be human in a manner that contests anthropocentrism, see Haraway (1991).

3 For an interesting critical attempt to contest this cultural discourse of the separation between the human and the material and the instrumental relationship of the former and the latter, see Bennett (2004).

4 For a counterpoint to my assertion that no one mourns the loss of ugly buildings, see Weiss (2000).

5 In this regard it is important to note that the European Administration of Mostar (EUAM) gave the task of reconstruction to an engineer/town planner, John Yarwood. The Department of Reconstruction was autonomous and given freedom from parallel departments dealing with the political questions raised by post-war Mostar. Reconstruction was thus seen as a 'tool to support political goals', an ancillary element of a project to establish new structures of governance in Mostar (Yarwood 1999, 25).

6 See, for example, Yarwood's diagram of the technical schema for determining extent of destruction and, hence, allocation of resources (Yarwood 1999, 114). Also interesting in this regard are Yarwood's accounts of the procedures formalised to provide reconstruction aid (*Ibid.*, 36–51).

7 Indeed, the fear was expressed that '[i]f it [the Old Bridge] is rebuilt ... the international community will walk away saying Mostar's OK, that's the problem solved' (Traynor 1994, 8).
8 For a general discussion of the contemporary security agenda, see Terriff, Croft, James and Morgan (1999). On new forms of war, see Kaldor (1999).
9 It is worth noting that security studies could be argued to have escaped the anthropocentric bias insofar as the sovereignty of the nation-state is, strictly speaking, a non-human referent object. However, in practice, traditional security discourses either anthropomorphise the state (viewing its security as the security of the 'body politic') or view the delivery of security to comprise the delivery of conditions of safety from harm for the individual citizens of the state.

Conclusion

1 In this regard the term 'warchitecture' – which captures the manner in which conflict is conducted in and through architecture – offers an interesting alternative to 'urbicide' (see Association of Architects of Bosnia-Herzegovina (1993); Association of Architects DAS – SABIH (1993); and Herscher (2000)). 'Warchitecture', however, does not capture the sense of the destruction of a particular existential characteristic that 'urbicide' entails.
2 See, in this regard, Machiavelli's comments regarding the problem the city poses for its rulers (Machiavelli 1988, 17–19).
3 In this regard, see Campbell's discussion of the manner in which civic conceptions of identity contest the logic of ethnic nationalism (1998a, 236–237).

Bibliography

Adams, N. (1993) 'Architecture as the Target', *Journal of the Society of Architectural Historians*, 52:4 (December), pp. 389–390.

Agamben, G. (2004) *The Open: Man and Animal*, translated by Kevin Attell, Stanford: Stanford University Press.

Amnesty International (2004) *Israel and the Occupied Territories: Under the Rubble: House Demolition and Destruction of Land and Property*, AI Index: MDE/15/033/2004, May. Online. Available HTTP:<http://web.amnesty.org/library/pdf/MDE150332004ENGLISH/$File/MDE1503304.pdf> (Accessed November 2004).

Andreopoulos, G. (ed.) (1994) *Genocide: Conceptual and Historical Dimensions*, Philadelphia: University of Pennsylvania Press.

Arendt, H. (1994) *Eichmann in Jerusalem: A Report on the Banality of Evil*, London: Penguin.

Association of Architects of Bosnia-Herzegovina (1993) 'Warchitecture', *ARH: Magazine for Architecture, Town Planning and Design*, 24.

Association of Architects DAS – SABIH (1993) *Urbicide – Sarajevo/Sarajevo, Une Ville Blessée*, Exhibition Catalogue, Paris: Warchitecture/Association of Architects DAS – SABIH/Arc en rêve centre d'architecture/Centre Georges Pompidou.

Bakic-Hayden, M. and Hayden, R. (1992) 'Orientalist Variations on the Theme "Balkans": Symbolic Geography in Recent Yugoslav Cultural Politics', *Slavic Review*, 51:1 (Spring), pp. 1–15.

Barthes, R. (1973) *Mythologies*, London: Paladin.

Bauman, Z. (1991) *Modernity and the Holocaust*, Ithaca: Cornell University Press.

Beaumont, P. (1996) 'Calling Out Around the World', *The Observer*, 30 June, p. 12.

Bennett, J. (2004) 'The Force of Things: Steps Towards an Ecology of Matter', *Political Theory*, 32:3, pp. 347–372.

Berman, M. (1983) *All That Is Solid Melts into Air: The Experience of Modernity*, London: Verso.

—— (1996) 'Falling Towers: City Life After Urbicide', in Crow, D. (ed.) *Geography and Identity: Living and Exploring Geopolitics of Identity*, Washington, DC: Maisonneuve Press, pp. 172–192.

Bevan, R. (2006) *The Destruction of Memory: Architecture at War*, London: Reaktion Books.

Bogdanovic, B. (1993) 'Murder of the City', *The New York Review of Books*, 40:10.

—— (1994) 'The City and Death', in Labon, Joanna (ed.) *Storm 6: Out of Yugoslavia*, London: Storm/Carcanet, pp. 37–74.

Botev, N. and Wagner, R. (1993) 'Seeing Past the Barricades: Ethnic Intermarriage in Yugoslavia During the Last Three Decades', *Anthropology of East Europe Review*, 11:1–2 (Autumn).

Bougarel, X. (1999) 'Yugoslav Wars: The "Revenge of the Countryside" Between Sociological Reality and Nationalist Myth', *East European Quarterly*, 33:2 (June).

Boyes, R. (2003) 'Bridge of Hope Spans the Ages', *The Times*, 24 April, p. 18.

Bringa, T. (1993) 'Nationality Categories, National Identification and Identity Formation in "Multinational" Bosnia', *Anthropology of East Europe Review*, 11:1–2 (Autumn).

—— (1995) *Being Muslim the Bosnian Way: Identity and Community in a Central Bosnian Village*, Princeton, NJ: Princeton University Press.

B'Tselem (2004) *Through No Fault of Their Own: Punitive House Demolitions during the al-Aqsa Intifada*. Online. Available HTTP: <http://www.btselem.org/download/200411_ Punitive_House_Demolitions_Eng.pdf> (Accessed 29 November 2007).

—— (2007a) 'Statistics on Houses Demolished for Alleged Military Purposes', *B'Tselem – The Israeli Center for Human Rights in the Occupied Territories*. Online. Available HTTP: <http://www.btselem.org/english/Razing/Statistics.asp> (Accessed 29 November 2007).

—— (2007b) 'Statistics on Demolition of Houses Built Without Permits in the West Bank (Excluding East Jerusalem)', *B'Tselem – The Israeli Center for Human Rights in the Occupied Territories*. Online. Available HTTP: <http://www.btselem.org/english/ Planning_and_Building/Statistics.asp> (Accessed 29 November 2007).

—— (2007c) 'Statistics on Demolition of Houses Built Without Permits in East Jerusalem', *B'Tselem – The Israeli Center for Human Rights in the Occupied Territories*. Online. Available HTTP: <http://www.btselem.org/english/Planning_and_Building/East_ Jerusalem_Statistics.asp> (Accessed 29 November 2007).

Campbell, D. (1998a) *National Deconstruction: Violence, Identity, and Justice in Bosnia*, Minneapolis: University of Minnesota Press.

—— (1998b) 'Why Fight: Humanitarianism, Principles, and Post-Structuralism', *Millennium: Journal of International Studies*, 27:3, pp. 497–521.

—— (2002a) 'Atrocity, Memory, Photography: Imaging the Concentration Camps of Bosnia – The Case of ITN versus *Living Marxism*, Part 1', *Journal of Human Rights*, 1:1, pp. 1–33.

—— (2002b) 'Atrocity, Memory, Photography: Imaging the Concentration Camps of Bosnia – The Case of ITN versus *Living Marxism*, Part 2', *Journal of Human Rights*, 1:2, pp. 143–172.

Campbell D. and Dillon, M. (eds) (1993) *The Political Subject of Violence*, Manchester: Manchester University Press.

Caney, S. (1992) 'Liberalism and Communitarianism: A Misconceived Debate', *Political Studies*, 40:2, pp. 273–290.

Casey, E. (1998) *The Fate of Place: A Philosophical History*, Berkeley: University of California Press.

Charny, I. (1994) 'Toward a Generic Definition of Genocide', in Andreopoulos, George (ed.) *Genocide: Conceptual and Historical Dimensions*, Philadelphia: University of Pennsylvania Press.

Connolly, K. (2007) 'Cracks Show in Rebuilt Mostar Landmark', *The Guardian*, 6 December, p. 30.

Connolly, W. E. (1991) *Identity\Difference: Democratic Negotiations of Political Paradox*, Ithaca: Cornell University Press.

—— (1995) *The Ethos of Pluralization*, Minneapolis: University of Minnesota Press.

Connor, W. (1994) *Ethnonationalism: The Quest for Understanding*, Princeton: Princeton University Press.

Council of Europe (1993) *The Destruction by War of the Cultural Heritage in Croatia and Bosnia-Herzegovina: Information Report*, Parliamentary Assembly Committee on Culture and Education, Council of Europe, Doc. no. 6756. Online. Available HTTP: <http://assembly.coe.int/main.asp?Link=/documents/workingdocs/doc93/edoc6756. htm> (Accessed 2000; November 2002).

—— (1994) *War Damage to the Cultural Heritage in Croatia and Bosnia-Herzegovina:*

Fourth Information Report, Parliamentary Assembly Committee on Culture and Education, Council of Europe, Doc. no. 6999. Online. Available HTTP: <http://assembly. coe.int/main.asp?Link=/documents/workingdocs/doc93/edoc6999.htm> (Accessed 2000; November 2002).

Coward, M. (2004) 'Urbicide in Bosnia', in Graham, Stephen (ed.) *Cities, War and Terrorism: Towards an Urban Geopolitics*, Oxford: Blackwell, pp. 154–171.

Critchley, S. (1999) *Ethics–Politics–Subjectivity: Essays on Derrida, Levinas and Contemporary French Thought*, London: Verso.

Culler, J. (1986) *Saussure*, revised edition, London: Fontana.

Davis, M. (1992) *City of Quartz: Excavating the Future in Los Angeles*, New York: Vintage Books.

—— (2002) *Dead Cities and Other Tales*, New York: The New Press.

—— (2006) *Planet of Slums*, London: Verso.

Deleuze, G. and Guattari, F. (1994) *What Is Philosophy?*, London: Verso.

Denich, B. (1993) 'Unmaking Multi-ethnicity in Yugoslavia: Metamorphosis Observed', *Anthropology of East Europe Review*, 11:1–2 (Autumn), pp. 43–53. Online. Available HTTP: <http://condor.depaul.edu/~rrotenbe/aeer/aeer11_1/denich.html> (Accessed January 2008).

Der Derian, J. (1992) *Antidiplomacy: Spies, Terror, Speed, and War*, Oxford: Blackwell.

Derrida, J. (1994) *Spectres of Marx: The State of the Debt, the Work of Mourning, and the New International*, London: Routledge.

—— (1997) *Of Grammatology*, corrected edition, Baltimore: Johns Hopkins University Press.

Devisch, I. (2000) 'A Trembling Voice in the Desert: Jean-Luc Nancy's Rethinking of the Space of the Political', *Cultural Values* 4:2 (April), pp. 239–256.

Dewey, R. (1960) 'The Rural–Urban Continuum: Real but Relatively Unimportant', *The American Journal of Sociology*, 66:1 (July), pp. 60–66.

Donia R and Fine, J. (1994) *Bosnia and Herzegovina: A Tradition Betrayed*, New York: Columbia University Press.

Drakulic, S. (1993) 'Falling Down: A Mostar Bridge Elegy', *The New Republic*, 13 December, pp. 14–15.

Dreyfus, H. (1991) *Being-in-the-World: A Commentary on Heidegger's Being and Time, Division 1*, London: MIT Press.

Eagar, C. (1995) 'So Many Tragedies in One Family', *The Observer*, 24 September, p. 19.

Elden, S. (2000) 'Rethinking the *Polis*: Implications of Heidegger's Questioning the Political', *Political Geography*, 19:4, May, pp. 407–422.

Eltringham, N. (2004) *Accounting for Horror: Post-Genocide Debates in Rwanda*, London: Pluto.

Farby, I. and Magnusson, M.-L. (1999) 'The Battle(s) of Grozny', *Baltic Defence Review*, 2, pp. 75–87.

Fein, H. (1993) *Genocide: A Sociological Perspective*, London: Sage.

Foucault, M. (1980) 'Two Lectures' in Michel Foucault, *Power/Knowledge: Selected Interviews and Other Writings 1972–1977*, edited by Colin Gordon, New York: Pantheon Books.

—— (1982) 'Afterword: The Subject and Power', in Dreyfus, H. L. and Rabinow, P., *Michel Foucault: Beyond Structuralism and Hermeneutics*, Brighton: Harvester Press.

—— (2000) 'The Ethics of Concern for Self as a Practice of Freedom', in Rabinow, Paul (ed.) *Michel Foucault: Ethics Subjectivity and Truth – Essential Works of Foucault 1954–1984, Volume 1*, London: Penguin Books.

Friedman, L. (ed.) (1972) *The Law of War: A Documentary History*, Vol. 1, New York: Random House.

Fukuyama, F. (1992) *The End of History and the Last Man*, London: Hamish Hamilton.

Gentleman, A. (1999) 'Russia's Shockwave of Terror', *The Guardian*, Tuesday 14 September.

Online. Available HTTP:<http://www.guardian.co.uk/yeltsin/Story/0,,200938,00.html> (Accessed 15 September 1999).

Goodson, L. (2001) *Afghanistan's Endless War: State Failure, Regional Politics, and the Rise of the Taliban*, London: University of Washington Press.

Graham S. (2002) 'Bulldozers and Bombs: The Latest Palestinian–Israeli Conflict and Asymmetric Urbicide', *Antipode*, 34:4 (September), pp. 642–649.

—— (2003) 'Lessons in Urbicide', *New Left Review*, 19 (January–February), pp. 63–77.

—— (ed.) (2004) *Cities, War and Terrorism: Towards an Urban Geopolitics*, Oxford: Blackwell.

Grodach, C. (2002) 'Reconstituting Identity and History in Post-War Mostar, Bosnia Herzegovina', *City*, 6:1.

Gunzburger Makas, E. (2005) 'Interpreting Multivalent Sites: New Meanings for Mostar's Old Bridge', *Centropa*, 5:1.

Gusic, B. (1995) 'Testimony of Mr. B. Gusic', *Oslobodjenje*, 16–23 March. Online. Available HTTP:<http://www.haverford.edu/relg/sells/banjaluka/gusic1.html> (Accessed February 2008).

Habermas, J. (1990) *Moral Consciousness and Communicative Action*, Cambridge: MIT Press.

Hage, G. (1996) 'The Spatial Imaginary of National Practices: Dwelling–Domesticating/Being–Exterminating', *Environment and Planning D: Society and Space*, 14, pp. 463–485.

Halper, J. (2007) 'Demolition Statistics Since 1967', *Israeli Committee Against House Demolitions (ICAHD)*, Online. Available HTTP: <http://www.icahd.org/eng/articles.asp?menu=6&submenu=2&article=402> (accessed 29 November 2007).

Haraway, D. (1991) *Simians, Cyborgs and Women: The Reinvention of Nature*, New York; Routledge.

Harvey, D. (1985) *Consciousness and the Urban Experience*, Oxford: Blackwell.

—— (1989) *The Condition of Postmodernity: An Enquiry into the Origins of Cultural Change*, Oxford: Blackwell.

Hass, A. and Harel, A. (2001) 'IDF Digs Trench to Keep 65,000 Villagers Out of Ramallah', *Ha'aretz*, 8 March.

Hayden, R. (1996) 'Imagined Communities and Real Victims: Self-Determination and Ethnic Cleansing in Yugoslavia', *American Ethnologist*, 23:4, pp. 783–801.

Heidegger, M. (1962) *Being and Time*, translated by John Macquarie and Edward Robinson, Oxford: Blackwell.

—— (1993a) 'Building Dwelling Thinking', in Martin Heidegger, *Basic Writings*, edited by D. F. Krell, revised edition, London: Routledge.

—— (1993b) 'The Question Concerning Technology', in Martin Heidegger, *Basic Writings*, edited by D. F. Krell, revised edition, London: Routledge.

—— (1993c) 'Letter on Humanism', in Martin Heidegger, *Basic Writings*, edited by D. F. Krell, revised edition, London: Routledge.

—— (1993d) 'The Origin of the Work of Art', in Martin Heidegger, *Basic Writings*, edited by D. F. Krell, revised edition, London: Routledge.

—— (1996) *Gesamtausgabe, Vol. 27: Einleitung in die Philosophie*, edited by O. Saame and I. Saame-Speidel, Frankfurt: Klostermann.

Herscher, A. (2000) 'Warchitecture', *Assemblage*, 41.

—— (2007) 'Urbicide, Urbanism and Urban Destruction in Kosovo', *Theory and Event*, 10:2.

Herscher, A. and Riedlmayer, A. (2000) 'The Destruction and Reconstruction of Architectural Heritage in Kosovo', *Bosnia Report*, 19/20 [New Series] (October–December). Online. Available HTTP:<http://www.bosnia.org.uk/bosrep/report_format.cfm?articleid=703&reportid=146> (Accessed January 2008).

Hewitt, K. (1983) 'Place Annihilation: Area Bombing and the Fate of Urban Places', *Annals of the Association of American Geographers*, 73:2, pp. 257–284.

—— (1987) 'The Social Space of Terror: Towards a Civil Interpretation of Total War', *Environment and Planning D: Society and Space*, 5, pp. 445–474.

Hills, A. (2004) *Future War in Cities: Rethinking a Liberal Dilemma*, London: Frank Cass.

Hoffman, D. (1999) 'Russians Bombard Chechen Capital', *Washington Post Foreign Service*, 27 November, p. A1.

Human Rights Watch (1995) *Russia's War in Chechnya: Victims Speak Out*, Online. Available HTTP: <http://www.hrw.org/reports/1995/Russia.htm> (Accessed 2 December 2007).

—— (1999) 'Russian Ultimatum to Grozny Condemned', 8 December. Online. Available HTTP: <http://www.hrw.org/press/1999/dec/chech1208.htm> (Accessed 9 December 1999).

Husarska, A. (1998) 'Without a Prayer? Rebuilding a Muslim Temple Is a Test of Bosnia's Peace', *The Washington Post*, 10 May, p. C01.

Huttenbach, H. (2005) 'From the Editor: Lemkin Redux: In Quest of a Word', *Journal of Genocide Research*, 7:4, pp. 443–445.

Huxtable A. (1972) *Will They Ever Finish Bruckner Boulevard? A Primer on Urbicide*, New York: Collier Books.

International Crisis Group (1997) *House Burnings: Obstruction of the Right to Return to Drvar*, London: ICG, 9 June. Online. Available HTTP: <http://www.crisisgroup.org/home/getfile.cfm?id=252&tid=1573&type=pdf&l=1> (accessed 14 November 2007).

—— (1998a) *The Konjic Conundrum: Why Minorities Have Failed To Return To Model Open City*, London: ICG, 19 June. Online. Available HTTP: <http://www.crisisgroup.org/library/documents/report_archive/A400163_19061998.pdf> (Accessed 27 November 2007).

—— (1998b) *A Tale of Two Cities: Return of Displaced Persons to Jajce and Travnik*, London: ICG, 3 June. Online. Available HTTP: <http://www.crisisgroup.org/library/documents/report_archive/A400160_03061998.pdf> (Accessed 27 November 2007).

—— (2003) *Building Bridges in Mostar*, London: ICG, 20 November. Online. Available HTTP:<http://www.crisisgroup.org/library/documents/europe/150_building_bridges_mostar.pdf> (Accessed 1 December 2003; 9 December 2007).

Inwood, M. (1999) *A Heidegger Dictionary*, Oxford: Blackwell.

Israel Defence Forces (2004a) *Rafah: A Weapons Factory and Gateway*, IDF Spokesperson Unit, May. Online. Available HTTP:<http://www1.idf.il/SIP_STORAGE/DOVER/files/5/31365.pdf> (Accessed November 2004).

—— (2004b) 'The Demolishing of Terrorists' Houses in the Aida Refugee Camp in Bethlehem', *IDF News*, Friday 27 February. Online. Available HTTP:<http://www1.idf.il/dover/site/mainpage.asp?sl=EN&id=7&docid=25146.EN> (Accessed November 2004).

Izetbegovic, A. (1997) 'Remarks Made by the Chair of the Presidency of Bosnia Herzegovina, Alija Izetbegovic on the Occasion of Being Awarded the 1996 International Democracy Award by the Centre for Democracy, Washington (25th March 1997)'. *Bosnet-digest*, 05:557, Monday 14 April.

Jay, M. (1992) 'Of Plots, Witnesses, and Judgements' in Friedlander, Saul (ed.), *Probing the Limits of Representation: Nazism and the "Final Solution"*, Cambridge: Harvard University Press.

Jezernik, B. (1995) 'Qudret Kemeri: A Bridge Between Barbarity and Civilisation', *Slavonic and East European Review*, 73:3.

Kaldor, M. (1999) *New and Old Wars: Organized Violence in a Global Era*, Cambridge: Polity.

King, M. (2001) *A Guide to Heidegger's Being and Time*, edited by John Llewelyn, Albany: SUNY Press.

Krell, D. F. (1993) 'Introduction to *Building Dwelling Thinking*' in Martin Heidegger, *Basic Writings*, edited by D. F. Krell, revised edition, London: Routledge.

Laclau, E. (1990) *New Reflections on the Revolution of Our Time*, London: Verso.
—— (1996) *Emanciaption(s)*, Oxford: Verso.
Lacoue-Labarthe, P. (1990) *Heidegger, Art and Politics: The Fiction of the Political*, Oxford: Basil Blackwell.
Lacoue-Labarthe, P. and Nancy, J.-L. (1997) *Retreating the Political*, edited by Simon Sparks, London: Routledge.
Lefort, C. (1986) *The Political Forms of Modern Society*, edited and translated by John B. Thompson, Cambridge: Polity Press.
Lein, Y. and Weizman, E. (2002) *Land Grab: Israel's Settlement Policy in the West Bank*, Btselem Report, May. Online. Available HTTP:<http://www.btselem.org/Download/200205_Land_Grab_Eng.pdf> (Accessed January 2008).
Lemkin, R. (1994) *Axis Rule in Occupied Europe: Laws of Occupation; Analysis of Government; Proposals for Redress*, Washington: Carnegie Endowment for International Peace.
Lieven, A. (1998) *Chechnya: Tombstone of Russian Power*, New Haven: Yale University Press.
McGreal, C. (2004) 'Hope Crumbles in Rafah as Homes Are Ground into Dust', *The Guardian*, 10 March.
Machiavelli, N. (1988) *The Prince*, eds, Quentin Skinner and Russell Price, Cambridge: Cambridge University Press.
Malcolm, N. (1994) *Bosnia: A Short History*, London: Macmillan.
Mamdani, M. (2001) *When Victims Become Killers: Colonialism, Nativism, and the Genocide in Rwanda*, Princeton: Princeton University Press.
Markusen, E. and Kopf, D. (1995) *The Holocaust and Strategic Bombing: Genocide and Total War in the Twentieth Century*, Boulder: Westview Press.
May, T. (1997) *Reconsidering Difference: Nancy, Deleuze, Levinas, and Derrida*, Pennsylvania: The Pennsylvania State University Press.
Miami Theory Collective (ed.) (1991) *Community at Loose Ends*, Minneapolis: University of Minnesota Press.
Modrcin, L. (1998) 'Urbs vs. Polis', in Plunz, Richard, Baratloo, Mojdeh and Conrad, Michael (eds), *New Urbanisms, Mostar: Bosnia and Herzegovina*, New York: Columbia Books of Architecture; Studio Works 6/MSAUD New Urbanisms Series.
Mose, G. (1996) 'The Destruction of Churches and Mosques in Bosnia-Herzegovina: Seeking a Rights-Based Approach to the Protection of Religious Cultural Property' *Buffalo Journal of International Law* 3:1, pp. 180–208.
Mulhall, S. (1996) *Heidegger and Being and Time*, London: Routledge.
Mulhall, S. and Swift, A. (1996) *Liberals and Communitarians*, second edition, Oxford: Blackwell.
Musabegovic, S. (1994) 'The Death of Vukovar', *The New Combat*, (Autumn), pp. 48–52.
Myre, G. (2005) 'Israel Halts Decades-Old Practice of Demolishing Militants' Homes', *New York Times*, 18 February. Online. Available HTTP: <http://www.nytimes.com/2005/02/18/international/middleeast/18mideast.html?_r=1&n=Top/Reference/Times%20Topics/People/M/Mofaz,%20Shaul&oref=slogin> (Accessed 29 November 2007).
Nancy, J.-L. (1991) *The Inoperative Community*, translated by Lisa Garbus, Peter Connor, Michael Holland and Simona Sawhney, London: University of Minnesota Press.
—— (2000) *Being Singular Plural*, translated by Robert D. Richardson and Anne E. O'Byrne, Stanford: Stanford University Press.
New York Times (2000) 'Campaign Poster', *New York Times*, 26 March. Online. Available HTTP: <http://www.nytimes.com/library/review/032600grozny-review.html#> (Accessed 27 March 2000; 2 December 2007).
Norberg-Schultz, C. (1971) *Existence, Space and Architecture*, London: Studio Vista.
North Atlantic Treaty Organization (1999a) 'Press Conference by NATO Spokesman, Jamie

Shea and Air Commodore, David Wilby', NATO HQ, 4 April. Online. Available HTTP: <http://www.nato.int/kosovo/press/p990404a.htm> (Accessed April 2000).

—— (1999b) 'Press Conference by NATO Spokesman, Jamie Shea and Air Commodore, David Wilby SHAPE', NATO HQ, 6 April. Online. Available HTTP: <http://www.nato.int/kosovo/press/p990406a.htm> (Accessed April 2000).

Ó Tuathail, G. (1996) *Critical Geopolitics: The Politics of Writing Global Space*, Minneapolis: University of Minnesota Press.

Office of the High Representative Reconstruction and Return Task Force (1998) *RRTF Report March 1998: An Action Plan in Support of the Return of Refugees and Displaced Persons in Bosnia and Herzegovina*. Online. Available HTTP: <http://www.ohr.int/ohr-dept/rrtf/key-docs/reports/default.asp?content_id=5612> (Accessed 27 November 2007).

Oliker, O. (2001) *Russia's Chechen Wars 1994–2000: Lessons from Urban Combat*, Santa Monica, CA: RAND.

Orentlicher, D. (1999) 'Genocide', in Guttman, Roy and Rieff, David (eds), *Crimes of War: What the Public Should Know*, London: W. W. Norton. Online. Available HTTP:<http://www.crimesofwar.org/thebook/genocide.html> (Accessed January 2008).

Oxford English Dictionary (1989) *The Oxford English Dictionary*, second edition, Oxford: Clarendon Press.

Oxford Paperback Dictionary (1983) *Oxford Paperback Dictionary*, second edition, Oxford: Oxford University Press.

Pasic, A. (1994) 'Why *Stari Most?*', *Journal Institute of Muslim Minority Affairs*, 15:1 and 2.

—— (1995) *The Old Bridge (Stari Most) in Mostar: Studies on the History and Culture of Bosnia and Hercegovina, No. 4*, Istanbul: Research Centre For Islamic History, Art, and Culture.

Pattison, G. (2000) *The Later Heidegger*, London: Routledge.

Peric, B. (1999) 'Rebuilding Ferhadija', *Institute for War and Peace Reporting, Balkans Crisis Report*, Issue 84, 15 October.

Plunz, R., Baratloo, M. and Conrad, M. (eds) (1998) *New Urbanisms, Mostar: Bosnia and Herzegovina*, Studio Works 6/MSAUD New Urbanisms Series, New York: Columbia Books of Architecture.

Porteous, J. and Smith, S. (2001) *Domicide: The Global Destruction of Home*, London: McGill-Queen's University Press.

Pratt, J. (2000) 'Commentary: Economic Change, Ethnic Relations and the Disintegration of Yugoslavia', *Regional Studies*, 34:8 (November), pp. 769–775.

Ramet, S. (1996) 'Nationalism and the "Idiocy" of the Countryside: The Case of Serbia', *Ethnic and Racial Studies*, 19:1 (January), pp. 70–87.

Ribarevic-Nikolic, I. and Juric, Z. (eds) (1992) *Mostar '92 – Urbicid*, Mostar: Hrvatsko vijece obrane opcine Mostar.

Riedlmayer, A. (1994) 'The War on People and the War on Culture', *The New Combat* (Autumn).

—— (1995a) 'Killing Memory: The Targeting of Bosnia's Cultural Heritage, Testimony Presented at a Hearing of the Commission on Security and Cooperation in Europe, U.S. Congress, April 4', *Community of Bosnia Foundation*. Online. Available HTTP: <http://www.haverford.edu/relg/sells/killing.html> (Accessed 14 March 1997).

—— (1995b) 'Libraries Are Not for Burning: International Librarianship and the Recovery of the Destroyed Heritage of Bosnia and Herzegovina', *Conference Proceedings: 61st International Federation of Library Associations and Institutions General Conference, Istanbul, Turkey, August 20–25, 1995*. Online. Available HTTP: <http://www.ifla.org/IV/ifla61/61-riea.htm> (Accessed February 2008).

—— (2001) '*Convivencia* Under Fire: Genocide and Book Burning in Bosnia', in Rose (ed.) *The Holocaust and the Book: Destruction and Preservation*, Amherst: University of Massachusetts Press, pp. 266–291.

—— (2002) 'From the Ashes: Past and Future of Bosnia's Cultural Heritage', in Shatzmiller, Maya (ed.), *Islam and Bosnia: Conflict Resolution and Foreign Policy in Multi Ethnic States*, Montreal: McGill-Queen's University Press, pp. 98–135.

Roberts, A. and Guelff, R. (eds) (2000) *Documents on the Laws of War*, third edition, Oxford: Oxford University Press.

Rogers, A. P. V. (1996) *Law on the Battlefield*, Manchester: Manchester University Press.

Routley, R. and Routley, V. (1979) 'Against the Inevitability of Human Chauvinism', in Goodpaster, K. E. and Sayer, K. M. (eds) *Ethics and Problems of the 21 Century*, Notre Dame: University of Notre Dame Press.

Safier, M. (2001) 'Confronting "Urbicide": Crimes Against Humanity, Civility and Diversity and the Case for a Civic Cosmopolitan Response to the Attack on New York', *City*, 5:3, pp. 416–429.

Said, E. (1991) *Orientalism: Western Conceptions of the Orient*, London: Penguin Books.

Saunders, P. (1986) *Social Theory and the Urban Question*, second edition, London: Routledge.

Savage, M. and Warde, A. (1993) *Urban Sociology, Capitalism and Modernity*, Houndmills, Basingstoke: Macmillan Press.

Seckinelgin, H. (2006) *The Environment and International Politics: International Fisheries, Heidegger and Social Method*, London: Routledge.

Segal, R. and Weizman, E. (eds) (2003) *A Civilian Occupation: The Politics of Israeli Architecture*, London: Verso.

Sells, M. (1996) *The Bridge Betrayed: Religion and Genocide in Bosnia*, Berkeley: University of California Press.

Shalev, A. (1991) *The Intifada: Causes and Effects*, Boulder, CO: Westview Press.

Shaw, M. (2003) *War and Genocide: Organized Killing in Modern Society*, Cambridge: Polity.

—— (2004) 'New Wars of the City: Relationships of "Urbicide" and "Genocide"', in Graham, Stephen (ed.), *Cities, War and Terrorism: Towards an Urban Geopolitics*, Oxford: Blackwell, pp. 141–153.

—— (2007) *What Is Genocide?*, Cambridge: Polity.

Silber, L. and Little, A. (1995) *The Death of Yugoslavia*, London: Penguin/BBC Books.

Skeates, R. (1997) 'The Infinite City', *City*, 8, pp. 6–20.

Taylor, P. (1986) *Respect for Nature: A Theory of Environmental Ethics*, Princeton: Princeton University Press.

Terriff, T., Croft, S., James, L. and Morgan, P. M. (1999) *Security Studies Today*, Cambridge: Polity.

Todorova, M. (1997) *Imagining the Balkans*, Oxford: Oxford University Press.

Traynor, I. (1993) 'Shells Destroy Mostar Bridge', *The Guardian*, 10 November, p. 10.

—— (1994) 'Ottoman Treasure Splits Turks and EU', *The Guardian*, 24 August, p. 8.

—— (2004) 'Mostar Reclaims Ottoman Heritage: Celebrations as Ancient Bridge Destroyed by Croats Is Reopened', *The Guardian*, 24 July, p. 19.

UN-HABITAT (2006) *State of the World's Cities 2006/7*, London: Earthscan.

Van Den Abbeele, G. (1991) 'Introduction' in Miami Theory Collective (ed.) *Community at Loose Ends*, Minneapolis: University of Minnesota Press.

Walker, R. B. J. (1993) *Inside/Outside: International Relations as Political Theory*, Cambridge: Cambridge University Press.

—— (1999) 'Citizenship after the Modern Subject', in Hutchings, Kimberly and Dannreuther, Roland (eds) *Cosmopolitan Citizenship*, Basingstoke: Macmillan.

Waltzer, M. (1992) *Just and Unjust Wars: A Moral Argument with Historical Illustrations*, second edition, New York: Basic Books.

Weiss, S. J. (2000) 'NATO as Architectural Critic', *Cabinet*, 1, Online. Available HTTP: <http://www.cabinetmagazine.org/issues/1/NATO.php> (Accessed 16 November 2007).

White, S. K. (1998) '"Critical Responsiveness" and Justice', *Philosophy and Social Criticism*, 24:1.

Williams, R. (1973) *The Country and the City*, New York: Oxford University Press.

Wirth, L. (1996) 'Urbanism as a Way of Life', in LeGates, Richard T. and Stout, Frederic (eds), *The City Reader*, New York: Routledge.

Yarwood, J. (1999) *Rebuilding Mostar: Reconstruction in a War Zone*, with contributions by Andreas Seebacher, Niels Strufe and Hedwig Wolfram, foreword by Sir Martin Garrod, Liverpool: Liverpool University Press.

Zijderveld, A. (1998) *A Theory of Urbanity*, London: Transaction Publishers.

Index

Adams, N. 8, 13
Adie, Kate 7, 21
Afghanistan, Russian 'rubbleisation' tactics 9
Agamben, G. 110
agonism 93–4, 125
    and antagonism 95–7
    and 'the political' 93–5
Amnesty International 10
Andreopoulos, G. 44
antagonism 95–7, 125–6
    territorialisation 97–100, 126
'anthropocentic bias' (Seckinelgin) 109–10
anthropocentrism 109–21, 126
    and the autonomous individual 111–12
    consequences and the priority of the person 113–14
    and globalisation 135–7
    and the material environment 109–11
    and reconstruction 114–19
Arendt, H. 13, 24, 139, 143
Aristotle 110
Association of Architects DAS – SABIH 8
Axis Rule in Occupied Europe (Lemkin) 8

Bakic-Hayden, M. and Hayden, R. 29, 141
Balkanisation policies 28–31
Balkanism 30
    and fragmentation 30–1
Bauman, Z. 33, 41, 45
Beaumont, P. 2
'Being' 143
Being-alone 76–7, 83–4
Being-in-common
    and community 81–3
    and shared community 86–7
Being-in-the-world (Dasein) 55–71, 73–6
Being-with-others (Mitsein) 71, 73–7, 111–12, 124–5

Being Singular Plural (Nancy) 80, 87, 122
Being and Time (Heidegger) 58, 62–3, 73
Berman, M. 10, 36, 131
Bevan, R. 24
Bogdanovic, B. 37
Bosnia
    cultural and symbolic significance 5, 31–2
    destruction of the Stari Most (Old Bridge – Mostar) 1–7, 11–12, 30–1, 99–100
    fragmentation and Balkanisation policies 28–31
    house-burning 101–3
'Bosniac' 138
Botev, N. and Wagner, R. 26
Bougarel, X. 37, 51
Boyes, R. 117
'the bridge' (Heidegger) 66–8
bridge-building, and hope rhetoric 32
bridges
    military significance and justifications 22–3
    see also Stari Most (Old Bridge – Mostar)
bridging motifs (Bosnia) 31–2
Bringa, T. 26
B'Tselem 10, 103–4
building
    and dwelling 63–4
    and spatiality 54–71
built environment
    collective memory and experience 6–7, 11–12
    meaning and symbolism 5–7, 11–12
    and survival 13
    as symbols of ethnic co-existence 26
    see also urbicide

built environment–heterogeneity relationship 127–30
built environment–urbanity relationship 130–1
Bulevar Nardone Revolucije (Mostar) 116–17

Campbell, D. 13, 116, 126, 133, 141
Caney, S. 111
Carthage 8
Casey, E. 59, 97
Celebi, Katib 2
Charny, I. 46
Chechen conflict (1994–96; 1999–2000) 104–7
    Russian 'rubbleisation' tactics 9
churches 8
cities
    Carthage 8
    Dresden 8
    Hiroshima 8
'city haters' (Bogdanovic) 37
closeness 58
collective memory, and acts of destruction 6–7, 11–12
collective punishment 10
Columbia University Gym (US) 36
'community' 81–3, 124, 126
    and 'being-in-common' 81–3, 124
    and collective shared experience 12, 14
    shared 85–7
concentration camps 13
'concepts' 41
conceptual stakes of urbicide 109–21, 145–6
    anthropocentrism and the autonomous individual 111–12
    anthropocentrism and the material environment 109–11
    consequences and the priority of the person 113–14
confrontation 95–7
Connolly, K. 118
Connolly, W. 94, 125, 133, 142, 144
Council of Europe
    on ethnic cleansing 24
    on targeting of non-strategic sites 21–2
The Country and the City (Williams) 50
Critchley, S. 79–80
Critique of Pure Reason (Kant) 110
cultural genocide 24–8
    cf. human genocide 24–5

cultural heritage
    concepts and designations 26–7, 140
    'protective' conventions 24
    see also cultural genocide

dam building 10
Dasein (Heidegger) 55–71, 73–6
Davis, M. 10, 29, 135
Dayton Agreement 101–2
De Anima (Aristotle) 110
de-severance 58
Dead Cities (Davis) 10
definitionalism 46
Deleuze, G. and Guattari, F. 41
Der Derian, J. 29
Derrida, J. 69, 143
destruction of built environments *see* urbicide
Dewey, R. 49–50, 52
direction 58–9
discourse ethics 145
distance 59–60
Donia, R. and Fine, J. 37
Drakulic, S. 11–12, 14, 17–18, 67, 139
Dreyfus, H. 55, 63, 74
Drvar (Bosnia) 101–3
Dubrovnik 113
'dwelling' 63–6

Eagar, C. 2, 4
Eichmann, Adolf 143
Elden, S. 65
Eltringham, N. 132
em-placement 57–9
    dimensions 58
'equipmental wholes' (Heidegger) 57–9
ethnic cleansing 24–8, 101–3
    myths of historical antagonism 25–6
    terminology and definitions 48
ethnic co-existence 26
ethnic nationalism 133
    and 'ancient hatreds' 25–6
    and identity 97
    origins 51, 133
European Administration of Mostar (EUAM) 116–17, 145
existential spatiality (Heidegger) 55–71

Farby, I. and Magnusson, M.-L. 105
Fein, H. 45
Ferhadija Mosque (Banja Luka) 8
'figuration' 82–4, 125, 143
    and territorialisation 99–100
Foucalt, M. 93–6, 125–6, 144

Friedman, L. 20
Fukuyama, F. 85

genocide 40
    cf. urbicide 39–40, 47–9
    conceptual logic 42–3
    and the 'ills of definitionalism' 46–7
    and intent 44–6
Genocide Convention (1948) 25, 139–40
Gentleman, A. 105
globalisation and urbanity 135–7
Goodson, L. 9, 37
Graham, S. 37, 103, 121
Grodach, C. 37, 51, 138
Grozny 104–7
Gunzburger Makas, E. 4, 138–9
Gusic, B. 8

Habermas, J. 145
*Hague Convention for the Protection of
    Cultural Property in the Event of Armed
    Conflict* (1956) 24
Halper, J. 103
Harvey, D. 130
Hayden, R. 26
Heidegger, M. 55–71, 72–7, 123–4, 126,
    128–9
    on *Dasein* 55–71, 73–6
    on 'enframing' 110
    on humanism 120–1
    on *Mitsein* 71, 73–7
    on space and spatiality 98
Herceg-Bosna 1–2
heritage lists
    designation criteria 26–7
    see also cultural heritage
Herscher, A. 37, 49
Herscher, A. and Riedlmayer, A. 27
heterogeneity 141–2, 142–4
    as being-with-others 70–1
    as characteristic of existence 124
    as distinctive feature of urbanism 39,
        72–3, 123
    'heterogeneity of' 87–9
    and the logic of urbicide 43, 123
    and political plurality 87–9
    relationship with built environment
        127–30
Hewitt, K. 37
Hills, A. 106, 121
historical animosities, myths of 'ancient
    hatreds' 25–6
Hoffman, D. 106
house-burning, Bosnia 101–3

Human Rights Watch 105–6
humanism, critiques 120
'humanitarianism' 115–16
'humanity' 81–2
Husarska, A. 8
Huttenbach, H. 40
Huxtable, A. 10, 36, 48, 131

iconic imagery, human suffering vs.
    destruction of buildings 11, 12–13
identity
    and assaults on alterity 96–7
    in relation to difference 91
    in relation to sharing 86
'idiocy of the countryside' (Ramet) 51
Imagining the Balkans (Todorova) 30
immanentism 83–4
individuality, and humanitarianism 116
The Inoperative Community (Nancy) 80,
    85
'intent' 44–6
International Crisis Group 100–1, 118
International Democracy Award (1996) 32
Inwood, M. 66, 88
Israel Defence Forces 9–10, 103–4
Israel/Palestinian conflict, house
    demolitions 9–10, 37, 103–4
Israeli Committee Against House
    Demolitions (ICAHD) 103
Izetbegovic, Alija 32

Jenin refugee camp (Palestinian territories)
    37, 103
Jezernik, B. 2–4, 138
Just and Unjust Wars (Waltzer) 22

Koschnick, H. 117
Kosovo Cultural Heritage Survey 27
Krell, D.F. 63

Laclau, E. 144–5
Lacoue-Labarthe, P. 93, 143–4
Lein, Y. and Weizman, E. 10
Lemkin, R. 8, 35, 39–40, 42–3, 44, 142
liberal political theory, on being-with-
    others 111–12
libraries 7–8
Lieven, A. 105
'locale' 67
    as shared space 68–70
'logic' of urbicide 40–4, 141–2
    key features 122–6
    see also urbicide
Lower Manhattan Expressway (US) 36

McGreal, C. 9
Malcolm, N. 2
Man and Space (Krell) 63
Markusen, E. and Kopf, D. 8, 37
May, T. 143
memory *see* collective memory
Miami Theory Collective 85
'military necessity' and urbicide 19–23,
  123
    critiques 23
'Mitsein' (Heidegger) 71, 73–7
Modrcin, L. 91
mosques 8, 22
Mostar '92 – Urbicid (Ribarevic-Nikolic
  and Juric) 35–6, 40
Mulhall, S. 56, 63
Mulhall, S. and Swift, A. 111
Musabegovic, S. 128
Musanovic, A. 13
Myre, G. 104

Nagasaki 8
Nancy, J.-L. 71, 72, 79–83, 111, 122,
  124–5, 132–3, 135, 143
    on community 79–83
    on the disavowal of the political 107
    on relational agonism 94
    on shared community 85–7
National Library (Sarajevo) 7, 22
National Museum (Sarajevo) 7, 21–2
nationalism 133
    and 'ancient hatreds' 25–6
    and identity 97
    origins 51, 133
NATO bombardments of Serbia 20–1
New Republic (Drakulic) 11–12
New York City, house clearance policies
  10
Newton, I. 59
Norberg-Schultz, C. 55
North Atlantic Treaty Organization 20–1

ontological statements 75
'ontopolitical claim' 132–3
ontopology 69
Orentlicher, D. 24
Oriental Institute (Sarajevo) 7, 22
orientalism 29–30
'orientation' 56
Ottoman Empire, construction of the *Stari
  Most* 3

Palestinian house demolitions 9–10, 37,
  103–4

Pasic, A. 4, 11, 118, 138
Peric, B. 8
'Philadelphi route' (Gaza–Egypt border) 9
'place' 56
planning policies, Israel 10, 103–4
Plunz, R., Baratloo, M. and Conrad, M.
  117
'political' 93
political stakes of urbicide 93–107, 144–5
    agonism and the political 93–5
    from agonism to antagonism 95–7
    the territorilisation of antagonism
      97–100
    revealing the stakes of urbicide
      100–7
        demolition of Palestinian homes
          103–4
        Grozny 104–6
        house-burning in post-war
          Bosnia 101–2
political violence 14, 35
    proliferation of terms 47–8
    see also genocide; urbicide
Porteous, J. and Smith, S. 10
post offices 22–3
post-war reconstruction, and
  anthropocentrism 114–19
'Presence' 143
'Presence-in-hand' 142

'The Question Concerning Technology'
  (Heidegger) 110

Rafah Refugee Camp 9
Ramet, S. 51
'Ready-to-hand' 142
reconstruction, and anthropocentrism
  114–19
returnees 102–3
Ribarevic-Nikolic, I. and Juric, Z. 35–6
Riedlmayer, A. 6, 7–8, 13, 21, 25–6
Robert Moses' Cross Bronx Expressway
  (US) 10, 36
Roberts, A. and Guelff, R. 24, 114
Rogers, A.P.V. 19
Routley, R. and Routley, V. 109
'rubbleisation' tactics 9, 37
rural–urban divide 37, 49–53
    stereotyping dangers 51–2
Russian Chechen campaigns 9, 104–7

Safier, M. 38
Said, E. 30
St Petersburg Declaration 20

Sarajevo, National Library 7
Saunders, P. 49–50, 130
Savage, M. and Warde, A. 49, 50
'scorched earth' tactics vs. 'rubbleisation'
    tactics 9
Seckinelgin, H. 109–10
Segal, R. and Weizman, E. 10
Sells, M. 1, 3, 5, 25, 31, 48, 141
Shalev, A. 104
shared community 85–7
shared spatiality
    and the built environment 60–3, 142
    see also spatiality
sharing 112
Shaw, M. 24–5, 44–5, 46–9, 101, 129,
    132
Simmel, G. 50, 52
Skeates, R. 52
space 59–60, 67–8, 97–8
spatiality 54–71, 97–8
    being-in-the-world as em-placement
        55–7
    and the bridge (Heidegger) 66–8
    of the built environment 60–3, 142
    dwelling, gathering and locales 63–6
    and existence 57–9
    the locale as shared place 68–70
    space, distance and public natures
        59–60
    thinking in the context of buildings
        63
    towards co-ontology 70–1
Stari Grad (Old Town – Mostar) 7
Stari Most (Old Bridge – Mostar) 1–7,
    138–9
    background history 2–3
    cultural importance 3–4, 5, 11–12,
        30–1
    destruction rationale 4–5
    elegies 11–12
    impact 5–7, 11–12
    reconstruction 118–19
    as shared public place 68–70
    territorialisation of antagonism 99
Sultan Suleiman the Magnificent
    (1520–1566) 3
symbolism of buildings 5–7
    see also iconic imagery

Taylor, P. 109
Telos 85
territorialisation
    of antagonism 97–100, 126
    of figuration 99–100

Todorova, M. 30
Tomasic, D. 51
totalitarianism 84–5, 142
Traynor, I. 1–2, 4, 118
Tudjman, Franjo 1, 29

UNESCO (United Nations Educational
    Scientific and Cultural Organization),
    designation of heritage sites 26–7, 140
Unis Co. buildings 141
United Nations Genocide Convention
    (UNGC) 44
urban, definitions 49–50
urban–rural divide 37, 49–53
    stereotyping dangers 51–2
urbanism, constituent elements 39
urbanity
    definitions 50–1
    threats in a global era 135–7
    see also built environment–urbanity
        relationship
urbicide
    anthropocentrism 109–21
        and the autonomous individual
            111–12
        consequences and the priority of
            the person 113–14
        and the material environment
            109–11
        and reconstruction 114–19
    conceptual definitions 38–9
        cf. genocide 39–40, 47–9
        and the community 89–90
        as deprivation of Being-with
            (Heidegger) 78–9
        and the destruction of
            heterogeneity 39, 43–4, 62
        inclusive of rural targets 49–53
        as killing of urbanity 54–5
        and 'logic' 40–4
    historical genesis of the concept
        35–8
    motivations and interpretations
        Balkanisation policies 28–31
        bridging concepts 31–3
        destruction of heterogeneity 39,
            43–4, 49, 62
        destruction of political
            possibilities and identities
            48–9, 61–2
        ethnic cleansing and cultural
            genocide 24–8
        and intent 44–6
        'military necessity' 19–23

political 14
wanton destruction and
vandalism 23–4
and ontopolitics 134–5
political stakes 93–107
agonism and the political 93–5
from agonism to antagonism
95–7
the territorilisation of antagonism
97–100
revealing the political stakes
100–7
symbolic dimensions 5–7
and urban renewal programmes 36
utility of term 131–2

vandalism and urbicide 23–4
violence *see* political violence; urbicide
Vukovar (Croatia) 37

Walker, R.B.J. 89, 100, 134
Waltzer, M. 22
'wanton destruction' 23–4
warchitecture 146
White, S. 142
Wilby, Air Commodore 20–1
Will They Ever Finish Bruckner
Boulevard? A Primer on Urbicide
(Huxtable) 36
Williams, R. 50, 128
Wirth, L. 39, 50, 52, 123
work, and shared community 85
World Trade Center (US) 10, 36, 37
World War II bombings 37
'wunian' 65

Yarwood, J. 32, 145

Zijderveld, A. 51